# Fired for Heresy!

## A Baptist History Professor's Career During the SBC Controversy

Slayden A. Yarbrough

*Fired for Heresy! A Baptist History Professor's Career During the SBC Controversy*
ISBN: Softcover 978-0-692639-32-0
Copyright © 2024 by Slayden A. Yarbrough

All rights reserved. No part of this book may be reproduced or transmitted in any form or by any means, electronic or mechanical, including photocopying, recording, or by any information storage and retrieval system, without permission in writing from the publisher.

Scripture references are from NASB New American Standard Bible®, Copyright © 1995 by The Lockman Foundation.

Parson's Porch Books is an imprint of Parson's Porch *&* Company (PP*&*C) in Cleveland, Tennessee. PP*&*C is a self-funded charity which earns money by publishing books of noted authors, representing all genres. Its face and voice is David Russell Tullock (dtullock@parsonsporch.com).

Parson's Porch *&* Company *turns books into bread & milk* by sharing its profits with the poor.

www.parsonsporch.com

*Fired for Heresy!*

# Dedication

To Dr. Michael Kuykendall, friend, fellow Baptist historian and religion professor. Mike has encouraged and critiqued my writing projects in retirement. He edited and contributed to *Southern Baptists: A History of Confessional People*. He volunteered as proofreader and critic of two of my books, *We Coulda Been Killed! Two Brothers and Others Growing Up*, and this, my final book. Soon after my arrival in the Northwest, Mike and I began to meet for a late breakfast and coffee every month or two to share stories, solve issues related to Baptist history matters, and to dream dreams of the future for a discipline for which we both have a passion. His friendship is treasured and enduring.

# Acknowledgements

To my teachers of Baptist history: Dr. H. K. Neely; Dr. Glenn O. Hilburn, Dr. J. M. Gaskin.

To all my fellow Baptist historians, who have shared the journey of researching, writing, teaching, and recording the history and principles of the people called Baptist. So many names, like Dr. Rosalee Beck, Dr. Carolyn Blevins, Dr. Charles Deweese, Dr. Pam Durso, Dr. Bill Estep, Dr. Bill Leonard, Dr. Alan Lefever, Dr. H. Leon McBeth, Dr. Morgan Patterson, and Dr. Walter "Buddy" Shurden.

To all of the younger Baylor Ph.D. graduates, who picked up the mantle of Baptist history in a number of colleges and universities.

To all of my students who endured my lectures and jokes and who pondered my interpretations of what it means to be Baptist.

To Dr. James Howard, fellow graduate student at Baylor University, who shared my fate of losing a teaching position because of criticism of his views on the Bible, which were based upon the quality education at denomination schools where we both learned to think.

And, as always, to Janis, my wife of 60 years, who supported me on the journey, typed countless papers, and openly critiqued my views and changes with courage and conviction.

> # *BAPTIST HISTORY & HERITAGE SOCIETY*
>
> Slayden A. Yarbrough, Executive Director (1996-1999)

In 1938 the Southern Baptist Historical Society organized to promote and preserve the history of Baptists. In 1951 the Historical Commission was organized by the Southern Baptist Convention, and the voluntary Society affiliated with the new agency. However, in 1995 the Convention voted to dissolve the Commission. The Society became an independent, self-supporting organization committed to continuing the important work of Baptist history. This book details many of the challenges and successes, which led to the preservation of the Society.

In 2001 a new name was adopted, the Baptist History & Heritage Society (BHHS), which reflects the expanded mission of the organization. The Society assists all Baptists worldwide in remembering, preserving, and interpreting Baptist heritage and identity for the present and future. The BHHS educates congregations and individuals about Baptist history through print and digital resources, conferences, seminars, training, consultations and other educational means.

The BHHS publishes the most important resource committed to Baptist history nationally and world-wide, *Baptist History & Heritage*. Through the Society's work and ministry, congregational identity is strengthened, and individual lives are transformed. The expanding work and ministry of the Society is dependent upon the generous financial support of Baptist individuals who are committed to the future of their faith. I ask you to become a member, provide support, and preserve Baptist history. The history of Baptists is essential to the future of Baptists!

Dr. Aaron Weaver, Executive Director (2024 -   ) - email: aweaver@thebhhs.org

Contact: https://thebhhs.org – today!

# Contents

Preface ..................................................................................................... 1
    The Importance of Baptist History
Introduction ............................................................................................ 4
Chapter One ......................................................................................... 13
    Becoming Baptist
Chapter Two ........................................................................................ 24
    How A "Conservative" Became A "Liberal"
Chapter 3 .............................................................................................. 42
    Fired for Heresy!
Chapter Four ........................................................................................ 61
    In Search Of A Teaching Position
Chapter Five ......................................................................................... 70
    Oklahoma Baptist University and the Rise Of the "Controversy"
Chapter Six .......................................................................................... 87
    Teaching at Oklahoma Baptist University during the "Controversy"
Chapter Seven ................................................................................... 100
    Publishing During The "Controversy" Part 1: Baptists And Books
Chapter Eight .................................................................................... 123
    Publishing During The "Controversy"
    Part 2: Encyclopedias, Dictionaries, And Editorials
Chapter Nine ..................................................................................... 141
    Publishing During The "Controversy"
    Part 3: Journal And Periodical Articles
Chapter Ten ....................................................................................... 162
    The "Controversy:" Success or Failure for the Southern Baptist Convention?
Conclusion ........................................................................................ 192
    A Young Professor's Defense of Diversity
Bibliography ..................................................................................... 195
Index .................................................................................................. 204

# Preface

# The Importance of Baptist History

"Nothing can be understood until you know its history. For that reason, the Baptist heritage matters." A quote from Walter B. Shurden, *Not a Silent People: Controversies That Have Shaped Southern Baptists* (Macon, GA: Smythe & Helwys Publishing, Inc., 1995), Preface.

## Introduction

Over fifty years ago I began teaching in the Courts Redford School of Theology at my alma mater, Southwest Baptist College (SWBC) in Bolivar, Missouri. On the day that I completed my oral exam for my Ph.D., at Baylor University (BU), I was in the office of my advisor, Dr. Glenn O. Hilburn. I was preparing to take documentation to the academic office as my final requirement to receive my degree. I happened to mention a lunch conversation with a former student at Southwest Baptist. He told me that G H Surrette, my former Old Testament professor, had been appointed Academic Vice-President at the school. I thought there might be a faculty opening. Dr. Hilburn immediately called Dr. Surrette and handed me his phone. Dr. Surrette told me that they were not planning a replacement, but asked if I would be interested in the Dean of Students position. I said the position out loud, and Dr. Hilburn quickly nodded" yes."

I had no idea what a Dean of Students did, but I replied "yes." I was invited for an interview in a few weeks. I was offered a contract to be Dean of Students and Associate Professor of Religion for the fall semester in 1972, a few months after receiving my Ph.D. My discipline was the history of Christianity. After four years in this position, I was appointed Associate Dean of the School of Theology, a position I held for three years. I continued to teach classes with the rank of Associate Professor of Religion.

During my seven-year tenure at the school, a conservative movement began to develop as an effort to seize control of the Southern Baptist Convention (SBC), affiliated state conventions, and organizations and institutions connected with all levels of denominational life. The initial focus was to gain authority over the convention and its agencies. The rationale was to purify the institutions by removing "liberals" from leadership roles, including professors at colleges and seminaries. The test of faith for orthodoxy was the correct interpretation of the Bible.

As a young, part-time professor I taught courses to freshmen in Old Testament history and New Testament history. I also taught upper-level courses in the Baptist denomination, church and state relations, and church history. I was optimistic, passionate, and inexperienced as I instructed my students. Many of them were preparing to serve as pastors and leaders in Southern Baptist churches.

I soon found myself under assault from a small number of theologically conservative pastors in southwest Missouri. They were convinced that I was teaching their students heresy. The general charge was that I did not believe the Bible. That was an easy accusation to make. What they meant was that I did not believe their view of the Bible. They were right on target on that count, although I always was careful to present options for my students rather than simply indoctrinate them in my views.

The primary accusation by the pastors was my treatment of Genesis, especially the creation accounts in the first three chapters. This question had been around for decades. But there were other issues as well, which I will detail in later chapters. The bottom line is that eventually in early 1978, upon receiving my annual contract for year seven (1978-1979) at the college, I raised a question about tenure. According to the faculty handbook tenure should have been automatic upon my signing and returning the contract. Instead, I provided the administration with a rationale to determine that I would not be offered tenure beyond the signed contract.

Based upon the continuous accusations from the select group of pastors, it was obvious to me that I was being "fired" based upon the charges of heresy thrown my way. The administration carefully avoided using that term. But I have no doubt that "fired" is an accurate description. I will make my case in this book. I need to add that as I look back on events that I moved on. I had a very productive and fulfilling career as a university professor, as a researcher and writer, and briefly even as a denomination executive.

This book will chronicle my journey as a professor of Baptist history and other religion courses. I will narrate my involvement in Baptist history organizations, my publication of books, articles, and other writings evolving out of the controversy in the denomination, and my contributions resulting from my career interests and activities.

I am indebted to my friends and colleagues, who encouraged and supported me. Dr. Warren McWilliams at Oklahoma Baptist University (OBU) was a model for my writings. Dr. Michael Kuykendall was a superb fellow Baptist historian, who not only provided a sounding board for my ideas, but who volunteered to edit this writing along with others, and who kept me committed to the challenge of staying with this project.

Above all, Janis, my spouse of sixty years, always stood by my side, always shared the consequences of my choices, and never wavered in believing in me and in what I was doing. As you read the pages that follow, many of you will recall your own involvement in the struggles for Baptist identity. May my story contribute to your self-understanding of your respective journeys.

Slayden A. Yarbrough

# Introduction

From the cowardice that shrinks from new truth,
From the laziness that is content with half-truth,
And from the arrogance that thinks it knows all truth
O God of Truth, deliver us.
—Ancient Hebrew Prayer, anonymous

### A Career and a Firing

Which are those events that shape our lives, that determine our identities, and that provide the context in which we frame the challenges that define who we are? In my case, it was a career that cannot be understood outside what is known in Southern Baptist life simply as the "Controversy." In *Fired for Heresy* I trace my roots in becoming a Christian and a Southern Baptist. I examine carefully the accusations against me by one pastor in Missouri, documented in a confessional call from him after I went to Oklahoma Baptist University in the fall semester of 1979. During our conversation I asked for and soon received his file of letters and phone transcriptions/summaries detailing his communications with administrators of SWBC.

I am convinced that during this denominational conflict starting in the 1970s, I became the first professor fired during this struggle. The movement would result in many more persons being removed from leadership or teaching positions in Southern Baptist organizations. They were either terminated, forced to resign, or chose early retirement. The battle resulted in the most radical changes and restructuring in the history of the Southern Baptist Convention, and its affiliated organizations and institutions. Supporters of the changes call it the "Conservative Resurgence." Opponents, like me, labeled it the "Takeover." I will use the terms "conservative" and "moderate" to describe the two movements in this volume. Neither are totally accurate. Many moderates were conservative in theology, while opposed to the politicized efforts to seize control of the convention. Some "conservatives" were either fundamentalists theologically, or moderates in their respect for diversity in the denomination.

The context of my entire twenty-nine-year academic career was framed by the rise of the Controversy, the battles fought, the restructuring of the Southern Baptist Convention, and the adoption of a significantly revised *Baptist Faith and Message* in 2000. The effects of the conflict continued through a creedal approach versus the historic confessional approach of Southern

Baptists. The final chapter is not close to being written. This book will contribute to the understanding and the effect of the struggle, and to the ongoing consequences of this period of denominational warfare in Baptist history.

## A Professor, a Baptist Historian, a Writer, and a Denominationalist

My journey as an academician at two denominationally affiliated schools is an insightful case study of one individual whose service was characterized by charges of heresy, challenges over tenure, opportunities to teach, and the publication of articles and books related directly or indirectly to the Controversy and the Baptist tradition of freedom and the commitment to higher education. During this period, I also participated in and led two Baptist historical organizations, while contributing to the preservation and study of Baptist history and theology. Reflective of the title of a book containing a composite of one of my favorite comic strips, *The Days Are Just Packed: A Calvin and Hobbes Collection* by Bill Waterson,[1] these were eventful yet surprisingly exciting years in my career. As a Baptist historian and professor, I was certainly never bored. In fact, I found the challenges during my journey to be invigorating and rewarding. That may sound strange coming from a fired heretic, but the events strengthened me and affirmed the significant principles of the people called Baptist.

Nearly all my service, challenges, and accomplishments were defined in the context of the ongoing conflict that divided the largest Protestant denomination in the United States. The battle would determine who Southern Baptists were going to become in the twenty-first century. Over fifty years after beginning my career at my alma mater in 1972, my journey through the greatest struggle in the history of the denomination outside the Civil War provides one example of one individual significantly affected by the Controversy. It also illustrates many of the issues that touched the lives of innumerable participants during the last three decades of the twentieth century, which were defined by religious, political, and theological conflict. Finally, my journey provides a perspective to evaluate the results of this "holy war"[2] in the convention after half-a-century from the initial rise of the

---

[1] Bill Waterson, *The Days Are Just Packed* (Kansas City, MO: Andrews & McMeel, 1993).
[2] A phrase used by Roy Honeycutt, president of Southern Seminary, on August 28, 1964 in a sermon entitled "To Your Tents O Israel." The sermon was a call to battle against the fundamentalists after Dr. Charles Stanley was elected president of the Southern Baptist Convention during its annual meeting two months earlier.

strategy to seize control of Southern Baptist institutions and organizations, and the consequential effects upon the movement.

I initially examine my journey in becoming a Southern Baptist. I then document and discuss my firing from Southwest Baptist College (SWBC). As indicated, this action is a case study foreshadowing future removals and replacements of leadership in the Southern Baptist convention through firings, resignations, and retirements of leaders. I participated in the restructuring of the denomination in my roles as trustee and executive director of the Historical Commission (HC) of the Southern Baptist Convention (SBC), which implemented changes that affected missions, finances, leadership, and programs of the longstanding agencies within the denomination. The restructuring flowed through state conventions, educational institutions, and related organizations under the Southern Baptist denominational umbrella. Few if any of the thousands of Southern Baptist churches were unaffected by the continuous conflict that defined convention life in the last few decades of the twentieth century and into the twenty-first century.

I also provide examples of the tensions created in the convention, especially in regard to educational institutions. Naturally, charges against religion faculty, and even administrators, took place in colleges, universities, and seminaries. The conflict also affected mission and ministry agencies at international, national, regional, and even local levels. My case included activity related to my role as a professor of Baptist history. My roles as a trustee and then executive director of the Historical Commission of the SBC cannot be understood outside the context of the Controversy. I would never have been selected the executive director of the orphaned, voluntary Southern Baptist History Society following the dissolution of the Commission. In 2001, the organization changed its name to the Baptist History & Heritage Society (BHHS).[3] This development reflected both the movement away from Southern Baptists and toward a more expansive connection with both moderate and progressive Baptist organizations.

I chronicle my career in academic and denominational life in the framework of the convention strife. I was not only a professor of religion, but I also began to publish articles and books that addressed the rising and ongoing conflicts reshaping the convention. And I document my service as a

---

[3] Information from the Baptist History & Heritage Society website: https://(thebhhs.org).

participant in the historical work at the state and national levels of the denomination. I worked alongside some of the most capable and committed historians in the denomination to proclaim, protect, and preserve the historical heritage of Baptists and Southern Baptists through and beyond the Controversy and into the twenty-first century. The opportunities and challenges that I faced in the Controversy opened doors of opportunity that shaped my identity as a Baptist historian, professor and contributor to the work of Baptist history, and in a real sense a restructuring of the Society, as it responded to the conflict in the Southern Baptist Convention.

I provide a thorough examination of Southern Baptists and those who demanded theological purity, or orthodoxy, in the Southern Baptist Convention. I conclude with my personal observations resulting from this continuous quest for orthodoxy in the SBC and the effects upon a once proud organization. In so doing, I provide my personal evaluation of the success or failure of the control of the denomination by those who planned and executed their strategy in seizing control of the boards and agencies of the convention.

**Why Should Anyone Read This Book?**

Upon completion of this book, I will have answered a question that lies behind this project. Why would anyone want to read the story about one professor of one small denominational school being fired almost fifty years ago? The answer should be evident when this single career is understood from the perspective of the most important internal conflict in denominational life in the United States, and most certainly in Southern Baptist history. The completed book itself will document the answer to this question.

Many individuals also had parallel experiences, such as losing their positions or facing assaults and challenges in their denominational service. However, I know of no one who was fired, or forced to resign or retire, but who also was chosen to take a leading role in their respective disciplines and organizations following such developments, as did I. Many became writers and speakers on Baptist history, and so did I as a professor of the discipline. At the same time becoming a leader within the SBC structure on one hand, and at the same time heading up an organization that found a new identity after the dissolution of the convention agency separates my story from so many of the moderate participants in the Controversy. The totality of my experiences makes my story worth telling, and provides a framework for the journeys of so many who defended the highest principles and practices of the people called Baptist.

## Methodology

The contents of this book will be drawn primarily from four sources. The context of my career is framed in the history of Southern Baptists during this time. During my twenty-nine-year tenure as a professor, I began to publish in the field of Baptist and Southern Baptist history. The following publications will be discussed in detail later in the book, but I will reference them at this time.

**Source 1 – Books**: My first source was publications of books on Southern Baptists. In 1984 I initially published a small volume that was a compilation of three articles, which appeared in *The Oklahoma Baptist Chronicle* beginning in the Spring, 1983 issue.[4] The title was *Southern Baptists: Who Are We?*

My first important book on Southern Baptist history appeared in 2000,[5] which I intentionally sent to the printer on the day after the Southern Baptist Convention adopted a revision of the *Baptist Faith and Message*. I edited my chapter on theology with the anticipation of the adoption of the revised confessional statement by the SBC during its annual meeting in 2000. As soon as the action was taken, I put my completed manuscript in the mail to the publisher. The 2000 revised *Baptist Faith and Message* became a tool for enforcing a developing creedalism in the denomination during the next two decades and beyond. This volume was edited and revised with the collaboration of Dr. Michael Kuykendall in 2021.[6] This book was an important revision to my 2000 volume because of its significant editing and updates.

Neither of these last two volumes was the most extensive history of the movement and the convention to appear before, during, or following the

---

[4] There were three successive parts on the history, theology, and practical topics in the *Chronicle*. The three were then combined by Dr. J. M. Gaskin and published by the Oklahoma Baptist Historical Commission into a single volume in 1984. I updated this small book in 1985 and 1990. The last edition provided a foundation for my expanded histories in 2000 and 2021.
[5] Slayden A. Yarbrough, *Southern Baptists: A Historical, Ecclesiological, and Theological Heritage of a Confessional People* (Nashville, TN: Fields Publishing), 2000.
[6] Slayden A. Yarbrough and Michael Kuykendall, *Southern Baptists: A History of a Confessional People* (Jefferson, NC: McFarland Books), 2021.

years of the Controversy and restructuring. However, their primary contribution and value are found in my treatment of the Controversy, the restructuring of the Southern Baptist Convention, and the chapter on theology in the history of the denomination. The latter chapter included a thorough examination of the history and the contents of the *Baptist Faith and Message* (1925) and its revisions in 1963, 1998, and 2000.

Although I was determined to be as objective as possible, my treatment of these topics was framed in my personal role in Southern Baptist life and institutions during the last decades of the twentieth century. The books were written from the perspective of one who was an actual participant in the events which resulted in the dissolution of a convention agency, and in the revitalization of a voluntary society, committed to the continuing work of Baptist history. The 2000 book, I believe, was also the very first history of the denomination published following the Controversy and restructuring, which I conclude ended with the adoption of the 2000 revision of the *Baptist Faith and Message*.

I also used numerous books and articles by established Baptist historians to provide background for so much that was going on during my career. In fact, many of these writings took place in the heat of the Controversy in the convention. These sources are too numerable to mention, but they will be referenced throughout this volume. Many of these men and women were active in the Southern Baptist Historical Society (SBHS), where I became acquainted with them. Many were fellow college and university professors, who accepted major responsibility for presenting and preserving the Baptist heritage. They often presented papers during the annual meetings of the Society, which provided me excellent examples of research and delivery of academic papers. I am thoroughly indebted to them for their influence and example throughout my career, especially during my time at OBU.

Finally, I need to mention a few other books that I wrote during my career and in retirement. I published a local church history.[7] I co-authored with three others an institutional history.[8] I self-published a book of monologues

---

[7] Slayden A. Yarbrough, *The Lengthening Shadow: The Centennial History of FBC, Shawnee, OK* (Shawnee, OK: First Baptist Church, 1992).
[8] Slayden Yarbrough, et al., *The View from Bison Hill* (Shawnee, OK: Oklahoma Baptist University, 1985).

and dramatic presentations.[9] I even wrote a humorous autobiography, which included a chapter on my Baptist experience.[10] I will discuss these writings more thoroughly in the context of the Controversy in a later chapter.

**Source 2 - Articles and Editorials**: The second source of information for this book was the numerous articles I published during my years at OBU (1979-2001). This period also included my years as trustee (1987-1995) and executive director (1995-1997) of the Historical Commission, and my role as executive director of the SBHS (1996-1999), following the dissolution of the Southern Baptist Historical Commission in 1997. My first important article was "Is Creedalism a Threat to Southern Baptists?" It appeared in the April 1983 issue of *Baptist History & Heritage*, and predicted many of the dangers facing Southern Baptists in the years during and following the Controversy and restructuring of the convention. I also will discuss this article and others more thoroughly later in the book.

Dr. Lynn E. May Jr. was the executive director of the Historical Commission from 1971 to 1995. Dr. Charles Deweese began working in publications and communications at the agency in 1973 and served as the assistant executive director of the Commission from 1990 to 1994. These two historians enlisted me to write on a potentially controversial topic, entitled "Biblical Authority in Southern Baptist History, 1845-1945." The article appeared in the January 1992 issue of *Baptist History & Heritage*. I also in retirement wrote an article for the journal entitled "Academic Freedom and Southern Baptist History," which appeared in the winter 2004 issue.

Additionally, I published numerous articles that directly or indirectly reflected the battle that was going on for the soul of the denomination. I also published articles related to Baptist history in other publications, including three on the topic of elders in Oklahoma Baptist churches in *The Oklahoma Baptist Chronicle*. I even published a monologue sermon entitled "I Am the Bible," in *Proclaim*, a Southern Baptist Convention journal for ministers, which covered the development of canon, text, and translations. Over many years I have edited and delivered this presentation in more than sixty churches, and as a

---

[9] Slayden A. Yarbrough, *I Am: Storytelling in Worship* (Rapid City, SD: New Harbor Press, 2020).
[10] Slayden A. Yarbrough, *We Coulda Been Killed! Two Brothers and Others Growing Up* (Vancouver, WA: Slayden A. Yarbrough, 2023).

method to emphasize issues which I deem essential in the Southern Baptist debate over the Scriptures.

During my years as executive director of both the Historical Commission and my first year as executive director of the SBHS (1996—1999), I served as editor of *Baptist History & Heritage*. Among the thematic topics which the journal addressed were subjects such as "Baptists and the White House" and "The Changing State of Church and State." *Baptist History & Heritage* also published two addresses that I presented at the last SBHS meeting in which I led as executive director. I treated the topic of the history of Southern Baptist history and the results of the restructuring on the new SBHS. Moreover, I shared with the participants my dreams and visions on Baptist history in the twenty-first century.

**Source 3 – Letters and Emails:** An extremely important resource for me is a collection of letters provided by Rev. Bill Dudley. He engaged in a campaign to get me fired from SWBC. Eventually, he was successful. After I relocated to OBU in 1979, he called me and apologized for his role in my removal from Southwest. He asked if there was anything he could do. I requested the file he kept on me. Dudley sent me a collection of his correspondence and phone conversations with key administrators at the institution. These documents were invaluable in telling my story, and were an example of the story of the rise of the Controversy in the Southern Baptist Convention.

I also communicated by email with several individuals who were a part on this narrative. They included Deweese, who was on the staff of the Historical Commission, and who succeeded me as executive director of the SBHS. Deweese helped fill in several blanks in my story. I also exchanged email with other friends who provided helpful information.

**Source 4 - Religious News Publications:** My fourth source of information is found in religious news publications, especially as they relate to current events leading up and through the 2024 Southern Baptist Convention. This included *Baptist News Global*. I also will look at state Baptist newspapers, and other religious and secular news journals. I use the internet to access many of the articles found in these publications.

**Source 5 - Memories and Recollections:** My fifth and final source is simply my memories of events and personalities in Southern Baptist life. Unfortunately, I did not a keep a diary during the twenty-nine years of my career. Nor did I keep most of my correspondence with leaders and even opponents. Significantly, however, as mentioned, I did have access to a file of letters, phone transcriptions and summaries, and conversations in which the pastor who attacked me at SWBC made available to me. I also recall many stories about my journey, which are included in this volume. I confess that my memories may not always be as accurate as possible in terms of minor details, but I believe that it is necessary to do the best that I can in recalling important events and impressions in my various roles related to being a Baptist and a professor of Baptist history.

## A Personal Journey in a Denominational Conflict and a Challenge

In summary, this book through the lens of one person's Baptist journey will be framed in developments within the Southern Baptist Convention, especially as they relate to the period called the Controversy. Throughout the book, I examine the issue of theology, the Baptist principle of confessions of faith, and the creedal approach to Baptist theology in the late twentieth and early twenty-first centuries. I also evaluate the effects and results of the creedalism upon the Southern Baptist Convention, its organizations, institutions, and its churches considering the pledges made by those determined to purify the convention. In so doing I will interpret the successes and failures of the conservative "resurgence" in the Southern Baptist Convention.

Finally, I believe that my journey will encourage others to recall their personal pilgrimages through the troubled waters of Southern Baptists beginning in the decades of the 1970s through the present. Perhaps some of these fellow pilgrims will also record for future generation the challenges and changes to their careers. There are lessons to be learned for future generations of Baptists from the personal stories of those who were reluctant participants in this historic period of denominational history.

## Chapter One

# Becoming Baptist

Galatians 3:11 - *The Just Shall Live By Faith*

"Baptists are a people of genuine faith. . . committed to the Lordship of Christ through faith. There is no doctrine. . . more crucial to the understanding of Southern Baptists."[11]

**Introduction**

I was not raised in a particularly religious family, at least not in terms of identification with a church or denomination. Betty, my older sister, through her friends became a Christian and joined Unity Roselawn Baptist Church in what is now Fairview Heights, Illinois. She encouraged me to go to church, and there was always that influence in my journey. She married John L. Hall, who later became a career chaplain in the U.S. Navy. Other than the influence of Betty, my experiences with religion is rooted in my friends who were connected to First Baptist Church of Washington Park, Illinois.

**Seeking Eligibility, Not Religion**

I had numerous starts and stops on my faith experience journey as I occasionally attended Sunday School classes and sometimes worship services at First Baptist Church. However, when I initially became an active participant, my reason was not to get "religion." I started showing up for worship with the aim to get "eligible" to play on the church's basketball and softball teams. Eligibility requirements included attending at least three worship services every month. Since most Southern Baptist churches held worship on Sunday morning, Sunday evening, and Wednesday evening for Bible study and prayer meeting, fulfilling this requirement was not too difficult. It goes without saying, that thanks to the athletes there was often a

---

[11] Yarbrough and Kuykendall, *Southern Baptists*, 7. As author I give permission to all citations from this book.

surge in attendance during the last three worship opportunities every month.[12]

The purpose of the athletic programs sponsored by First Baptist Church was evangelistic. They were intended to lead the young people to a faith experience in Christ. At the same time, their concern about providing good opportunities for young people to enjoy fellowship through sports was an important contribution to our lives, especially since most of us lacked the ability to play on the public-school sponsored teams at our particularly large junior high schools and our city high school, East St. Louis Senior High. So, First Baptist Church provided a great environment for us not only to develop a faith experience, but also to socially interact with others our own age.

I am quite certain that I was a Baptist before becoming a Christian. I participated in a lot of Baptist programs before "walking the aisle" in the first public "confessional act" in becoming a follower of Jesus. Most young people at First Baptist Church attended Sunday School classes for specific age groups. They were segregated into male and female classes, and taught by volunteers. These poor (a term of empathy, not criticism) teachers often had a challenging time keeping us in check. We chatted, we laughed, we threw things back and forth during the lessons being taught. But there were no theological litmus tests for us to pass to move on the next level of classification.

The teachers genuinely cared for us, as did the coaches of the athletic teams of the church. The bottom line is that First Baptist Church provided an atmosphere that addressed at various levels spiritual, mental, social, and physical needs of developing young people. Kind of like Luke 2:52, where the author told us that Jesus grew in wisdom and stature, in favor with God and man. I do not know if that was the intention of First Baptist Church toward young people in the athletic programs, but it was the result for many of us.

When it came to becoming a Christian and a member of a Baptist church, here is what I remember. I remind you that I may express a little hyperbole in my descriptions. At the same time, most Baptist preachers provide excellent models of this approach in proclaiming their own stories.

---

[12] Yarbrough, *We Coulda Been Killed!* 179. Chapter 9 was titled "Being Baptist," 179-90, and provides an overview on my journey as a Baptist. As author, I give permission to all citations from this book.

## Baptist Worship, Theology, and Ethics for a Teenager

Baptist worship services followed a consistent pattern. The sermons, the music, and the prayers usually followed a basic theme. The goal was to make converts out of sinners, especially teenagers. The first Scripture passage that I recall memorizing from the King James Version probably was not that God and Jesus loved me nor that Jesus was central to my faith. Rather, it was the one that easily induced guilt. That passage was "For all have sinned and fall short of the glory of God!" (Romans 3:23, NASB). That got my attention. Like most teenagers, I could personally document it.

A close second was John 3:16 "For God so loved the world, that He gave His only begotten Son, that whoever believes in Him shall not perish, but have eternal life" (NASB). Everyone in our church used the KJV. In fact, I did not know that there were other Bible translations. Nor did I know that the Scriptures were written primarily in Hebrew in what we called the Old Testament, and in Greek for the New Testament.

Guilt was the most effective method to guide a teenager down the path to becoming a follower of Jesus! Many pastors were very good at making a teenager feel guilty. Teenagers experience so many changes in life. Add to guilt the thought of spending eternity in hell certainly encouraged us to look for a way to escape the eternal fires of punishment. The next step of accepting Jesus as Lord was actually easy. Confess one's sins, ask for and receive forgiveness, and then symbolically follow and confess Jesus in baptism by total immersion in the baptistery as a new way of life.

"Confessing" one's faith became a key characteristic in my understanding of Baptists over the many years of my journey. Personal testimony, symbolic witness, theological expression, worship, service, and many additional principles and practices all resulted from efforts to "confess" that one was a follower of Jesus. There was a genuineness in this journey for so many of the young people in First Baptist Church of Washington Park, myself included.

Following the path of faith shaped our ethical decisions, which were quite simple. These standards were easily defined. We were instructed to avoid alcohol, smoking, and most importantly, dancing. Danger from dancing was the riskiest route to becoming a "backslider." If you danced, you would have physical contact with a member of the opposite sex. Such activity would surely lead to impure thoughts, endanger your salvation, and potentially result in spending eternity in hell. Why risk eternal damnation for a few moments shuffling your feet while closely holding your dance partner as the music played?

Fortunately, in regards to dancing, I turned out to be an excellent Baptist. I had two right feet. In my case clumsiness was a virtue! Sometimes I did attend dances with my reprobate friends. I once even considered asking a girl to dance. But I was awkward and simply not coordinated enough to make my feet move in any uniform pattern. Dancing was almost an impossible task for me. Furthermore, I was extremely shy. I feared rejection by any girl desperate enough to say "yes" to my invitation to dance. Therefore, when evaluated according to this particular sin, I was a good Baptist. Besides, the young lady turned me down. Either she did not like me or she feared having her toes stepped on, or both.

I, however, did experience some guilt related to dancing. I got a job working at a dance sponsored by a local disk jockey named Dick Farrell. He had silver-colored hair that stylistically looked like that of the Fonz on "Happy Days," a later successful television series remembering earlier times. The dance took place every Saturday evening in the Greek Orthodox Fellowship Hall in East St. Louis. A band named "Eugene Neill and the Rocking Kings" played live music.

I was assigned to watch a side door to keep teenagers from re-entering. They could leave the building at the door but not return through it. Instead, they were required to go through the main entrance. I suppose the reason was to prevent them from bringing alcohol back into the dance hall, since a policeman named Lou manned the front door. I made $4 every Saturday evening. I felt guilty for engaging in such a promiscuous enterprise, even if I never actually danced. I am sure I tapped my feet to some of the music. I wondered if my job might result in my being sent to hell after all. But I needed the money ($4 a night was big money in those days), so I took the chance despite my guilty feelings. I suppose I was practicing a teenage version of "situation ethics," a term I learned while in graduate school, and one condemned by many Baptists. But at the time I was a typical Baptist teenager, for sure.

If a teenager succumbed to dancing or any other temptations or sins that might stain our Christian witness, we faced another dilemma as Baptists. We were taught about the "security of the believer." On one hand, this provided us with great comfort in terms of eternal life. This staple Baptist belief was one of my early introductions to a Baptist theological principle. Most Southern Baptists believed that once a person had a genuine faith experience, they could not lose their salvation. To phrase it another way, Baptists believed that "once saved, always saved." Candidly, I have always questioned this position. It always seemed illogical to believe that once a person got "saved," then it did not matter what you did afterwards. At least, that was the interpretation that many Baptists held.

Over the years my study of this idea led me to the conclusion that the doctrine was rooted in the Reformed or Calvinistic influence upon Baptists, which teaches that true believers were chosen by God before "the foundations of the earth" to be saved. Once God saved you, you stayed saved no matter what you did. Hence, the security of the believer, or according to Reformed theology, "the perseverance of the saints." If you were really elected by God and saved, you would persevere.

For me and other teenage believers this presented a problem. If we failed, then what? Well, the answer was obvious. We apparently must not have been true believers. So, we went through the conversion experience all over again. This time it should really should take. But it always did not. So, I and others would enter the baptismal waters once more. In my case I went under three times. Usually, the church membership roll was padded with the additional conversions of the same person. It is difficult to be thrown off a Baptist church membership roll. Few churches seldom corrected their numbers. But we always were good at counting conversions and members.

However, there was one other option. I, like many, used it from time to time. When we stumbled, we were "backsliding." Backsliders would fall away, but always could once more "confess" their sins and start all over with a clean slate. However, in my case, after taking this approach a few times, I soon began to feel guilty even more.

Whatever my reason for attending First Baptist, in the end they tricked me by requiring me to attend services so I could become eligible to play basketball and softball on the church teams. In the end, they kept confronting me with the good news and reminding me that I was a guilty sinner. And, they kept pointing me to the grace of God as manifested in the redemptive grace of Jesus. A combination of guilt and hope induced me to walk the aisle (more than once) during the "invitation" near the end of the service, confess my sins, and once more put my faith in Jesus. Looking back, this was a part of my journey through life. You go through many stages, and this was one of those.

Slayden A. Yarbrough

**Enduring influences of the Baptists**

I am indebted to the Baptists in many ways. They gave me confidence in myself. The First Baptist Church Baptists I grew up with were encouragers. They affirmed the good and the potential that I and my friends had buried beneath the surface. Moreover, I met many lifelong friends at First Baptist.

In addition, the Baptist influence affected some of the most important developments in my pilgrimage. Through my Baptist roots in becoming a Christian, I continually experienced change and focus. I discovered through the years that Baptists emphasized freedom. Paul's statement in Galatians 5:1 states "Stand fast therefore in the liberty wherewith Christ hath made us free" (KJV). Sometimes this is translated "It was for freedom that Christ set us free." (NASB). It became one of my favorite biblical passages. Baptists at their best emphasize faith freedom, which I will comment on later. When I examine my teachings on a variety of subjects, freedom in Christ and freedom as a Baptist directs my focus.

My local church encouraged me to go to college. My pastor helped me to gain a scholarship to play basketball at Hannibal LaGrange Junior College (HLG) in Missouri. I successively graduated from there with an Associate of Arts (A.A.) degree in 1965. Then I received a Bachelor of Arts (B.A.) degree in 1967 from SWBC (SWBC) in Bolivar, Missouri. Finally, I earned a Doctor of Philosophy (Ph.D.) in Religion from BU in Waco, Texas, in 1972, where I focused on the History of Christianity.

While a student at HLG, I met and married Janis Sue Lane. We will celebrate sixty years of marriage in the fall of 2024. We met in the back row of an economics class. Significantly, Janis has always asked open and honest questions, especially in matters of religion. She has kept me grounded and honest through these many years. Because of her, I never became complacent. Exercising Baptist and Christian freedom in the context of the Baptist emphasis on education, I always found myself reevaluating simple answers to challenging questions. I do not underestimate the importance of the candor and inquisitiveness of Janis in my continual change in my understanding of life and faith.

The Baptists also provided me with opportunities to serve. I initially served as an administrator for seven years (1972-1979) at SWBC, as well as teaching part-time every semester in the department of Christianity. This experience ended with my eventual dismissal for heretical teaching at my alma mater. I then taught for twenty-two years at OBU from 1979 to 2001. Then Janis and I took early retirement and moved to Denver, Colorado. In 2009, we moved to Vancouver, Washington, to watch Kellan, our only grandson, grow up. During all stages of our journey, we remained Baptists. At the same time through Baptist freedom, we constantly reshaped our understanding of what it meant to be Baptist. We still do.

## Disenfranchised as a Southern Baptist and Becoming an American Baptist

Because of conflict within the Southern Baptist Convention from 1979 through the restructuring of the Southern Baptist Convention in 1997, I felt disenfranchised from the denomination that nurtured me through many years. Janis and I became American Baptists (ABCUSA) after retiring to Denver in 2001. While attending First Baptist Church of Denver, an interesting development took place related to my credentials as a Baptist historian. I decided to seek having my Southern Baptist ordination recognized by American Baptists. I proceeded with my application, and began the process. I met with a ministerial committee of the American Baptist Churches of the Rocky Mountain region. In my first meeting, they detailed the requirements for a person seeking recognition from another Baptist denomination. They included writing a paper (10-12 pages) on a variety of questions related to beliefs and practices. Dr. Gary Bowser, my pastor, previously told me of this requirement. He also provided me with a list of the questions. By the time that I met with the committee, I had written my paper. For a retired professor of religion this was an easy assignment. It also proved to be an enjoyable experience.

I also was required to take a course called "American Baptist Polity and History." The chairman of the committee, Dr. Nancy Darnell, pastor of First Baptist Church of Boulder, Colorado, stated that there were absolutely no exceptions to this rule. However, because of my twenty-nine years of college teaching of Baptist history, and my experience as executive director of both the Historical Commission and the SBHS, they decided to ask me to teach the course instead of take it. I found this to be an amusing development in circumventing a hard-set rule. But my credentials, and the law of common sense, overcame this legalistic requirement.

During retirement I continued to serve in two regions by teaching the American Baptist Polity and History course required of ordination candidates and ministers from other denominations who sought ABC recognition of their ordinations. Even after turning eighty years old, I continued to serve local churches in pulpit supply and as interim pastor during leadership transitions. A lot of my sermons, or as I learned to call them "reflections," related to the history, polity, and theology of Baptists.

Slayden A. Yarbrough

## Concluding Influences and Thoughts on Being Baptist

My journey as a Baptist has covered more than sixty years, and probably closer to seventy, if I consider my initial contacts with First Baptist Church of Washington Park. It has been characterized by challenges and changes, ups and downs, advances and regressions, and numerous unexpected and unintended consequences.[13] However, the core of the Baptist heritage has been affirmed time and time again. I believe that my journey is not unique, but normal.

Strangely, out of my negative experiences and setbacks as a Baptist, and out of the conflicts and controversies within the Baptist heritage, I have become an apologist for the best of Baptists. The bottom line for me after all the miles and memories is that when Baptists are at our best, there is no group with which I would rather be connected. At the same time throughout our history, Baptists have more-often-than-not stumbled and failed in trying to reach our highest ideals.

In graduate school at BU, I came across a line that applied to the church in general but seems to fit Baptists in my own experiences. I do not remember the source, but it went something like this in the Yarbrough paraphrase: "Baptists are like Noah's ark. If it were not for the storm on the outside, you could not stand the smell on the inside!" My experiences as a freedom-loving Baptist can document this description.

Let me elaborate. In terms of ideals, Baptists taught me to believe in and appreciate freedom. Walter "Buddy" Shurden's wonderful, short volume *The Baptist Identity: Four Fragile Freedoms*[14] provides defense of one of the greatest and most vital contributions of Baptists—freedom. Shurden examines soul freedom, Bible freedom, church freedom, and religious freedom. I love Baptist freedom.

As a Baptist historian, I would add theological freedom to Shurden's list, especially considering the demands for orthodoxy by many Baptists today, who claim certainty of their doctrinal convictions. Shurden includes theological freedom within the context of his four major Baptist freedoms. From my personal experience and my studies in Baptist history, I believe that

---

[13] Yarbrough, *We Coulda Been Killed!* 179-90.
[14] Walter B. Shurden, *The Baptist Identity: Four Fragile Freedoms*, (Macon, GA: Smyth & Helwys, 1993). This small volume is excellent on the discussion of the most important Baptist freedoms, and is used by many churches in many different Baptist denominations.

theological freedom deserves an equal status alongside Shurden's four important freedoms, especially as contemporary Southern Baptists have seriously eroded the definition of confessional theology into a test of faith on a variety of topics.

My first introduction to freedom was in the early 1970s, when I read Shurden's delightful, small volume entitled *Not a Silent People: Controversies That Have Shaped Southern Baptists.*[15] He examined the numerous controversies in Baptist life over several centuries. Buddy left me with the impression that if we were fighting, we were alive. Controversy in this regard is not a vice but a virtue! At least, until one of the combatant parties gains the power to insist upon its version of orthodoxy, and in so-doing, deny diversity.

Biblically, I trace my Baptist freedoms back to the New Testament. The Apostle Paul, after his magnificent defense of "justification by faith alone" in his "Letters to the Churches of Galatia," tells of the results of this doctrine. As previously stated, he writes in Galatians 5:1, which can be translated "It was for freedom that Christ set us free; therefore, keep standing firm and do not be subject again to a yoke of slavery." (NASB). Unfortunately, I find too many Baptists speak of freedom on one hand, but then revert to various forms of legalism on the other hand. Or, they simply shy away from going too far in expressing Christian freedom, which in my opinion restricts the possibilities of being relevant in a changing society.

I also am deeply indebted to Baptists for providing the institutions of higher education, where I received three different degrees from three different, liberal arts Baptist colleges and universities. Each institution was different from the other two. The faculty in all of these schools encouraged me to think, to study, to learn, to dialogue, and constantly to be willing to go where my studies took me. They provided me with a solid foundation of knowledge and research skills from which to continue learning and growing throughout my career.

Combined with the emphasis of Baptist freedom, I continue to learn even after becoming an octogenarian. These educational institutions also affirmed a lasting principle that the pursuit of a college degree is for education and preparation rather than indoctrination. In the twenty-first century, that is an ongoing challenge at smaller Baptist institutions of higher learning, especially

---

[15] Walter B. Shurden, *Not a Silent People: Controversies That Have Shaped Southern Baptists* (Nashville, TN. Broadman Press, 1972). A revised edition was published by (Macon, GA: Smyth & Helwys, 1994).

when certain pastors serve on boards of such schools, and attempt to place their own theological formulas on the quest to examine all subjects as objectively as possible.

My initial confrontation with this perspective came from a deacon at First Baptist Church, Washington Park. He called me aside and encouraged me as I prepared to head for college in Hannibal, Missouri. But he also warned me to be careful in what I learned. In other words, he was telling me to "watch out for those liberal professors. They will try and destroy your faith." Well, I apparently did not follow his advice. In fact, in the minds of many as expressed in the title of this book, I became one of those "liberal professors."

Beginning with my enrollment in 1963 at Hannibal-LaGrange, I began to develop my own understanding of higher education. I primarily shaped my views from a variety of professors over nine consecutive years as a college and university student, during which eventually I earned a Ph.D. I found myself appreciating the excellence of my teachers. At the same time, I was influenced by their compassion and patience with me and my fellow students. So many of them served as models for what a professor should be.

I have changed over the past sixty years. Baptists that I have encountered over that time have changed. Many, like me, have changed a lot. Many of my changes are traced to the important principles rooted in freedom that I continue to hold and practice. I am also convinced that many Baptists and Baptist leaders abandoned these foundational principles for numerous reasons. Freedom leads to change. Change leads to diversity. Diversity leads to disagreement. The result is conflict, or as I like to say, "meaningful dialogue" within the Baptist heritage. And, division often follows.

Attending three Baptist institutions of higher education opened my mind. It also opened doors of opportunity. At these Baptist schools I learned to appreciate honest and open inquiry. I embraced constructive change. I continue to be curious and open to new insights and new learning. For the foundation and freedom to think, I owe the Baptists my deepest gratitude. At the same time, many in Baptist authority did not like what I wound up thinking.

Choosing education over indoctrination, I rejected many beliefs and practices that can bind believers and churches. The Baptist emphasis on freedom shaped my commitment to think, to act, to change, and even to challenge the powers that be. In my own religious pilgrimage, I eventually rejected those who demanded theological orthodoxy, binding rules, and regulations as means to define one's faith. Furthermore, I recognized that this approach based upon freedom is an essential factor in the expansion and influence of Baptists over more than four centuries.

A significant result of my Baptist faith is the realization that change is a sign of life. It often leads to conflict and controversy. When this happens, the opportunity for growth becomes a possibility. Possibility opens the path to reality. Even in what seems to be our worst moments, when in our diversity we engage in major battles with each other, Baptists demonstrate that we are alive and energetic and involved. On the other hand, when we retreat to imposed conformity, the result more often than not is stagnation and potential irrelevancy. These principles from my journey will guide the basic arguments in this volume.

Finally, Baptists provided me the opportunity for service in terms of teaching at two institutions of higher learning. In summary, not only did I teach, as a professor I also became a researcher and publisher of both scholarly and practical articles and books. Additionally, I became active in organizations committed to the history of Baptists. My professional experiences provide the background for the chapters that follow.

All along the way of my journey and currently, I continued to serve in churches in terms of pulpit supply, interim pastor, and teacher. I point out that I recall no instances where any member of the churches where I served complained or challenged me in my teaching or preaching on any important principles of being a Baptist. I had many discussions and answered many questions from Baptists in these congregations. But we always finished our debates with a respect for each other, and an appreciation for the freedom to have diverse opinions.

Looking back, I am indebted to Baptists for believing in me, and for encouraging me to learn, grow, and contribute. The one constant in my journey was the belief that freedom, even (and perhaps, especially), as it challenges accepted norms, is the pathway to consistently becoming. The Baptists, both past and contemporary who know and practice this, have made a lasting contribution to who I am and what I have accomplished.

Chapter Two

# How A "Conservative" Became A "Liberal"

## LABELS, LIBEL, AND LIBERAL

"To label is to libel. Labels are dangerous. They oversimplify a viewpoint and the label sticks for a long time." From Dr. Warren McWilliams, a colleague at OBU.

**Introduction: An Early Morning Call from an Old Antagonist**

In July 1979 at the last minute, I was hired by OBU after my contract with SWBC in Missouri ended, completing a long period of controversy over my "liberal" teaching at the Missouri Baptist institution. During the fall of 1979, I was in my first semester as associate professor of religion at OBU. One morning in November, the phone rang before the sun came up. I was preparing to head for my office to begin another school day. I answered. On the line was Rev. Bill Dudley, a pastor who actively, aggressively, and successfully sought my termination at Southwest. Bill was the pastor of Carpenter Street Baptist Church in Moberly, Missouri. During my tenure at Southwest, he pastored the Westside Baptist Church in Wentzville, Missouri. His efforts to get me fired, along with those of several others, had proven successful. He quickly stated that his call was to apologize to me for his role in my firing, as both he and I interpreted it, from the school.

Bill explained that earlier in his pastoral career he left fundamentalism because of its negativity but found himself falling back into the same pattern in my situation. He also related that he continued to have disagreements with me but should not have participated in the effort to have me terminated. He asked for my forgiveness.

Based upon my Christian commitment, I have tried to be a forgiving person. I would much rather have friends than enemies. Bill's request was no exception to my perspective. So, I honestly told him "Yes." I am sure that the fact that I had found a new position made my answer much easier, but it was not the determining factor. Bill also showed his sincerity by asking me to teach a study of Baptist history at his church. Since he earlier had stated that he would never allow his son to take a course under me, this was a significant advancement.

As our conversation was ending, Bill asked if there was anything he could do to make it right in terms of his activity against me during my time at Southwest. I had not anticipated this offer. But I replied that there was something that he could do. I surmised that he was the type who would keep a record of his communications with the college administrators. Assuming this to be the case, I asked if he would send me a copy of his files. He agreed to do so, although I was not certain he would. If he followed up on his promise, it would confirm the sincerity of his regrets in my firing.

A few days later I received a large, manila envelope in the mail. It was from Bill. It contained just under forty pages of letters and phone transcripts or recollections between Bill and Dr. Jim Sells, president of Southwest, and Dr. G H Surrette, academic vice-president of the school. Bill also had numerous references to other pastors who were also in communication with the school during my time there.

It is important for historical context to point out that in a conversation with Dr. H. K. Neely, my dean and a longtime friend, Bill described attending a conference of the Criswell School of Prophecy in Dallas. The institution was named after the longtime pastor of First Baptist Church, Dr. W. A. Criswell. The president of the school and a leader of the conference was Dr. Paige Patterson. He and Judge Paul Pressler, an appellate federal judge, were engaged in the developmental stage of orchestrating a movement to gain control of the Southern Baptist Convention. They would be successful by the end of the twentieth century.

In one session of the conference, Patterson gave the marching orders to the audience comprised primarily of pastors who were committed to stamping out the perceived liberalism in the convention. Patterson told his eager listeners that basically "If you have liberals in your schools, call, write, write, call, keep at it until you get them removed." Bill took this challenge to heart and returned with a commitment to either have me silenced or fired. He stayed persistent until action was taken against me. My request in 1978 for tenure was rejected. Bill succeeded.

I write all of this to let readers know that I, like few if any others, obtained primary source documentation from an opponent of communications between the two parties, the accuser and the administration. These documents contributed significantly to my termination from SWBC (now Southwest Baptist University, or SBU). The letters and phone conversations provide much of the material in the paragraphs that follow, as I describe important events which resulted in my eventual firing. Follow-up correspondence between Bill and myself adds to the clarity of his file.

Slayden A. Yarbrough

My story is that of one person who was greatly affected in the struggle for the soul of the largest, non-Catholic denomination in the United States. Based upon my experience in the battle that took place, I gained important insights and observations, which I believe are relevant in evaluating not only Southern Baptists, but all Baptists and other denominations who have felt the effects of an aggressive struggle for theological purity in the contemporary environment.

At the same time my experiences were not isolated to one person. Countless other Southern Baptists found themselves attacked, criticized, and even fired, forced to resign, or retire early from positions of longtime service to a denomination, which had nurtured and educated them during their religious journeys. Slowly but effectively, they found themselves, as did I, disenfranchised from their community of faith, and forced to seek new directions and affiliations.

**How Did I Become a "Liberal?"**

My roots as a Christian and a Baptist are grounded in my journey of faith starting at First Baptist Church, Washington Park, Illinois. Overall, it was an enjoyable journey. We all begin somewhere in the significant and defining steps in our lives. Mine began as I was taught and influenced by people and friends who made up First Baptist Church of Washington Park. Basically, I experienced a positive pilgrimage as I established an essential foundation from which to develop.

Important in the resulting steps forward, although I was not aware of it at the time, were the Baptist emphases on education and freedom. So many of the Baptist people in my home church encouraged me and my friends to gain an education beyond high school. In the larger picture Southern Baptists during my early teaching years had either established or affiliated with more than fifty universities, colleges, and junior colleges across the United States. This system kept many Baptist young people connected with the church. At the same time, these institutions funneled back into the congregations educated people as leaders who could influence relevant change in local congregations.

Usually connected with state or regional conventions, these organizations often approved the boards of these educational institutions. As I completed my education and entered the teaching profession, the state conventions affiliated with the Southern Baptist Convention were contributing percentage-wise and dollar-wise a declining amount toward the overall cost of operation of the schools. At the same time as the Controversy was gaining steam, the boards of trustees, comprised of many conservative pastors and laymen, were gaining a much larger influence in the operation at many of these institutions. This trend continued as I entered the teaching profession.

Rev. Dick Belcher, pastor at First Baptist Church during my teenage years, helped me receive an athletic scholarship to Hannibal-La Grange Junior College (Hannibal-LaGrange) in Missouri. Although I did not make my high school basketball team, First Baptist Church sponsored a team in both the Baptist league and the YMCA League in the East St. Louis area. In the YMCA League I played against former college players, and this experience contributed to advancing my skills. In a game against the HLG junior varsity basketball team, I scored forty-four points, and received a scholarship offer to attend college and to play basketball. Running on the track team was added to my athletic commitment during my freshman year. I had been a factory worker for two years after high school graduation. An entirely new opportunity based upon an athletic scholarship came my way, and I am indebted to the many Baptists who made this possible.

I took advantage of the Southern Baptist commitment in providing so many educational institutions, and attended in succession HLG College, SWBC, and BU. As previously stated, I earned respectively, A.A., B.A., and Ph.D. degrees at these institutions. I completed my terminal degree in the summer of 1972, and soon began my career in higher education at SWBC. While a student over a consecutive nine-year period at these three institutions, I was exposed by numerous teachers to new ideas and interpretations, or perhaps put another way, new possibilities. None of these destroyed my faith. Rather, they challenged and enriched it. Moreover, they enabled me to continually redefine my faith in significant ways.

During my undergraduate years it seems that most of my learning was simply building a knowledge base from which to respond to future questions and issues. My major during these times was in the field of religion. Courses in Bible subjects primarily looked at content of specific collections of books. As far as I can remember, background and contextual examination was fairly-limited. At the same time my knowledge base expanded greatly. I took a variety of courses in religion topics, such as Old Testament and New Testament history, church history, Baptist history, comparative religions, philosophy, doctrine, and Greek.

I developed a deep interest in church history. I took my first church history course in my junior year, and a Baptist history course during my senior year. Both courses were taught by Dr. H. K. Neely, a superb and demanding teacher, and the fastest lecturer under whom I ever studied. My introduction to Baptist history previously came when Dick Belcher, my pastor in Washington Park, gave me a small, red-covered booklet by J. M. Carroll. It was titled *The Trail of Blood*. It was a compilation of lectures by the brother of B. H. Carroll, who led in the founding of Southwestern Baptist Theological Seminary. J. M. Carroll would become the first president of OBU, where I would teach for twenty-two years.

The pamphlet advocated the polemical and inaccurate view that Baptists could trace their beginnings back to the baptism of Jesus by John the Baptist in the Jordan River. It even had a pullout chart, which used little colored dots to trace the chronological movement of Christianity and Baptists. Non-Baptist movements were black dots. The Baptists and similar movements with different names that Carroll considered Baptists were represented by red dots (symbolic of Baptist history all the way back to the baptism of Jesus, and representative of the "trail of blood"). The influential theory sounded great, but could not stand up to the rigors of quality research.

Furthermore, the teaching may have been a response to the position of Dr. William H. Whitsitt, president and church history professor at Southern Seminary in Louisville, Kentucky. Whitsitt traced Baptist origins back to the sixteenth-century English Separatists. Whitsitt's removal as president of the seminary was led by B. H. Carroll, brother of J. M. Carroll. B. H. Carroll, thanks in large part to his defense of the "successionist" position tracing Baptists back to the Jordan River, became the first president of Southwestern Seminary in Fort Worth, Texas.

H. K.'s course was called the "Baptist Denomination." It provided an excellent foundation for understanding the history, theology, and organization of Baptists and Southern Baptists. It also served as a foundation for my further study of the Baptists, for teaching Baptist history, for research in Baptist topics and issues, and for publication of articles and books on the people called Baptist. Furthermore, the course was a major, contributing factor to my qualifications to serve in both denominational and societal organizations related to the discipline of Baptist history, especially in the years during the last two decades of the twentieth century, during a period labeled simply "The Controversy." This was the most defining influence in my lifetime in terms of shaping the identity of Baptists. And, my firing as a so-called liberal set the stage for my commitment to the Baptists during the last twenty-plus years of my career.

The roots of my changing views came during my educational journey, especially my time as a graduate student at Baylor. At BU I expanded my understanding of the options before me as a Christian and a Baptist. There were several defining moments.

Initially, I discovered that my fellow students and my professors reflected a diversity of thought and positions that I had not considered. I quickly decided it was better for me to ask questions, but also to listen to others and to learn and shape, or perhaps reshape, my own views. I observed that most if not all my fellow students and professors remained committed to their personal faith regardless of differences. I concluded that there was not a right or wrong in the diversity. In fact, I realized that such diversity was healthy and essential in the continual efforts to understand the place and dimensions of the importance of faith. In other words, the educational process was much more than simply an "academic" study of the variety of disciplines in the religion department.

During my first year at BU, I took about thirty hours of graduate courses. I found it interesting that BU did not require a Master's degree for acceptance into its rather new Ph.D. program. Thirty hours of graduate courses were required to enter the terminal program. Furthermore, admittance into the Ph.D. program required passing "qualifying exams" in nine different religious subjects. The topics included Old Testament history; New Testament history; biblical theology; systematic theology; historical theology; comparative religions; psychology of religion; ethics; and of course, church history.[16]

During my first two semesters I took courses which prepared me for the grueling exams that took place in the summer of 1968. Each exam was two hours long, and the nine exams were taken over a five-day period. It was a major grind, and resulted in a lot of anxiety, along with extensive preparation. After completion of the qualifying exams, I fortunately passed all nine tests and was admitted as a candidate to the Ph.D. program.

Of course, in preparation for the tests, I and other potential Ph.D. candidates seeking acceptance quizzed students who had already taken the qualifying exams about possible questions. In the two biblical courses it seemed that an essay was always asked about biblical backgrounds, especially in terms of canon, text, and translations. I dug into the topic and discovered a new world of knowledge, which shaped my understanding and approach to the biblical canon. This advanced study radically changed my perspective on the

---

[16] Thanks to Dr. Lynn McMillan, a fellow student at BU, who in 2023 confirmed the exam subjects.

Scriptures. How we got the Bible, and what this meant for interpreting it, became essential for my teaching approach in the years ahead. I became committed to learn more, and to share that learning with my future students.

This was my first important step in becoming a "liberal" in the minds of my conservative opposition in Missouri. For me, it was simply the outcome of gaining that good education which the Baptists in my home church had envisioned for me. In terms of the future Southern Baptist Convention Controversy, it moved me into a category of those called "moderates" during the historic conflict in the late-twentieth century.

While at BU I consecutively pastored two small churches. The first was Marquez Baptist Church in, where else, Marquez, Texas. This church in a small central Texas town was conservative theologically, yet also reflected a culture to which I was not accustomed. African Americans in the community were treated kindly by the members of the church. At the same time, they seemed to be relegated to a second-class citizenship. I first noticed this at the memorial service for one of the church's deacons. He was highly regarded in the Black community. Before the service many of them came to view the body and show their respect. However, just before the service began, all departed. I found this to be unusual and sad that they did not remain for the memorial of their good friend. My assumption was that it was not appropriate to do so, although I have no evidence of any official barriers.

The second incident related to the assassination of Dr. Martin Luther King Jr. on April 4, 1968. When I arrived at the church on the following Sunday, several deacons were in the parking area in front of the church. They were telling jokes about King and his assassination. I found this extremely disturbing, but said nothing and went inside to prepare for worship. I was bothered all week by what I had observed. The next Sunday I offered my resignation and did not return. This was not an act of courage. Rather, it resulted from confusion and the need to respond in the only way I knew how. I left. I suppose this was another defining moment in my movement toward a position of ethical liberalism.

My next pastorate was at First Baptist Church in Cranfills Gap, Texas. Overall, this turned out to be a positive and constructive experience. The first settlers in the community were Norwegian, and the Lutheran church was the largest congregation in the town of about 400 people. First Baptist was also a fairly-conservative congregation. I supplied the pulpit for several weeks, and the pastor search committee asked to interview me as a candidate. The first question they asked was whether Janis played the piano. My answer was "Yes." They swiftly moved to ask me to be the pastor. It seemed that good music was more essential than theological orthodoxy in terms of the needs of the congregation. After accepting the invitation to be pastor, Janis and I, along with our infant son Scott, moved into the church parsonage. I began to commute daily about fifty-five miles to BU.

During this time, I continued to be exposed to new ideas in my classes. In an Old Testament class taught by Dr. Edward Dalglish, we studied in-depth the book of Genesis. I had to rethink my simple and rather literalistic interpretation of the early chapters. I found myself challenging my traditional approach, where the creation narrative was seen as religious, scientific, and historical, all in one. That was what I was taught, and no other options were considered. In my church office one day, feeling the pressure of too many responsibilities, including student, pastor, husband, and father, I banged on my desk and cried out "What in the hell is going on here?" I surprised myself, but it was the most honest prayer to God I had ever uttered. I immediately began to refocus and put things into perspective.

I realized I could not do everything, but I could do some things that I could control. In terms of my views, I decided to go back and restudy Genesis 1-3 to reach my own conclusions. For starters, I simply kept rereading the text. By comparing Genesis 1 and 2, I soon accepted the position that there were two accounts of creation. I also determined that they were not nor were they intended to be scientific or historical accounts. They were what some called theological affirmation.

I also recognized that there were differences in the name used for God (*Elohim* translated "God" in Genesis 1:1-2:4a; and *YHWH Elohim* translated "Lord God" in the following verses of chapter 2). Just by reading and comparing the text, I realized that the order of creation was different in the two accounts and the emphases of a more universal view over against a more personal view was present. In Genesis 1 mankind was the culmination of creation. In chapter two Adam was the first of creation, followed by plants, animals, and then Eve. I had to ask myself why they were different.

In the end I moved away from literalism to a realization that there were many types of literature in the Scriptures, and this required different perspectives on the material. It was an eye opener, and quite liberating. I shared my changes in a sermon at First Baptist Church of Cranfills Gap. I no longer interpreted the Garden of Eden story literally, but symbolically. Adam and the translation of *"adam"* represented man, and Eve represented woman, or translated *"Mother of Living."* Interestingly, Ovie Dittrich, a lay preacher in First Baptist Church, Cranfills Gap, told me he could not accept my interpretation, but he continued to support me. Evelyn Sorenson, a grade school teacher who shared the same birthday with me, said that my views made sense to her for the first time, and she was glad to hear them.

The bottom line is that I practiced good Baptist freedom in studying and making up my own mind. I also recognized that Baptists could and should have dialogue over diverse opinions. I continue to treasure that understanding over fifty years later. From that time forward I would not fear asking questions, was open to new possibilities, and realized that the ability to change was a significant characteristic of growing. Furthermore, I concluded over the years that my new approach was an expression of being a good Baptist. I continue to practice these principles even in my twilight years.

## Teaching and Charges of Liberalism

BU was a life-changing but certainly not a not faith-destroying journey. In fact, my faith was much stronger, a result of my Baptist foundations that emphasized education and freedom. I received my Ph.D. in Religion with an emphasis on the History of Christianity during summer graduation in 1972. The next step came quickly.

I began teaching at SWBC in Missouri in the fall semester of the same year. I taught Old Testament history during the fall, and then New Testament history in the spring, along with an additional course each semester. At the beginning of both survey courses, I emphasized the development of the canon, text, and translation of the Scriptures. Like me, most of my students had been given a Bible, told it was the Word of God, and encouraged to study it to know the truth. I sought to impress upon my students the importance of understanding "how" the Scriptures came together. I taught about the development of the Old Testament and New Testament canons and the multitude of translations. My purpose was to assist them in interpreting the Bible as they sought to apply its teachings.

When arriving at the scriptural text, the orderly place to begin was Genesis. The book is a challenging place to initiate a study of the Old Testament, or more accurately the Hebrew Bible. Baptists and many other groups have engaged in polemical debate over creation and science throughout their history. In fact, major controversies in Baptist life have centered around creation, science, evolution, and other topics in a faith versus a scientific approach to biblical interpretation. It is a challenging book to begin a study of the Scriptures and the Old Testament, simply because of the literal foundations of many students, and the historical conflict in denominational life over Genesis and the creation stories. I was sensitive to where my students were in their respective journeys. At the same time, I exposed them to different and acceptable possibilities. Most of my students accepted my approach to examine different interpretations, but many did not.

During these early days of teaching, I began to point out that religion and science ask different questions. Religion wants to know "Who?" and "Why?" Science asks "How?" The questions are not necessarily contradictory. In fact, through the eyes of faith they can be seen as complementary.

Southern Baptists, however, have a history of disagreement over the questions related to Genesis and the creation textual material. Controversy often arose in the denomination, and the result was the adoption of confessional theological documents, which were intended to address concerns on one hand, and to ease tensions on the other.

In 1925 Southern Baptists, after eighty years of existence as a convention, produced their first confession of faith, the *Baptist Faith and Message*. The document resulted from conflict over evolution and science. Dr. E. Y. Mullins, president and theology professor of Southern Baptist Theological Seminary, led the convention through the dialogue and the attempt to impose a rigid theological approach over the interpretation of the Scriptures. A committee chaired by Mullins produced a statement which allowed for diversity by the adherents, while affirming the central place of the Bible in denominational life.

The storm abated for almost forty years but arose again in 1961. The first *Baptist Faith and Message* also included a preface which defined confessional theology. The statement would be included in the future revisions of the *Baptist Faith and Message*. It has been essential in understanding the role of confessions of faith in Baptist life.

Once again, a controversy arose over Genesis ignited over a publication in 1961 by the Southern Baptist Convention Sunday School Board's Broadman Press. Ralph Elliott's *The Message of Genesis*[17] immediately stirred up conflict. Elliott was a professor and chair of the Old Testament department at Midwestern Baptist Theological Seminary in Kansas City, Missouri. An uproar over his book took place during the 1962 Southern Baptist Convention annual meeting. A committee was appointed with Herschel Hobbs, pastor of First Baptist Church of Oklahoma City, as chair. A revised

---

[17] Ralph Elliott, *Message of Genesis* (Nashville: Broadman Press, 1961).

version of *the Baptist Faith and Message* was adopted without challenge in 1963. Again, the theological statement was a compromise effort to satisfy the diverse elements among Southern Baptists. It did for a few years, at least on the surface.

The Sunday School Board withdrew the publication of Elliott's book. He was directed by Midwestern Seminary not to seek a new publisher. However, Beacon Press published a paperback version. Interestingly, the company considered the book to be very conservative, but justified its publication based upon the need for academic freedom. Elliott was fired, not for heresy, but for "insubordination." He became an American Baptist pastor. He died at age ninety-seven in 2022.[18]

The Elliott controversy was my first exposure as a Baptist to theological controversy. Dick Belcher, my pastor of First Baptist Church, Washington Park, announced that he was attending the annual Southern Baptist Convention meeting in 1962. I remember that he was excited about dealing with the Elliott book and its controversial positions at the annual meeting. He returned from the meeting and reported to our church the success of the action taken by the messengers.

The 1963 *Baptist Faith and Message* became a confessional litmus test for both the "conservative" and "liberal" wings of the Southern Baptist Convention for many years. During the later years of my teaching career, I would often point out that I was initially considered a conservative for my affirmation of the 1963 *Baptist Faith and Message*, but during the years of the Controversy I was considered a "liberal" for taking the same position. Yesterday's orthodoxy became tomorrow's heresy, as evidenced when the years of conflict became a reality in Southern Baptist Convention life.

I find it ironic that in 1963 when the Southern Baptist Convention approved the first revision of the 1925 *Baptist Faith and Message*, I began my academic pursuit in the fall semester at HLG. A smoldering fire would continue beneath the surface in the ensuing years. Only in my early years as a professor at SWBC would I begin to recognize that a flame was about to burst forth in

---

[18] Mark Wingfield, "Ralph Elliott, Author of Genesis Commentary that Began the Southern Baptist Convention's Battle for the Bible, Dies," *Baptistnews.com*, 27 October 2022. Moreover, Brian Koonce noted that a panel of three conservative historians considered Elliott's book to be poison, as one panelist described it: Brian Koonce, "1961 Controversy over 'The Message of Genesis' Gets Baptist Historians' Reflections," *Baptistpress.org*, 16 September 2013.

more than two decades of theological and political controversy in the Southern Baptist Convention. I would find myself right in the middle of that fire.

After the Elliott controversy, conflict abated for a brief period. However, in 1969 while I was in the middle of my graduate school program at BU, controversy surfaced again over two Broadman Press publications. During that year the Sunday School Board published W. A. Criswell's *Why I Preach That the Bible Is Literally True*. Criswell was pastor of First Baptist Church of Dallas, Texas. The Association of Baptist Professors of Religion, an organization composed of Southern Baptist professors who taught at Baptist colleges, universities, and seminaries, criticized the book. Most of these educational institutions were in the eastern and southeastern United States. The action of the educators' organization resulted in developing suspicion of affiliated colleges and universities by Southern Baptist conservatives.[19]

Even greater controversy arose following publication of Volume 1 of the *Broadman Bible Commentary*.[20] G. Henton Davies, principal of Regent's Park College in Oxford, England, authored the commentary on Genesis. Major concern was directed toward Genesis 22:1-9. Davies advocated that God did not command Abraham to sacrifice Isaac. In 1970 during the annual meeting of the Southern Baptist Convention in Denver, the Sunday School Board was instructed to withdraw Volume I. Action by the convention messengers insisted that the Genesis commentary be "rewritten with due consideration to the conservative viewpoint." The Board asked Davies to rewrite the Genesis commentary. This did not resolve controversy. The St. Louis convention of 1971 narrowly voted to ask for a new writer. The Board enlisted Dr. Clyde T. Francisco of Southern Seminary. The revised edition of Volume 1 was published in 1972.[21]

I subscribed to a pre-release program to receive copies of the *Broadman Bible Commentary* series as volumes were published. I was still a student at Southwest Baptist. So, I received both the original volume followed by the revised version when it became available. I kept both volumes, as well as all the remaining set. Upon retirement from OBU in 2001, I forwarded to a

---

[19] W. A. Criswell, *Why I Preach That the Bible Is Literally True* (Nashville, TN: Broadman Press, 1969).
[20] G. Henton Davies, "Genesis," *Broadman Bible Commentary*, Vol. 1 (Nashville, TN: Broadman Press, 1969).
[21] Clyde T. Francisco, "Genesis," *Broadman Bible Commentary*, Vol. 1, rev. ed. (Nashville, TN: Broadman Press, 1972).

colleague the complete set, plus a copy of two other "heretical" or "banned" Broadman projects to a colleague and former student at OBU, Dr. Jerry Faught. One was the Broadman Press hardback version of Elliott's *Message of Genesis*.

The other writing was a copy of the galley proofs of H. Leon McBeth's centennial history of the Sunday School Board, *Celebrating Heritage and Hope* (1991). McBeth, a recognized Baptist historian at Southwestern Seminary, was enlisted by Broadman Press to write the centennial history. The volume was within a few weeks of being published and released when a controversial decision was made by the trustees of the Sunday School Board to stop the project from going forward. Conservatives criticized McBeth's treatment of the Board's president, Lloyd Elder. They wanted McBeth to provide a more critical evaluation of Elder, who was under fire resulting from the "Controversy" in the Southern Baptist Convention. Conservatives sought to control convention publications. Elder was eventually forced to resign, another casualty of the struggle for authority over Southern Baptist Convention agencies between the conservatives and the moderates in the convention.

Surprisingly, I obtained a copy of the galley proofs while teaching at OBU. One day I unexpectedly received in the mail a large, manila envelope holding a copy of the proofs of McBeth's writing. There was no information on who sent it. I read the entire 400-page plus document over the weekend. Then I had it bound. Upon retirement I passed it on to my younger colleague. I might add that as I read the unpublished material, I found it consistent with McBeth's reputation as a respected Baptist scholar whose writing and research reflected the highest standards of academic publications.

The controversies over these publications resulted from the organized concern within the convention for theological orthodoxy. My firing from SWBC, which resulted in the culmination of my contract in 1979, foretold things to come. It was an early warning of assaults upon educators and leaders in Southern Baptist life leading to open conflict in the convention in the next two decades.

Calls of doctrinal concern began to increase in the denomination. A group organized in March of 1973. The *Baptist Faith and Message* Fellowship arose in Atlanta, Georgia. The organization called for rigid adherence to the 1963 *Baptist Faith and Message*. It published the *Southern Baptist Journal*, an independent newspaper. Moderates in the convention, including myself, responded to these attacks by appealing to the preface of the 1963 *Baptist Faith and Message*. Although the revised confessional statement, especially the preface, was interpreted as a defense against encroaching creedalism, the attacks increased. In fact, Judge Paul Pressler, a major leader of the orthodoxy group, proposed that acceptance of the 1963 *Baptist Faith and Message* was a sure sign that a person was a liberal. The goal posts not only kept moving, they were getting narrower and narrower.

Anti-confessionalism continued to rise. Calls for orthodox theology affected educational institutions and Sunday School Board publications. Organized political activity gained momentum. Creedalism became the test of faith for many conservatives.

In 1979 Walter Shurden, church history professor of Southern Seminary, examined the thirty-one (at the time) Southern Baptist state conventions, and reported that only seven had officially adopted the 1963 *Baptist Faith and Message*. None required its employees to sign the statement. The Annuity Board used the 1963 *Baptist Faith and Message* as "guidelines." I am sure that recipients of monthly checks had doctrinal orthodoxy as a priority of the agency's distribution of funds. Even candidates for service under the Foreign Mission Board were not required to sign it. There were some restrictions for some employees in key positions at the Sunday School Board. Southern Baptist Convention seminaries demonstrated a growing sensitivity to the statement. Furthermore, none of the six convention commissions adopted the confession.[22]

Importantly, the preface to both the 1925 and the 1963 confessions, as well as the 2000 revision, affirmed the place of such statements in the denomination:

1. That they constitute a consensus of opinion of some Baptist body, large or small, for the general instruction and guidance of our own people and others concerning those articles of the Christian faith which are most surely held among us. They are not intended to add anything to the simple conditions of salvation revealed in the New Testament, viz., repentance towards God and faith in Jesus Christ as Saviour and Lord.

2. That we do not regard them as complete statements of our faith, having any quality of finality or infallibility. As in the past so in the future Baptists

---

[22] Walter B. Shurden, "Southern Baptist Responses to Their Confessional Statements," *Review and Expositor* 76, no.1 (1979): 80-81.

should hold themselves free to revise their statements of faith as may seem to them wise and expedient at any time.

3. That any group of Baptists, large or small, have the inherent right to draw up for themselves and publish to the world a confession of their faith whenever they may think it advisable to do so.

4. That the sole authority for faith and practice among Baptists is the Scriptures of the Old and New Testaments. Confessions are only guides in interpretation, having no authority over the conscience.

5. That they are statements of religious convictions, drawn from the Scriptures, and are not to be used to hamper freedom of thought or investigation in other realms of life.[23]

The prefaces of the 1925 and 1963 confessions additionally stated that "Baptists are a people who profess a living faith. This faith is rooted and grounded in Jesus Christ who is the 'same yesterday, today, and forever.' Therefore, the sole authority for faith and practice among Baptists is Jesus Christ whose will is revealed in the Holy Scriptures."[24] Unequivocally, theology for Southern Baptists arose from the faith commitment to the Lordship of Christ.

The 2000 *Baptist Faith and Message* deleted the position that the Lordship of Christ and his will is revealed in the Bible as the supreme authority for faith and practice among Baptists. It intentionally removed the statement that confessions have "no authority over the conscience." Significantly, these revisions affirmed that the authority of the Scriptures superseded the authority of Jesus. This in my opinion was a crucial change. For me, this reversal was "heretical," if you want to use the term. I will discuss this further in a later chapter.

Another creedal emphasis was evident. It stated that "Baptist churches, associations and general bodies have adopted confessions of faith as a witness to the world accountability. We are not embarrassed to state before the world that these are doctrines that we hold precious and essential to the Baptist tradition of faith and practice." The word "essential" affirms that the ultimate

---

[23] William L. Lumpkin and Bill J. Leonard, eds., *Baptist Confessions of Faith*, 2nd rev. ed. (Valley Forge, PA: Judson Press, 2011), 409-10.
[24] *Baptist Confessions of Faith*, 1963, 5.

test of faith for believers was changed from the authority of the Lordship of Jesus.

One only needed to follow the Scripture's teachings (as interpreted by the leaders of the convention) to be theologically correct. Who needed the leadership of Jesus through the promised Spirit in addressing contemporary issues not discussed in the Bible?[25] A pattern was now evident, which resulted in a more creedal understanding of confessions of faith. The Baptist emphasis on the positive attitude of such statements was now rejected as they became litmus tests for orthodoxy. Instead of the Baptist freedom to confess one's faith theologically, theology now was a test of doctrinal orthodoxy. Again, this theology would be defined by those in leadership positions.

Two other developments took place, which confirmed the replacement of a confessional approach to theology with creedalism. In 1998 there was debate over the addition of Article XVIII on "The Family." This was followed with the adoption of important revisions in the adoption of the 2000 *Baptist Faith and Message*. Both reflected moves away from traditional confessional theology toward more authoritative creedal interpretations of doctrinal statements. Decisions were based not upon history and tradition but by majority vote. Creedalism became the new norm in the Southern Baptist Convention.

In 2023 the Southern Baptist Convention's annual meeting held in New Orleans drove the final nail in the coffin of confessional theology. The votes of messengers legitimatized the creedal victory in the denomination's turn to usurp the authority of the local congregation in theologically expressing its faith. Messengers approved the first reading of a constitutional amendment prohibiting women to serve as pastors, adopted two supportive resolutions on the issue, and affirmed the expulsion of two churches from the convention—Saddleback Church in California and Fern Creek in Kentucky. Southern Seminary President R. Albert Mohler defended the action on biblical grounds, although former Saddleback pastor Rick Warren and Fern Creek pastor Linda Barnes Popum cited the same Bible to defend the practice of their respective congregations.

Not only were women senior pastors rejected but also the title was not to be used for women serving as children's pastor, youth pastor, associate pastor, and missions pastor. Both Warren and Popum "confessed" their

---

[25] Yarbrough and Kuykendall, *Southern Baptists*, 145-46.

conservative principles, but "Complementarianism" became the non-negotiable, orthodox interpretation of the churches affiliated with the Southern Baptist Convention. The preface of the *Baptist Faith and Message* was deemed unacceptable on matters voted on by the convention. Remarkably, the voting was not close. Fern Creek was considered no longer a part of the convention by a 91 percent majority. Saddleback was ousted by an 88 percent majority.[26] Not only had the Scriptures been elevated above the Lordship of Jesus in matters of theology, but in 2023 the messenger became more important than the message. The implications of this position will be discussed in Chapter 10.

I need to remind readers that in 2000 I published *Southern Baptists: A Historical, Ecclesiological, and Theological Heritage of a Confessional People*. In 2021 with the assistance of Dr. Michael Kuykendall, we edited and updated my earlier volume. *Southern Baptists: A History of a Confessional People* was published by McFarland Books in Jefferson, North Carolina. Kuykendall added the history of Southern Baptists between 2000 and 2021.

These two books cover thoroughly the following topics. The chapters on "A Heritage of Conflict (The Controversy)," "A Heritage of Change (The Restructuring of the Southern Baptist Convention)," and "A Theological Heritage (A Confessional People)" are essential sources in the following discussion, and in other parts of this volume, which discuss the context of my own pilgrimage and my interpretation of so much of not only my journey, but developments within the Southern Baptist Convention. Anyone who seeks to understand the history of the denomination conflict beginning in the 1970s, and the convention's restructuring in the 1990s is encouraged to read these chapters, plus the conclusion, which predicts the issues currently facing the contemporary Southern Baptist Convention.

During these challenging days I made my choices on who I was by what was going on in Baptist life. I understood Baptist history and applied that understanding to the courses which I taught at SWBC. During my subsequent years at OBU, I identified with the moderate movement in the Southern Baptist Convention. Those critical of me considered me a bleeding-heart liberal out to destroy the faith of my students. My colleagues and friends understood me to be a Southern Baptist committed to a rich denominational heritage, a capable Baptist historian, and an outspoken defender of both

---

[26] Mark Wingfield. "Anti-Egalitarian Forces Make Clean Sweep at Southern Baptist Convention Annual Meeting," *Baptistnews.com*, 14 June 2023.

biblical and Baptist principles. The context of my career was shaped significantly by what quickly became simply Controversy.

# Chapter 3

# Fired for Heresy!

Lessons Learned about Being Fired for Heresy

"There are worse things than being fired for heresy. One is not being fired. Two is actually being burned at the stake, when you are fired. Three is the idea that when someone accuses you of heresy, you must be doing something wrong." Slayden Yarbrough[27]

**Introduction: A Career in a World of Conflict**

Between the fall semester of 1972 and my retirement from teaching in 2001, my entire academic career took place as a rising controversy over theology and demands for orthodoxy developed in the Southern Baptist Convention. I consistently taught courses in Baptist history. Although most disciplines would produce anxiety on the part of professors of different disciplines, especially biblical studies, as a professor of Baptist history, I found the environment both invigorating and challenging. I felt compelled to examine the heritage of Baptists and Southern Baptists in greater depth each passing year. Furthermore, I felt the responsibility to confront the crises brought on by the Controversy in the Southern Baptist Convention by communicating in the classroom, in churches, and in publishing with as much clarity and conviction as possible, the history of Baptists and Southern Baptists.

Surprisingly, these years were the very best time to be a teacher and practitioner of Baptist history. I had to study Baptist history. I had to understand Baptist personalities and principles. I had to teach clearly who the Baptists were. And, I had to interpret what Baptist history had to offer to a denomination in conflict.

My journey through Baptist history and life raises the question. "Have you ever been fired for teaching heresy?" Probably not. But as I interpret events that occurred during my tenure at SWBC, I concluded that I was. In

---

[27] A paraphrase from Yarbrough, *We Coulda Been Killed!* 190.

retrospect, my loss of a teaching position was one of the best things professionally that ever happened to me, although considering a period of uncertainty as to my future, it did not seem so at the time.

## Principles of Teaching

Beginning in the fall semester of 1972 at SWBC I usually taught two religion courses every semester. Added to my teaching load was a course during a special one-month January term. I also often taught a course or two in summer school. My teaching career at Southwest Baptist for seven years covered a variety of courses. Included among my teaching assignments was an Old Testament History and Literature course. This description of the offering resulted from the need to avoid too much emphasis upon the biblical nature in the course title. If a student transferred to a public college or university, that student could receive transfer credit as a history offering. If the course had been classified as a religion offering, the class might not have been accepted for credit at a state institution. Of course, at a Baptist school a whole lot of Bible was included in the class. At the same time, I framed the biblical narrative in terms of the historical context of the ancient world.

I enjoyed teaching the Old Testament course, especially in terms of background in canon, text, and translation. Understanding these issues was important to me in my own development. I concluded that it would be to my students as well. They needed to understand how the current translations of the Bible came to be. Where did we get the Bible in terms of the selection of available writings over several centuries?

Furthermore, these texts were in Hebrew, and a little Aramaic. The New Testament books, of course, were written in Greek. Since most, presumably all, of my students were unable to read any of these languages, the question was "how did biblical manuscripts get into English?" A lecture on translations became an important part of the course. Studying all these topics would assist in students' understanding and the application of the Scriptures in their individual journeys of faith.

The results of my commitment to biblical backgrounds became evident early on. I quickly found myself in trouble. Literalism was demanded by many Baptist pastors and their churches. But my First Baptist Church of Washington Park friends had encouraged me to get an education. My Baptist professors had encouraged and taught me to think, and they contributed greatly to my personal development. I did both. The influence of these Baptists proved to be dangerous in the developing crisis in the denomination.

Slayden A. Yarbrough

I am not exactly sure when I began to be attacked for heretical teachings. I do remember a few incidents where I was called in to discuss some of my statements during my initial semester of teaching. I also must confess that I probably did not use the best judgment at times in terms of conversations with students, nor in my approach in lecturing. I was a student during a time when professors purposefully made controversial statements in class in order to grab the attention of students. Usually, meaningful dialogue would take place, and the result was a good educational experience. I followed this pattern in the classroom when I became a professor. But the educational world was changing in response to new challenges.

## Initial Accusations

The first charge against me came not from a class session but rather from a coffee break with students at the Student Union on the campus of SWBC. We were discussing worship and church services in a general sense. I commented that there were times that I could feel closer to God by withdrawing to the outdoors, perhaps even seeking solitude on a lake on Sunday morning. My position was to make the point that structured worship in a church setting was not the only option to seek and sense the presence of God. Nature was a viable option on occasion.

Shortly thereafter, Dr. H. K. Neely, my dean, called me into his office. Rev. Bill Dudley had contacted him. He charged me with saying that one did not need to go to church on Sundays to worship God. Of course, the statement was true. But it was taken totally out of context and missed my point completely. I never advocated not attending church worship. I simply said that there might be a time that one could experience and worship God in the world surrounding us, rather than only by gathering in a sanctuary. I am confident this initial complaint came very early in my career at SWBC, during my first year and probably during my first semester at the college.

As controversy over me developed, looking back it seems clear that a strategy of right-wing pastors was to use ministerial students at Baptist institutions as spies against suspected liberals in the religion department. Such an approach is unethical. It shapes the character of students into heresy hunters rather than learners. It results in students reporting back information that is usually taken out of context and often misunderstood. A pattern of students seeking unacceptable statements made by me and reporting them back to their pastor was now established. Of course, I obliged by raising issues that seemed important to me in terms of leading the students to develop as critical thinkers in their educational pursuits. My own professors had provided good models for me in this regard.

Another example occurred during my last few years at SWBC. I was lecturing on the biblical canon and how it came to be. In terms of the New Testament, I pointed out that there were some Christian leaders in the second, third, and early fourth centuries, who disputed certain books as authoritative, such as Hebrews, James, 2 Peter, 2 & 3 John, Jude, and Revelation. At the same time some early theologians accepted the authority of non-canonical books, such as *The Didache (The Teachings of the Twelve Apostles)*, the *Epistle of Barnabas*, and the *Shepherd of Hermas*.

Within thirty minutes after the class ended, I was called into the academic vice-president's office. Dr. G H Surrette immediately asked me why I was teaching that the *Epistle of Barnabas* should be included in the New Testament canon. Of course, I had not said that. This charge confirmed the truth of a line from Simon and Garfunkel's "The Boxer," which stated "a man hears what he wants to hear, and disregards the rest."[28] The student heard what he wanted to hear and reported it back to his pastor. I immediately defended myself by denying that I had said this. I pointed out to the academic vice-president that I concluded the lecture by stating that I believed not only in inspiration of the writings of the twenty-seven New Testament books, but also in the collecting and preservation of them. You cannot be any more orthodox than this on the New Testament canon. But the issue was becoming not my positions, which I was able to defend well, but simply the continued accusations.

**Letters and Phone Conversations**

I mentioned at the beginning of the previous chapter two things related to a telephone call during my first semester teaching at OBU. First, after a call from Bill Dudley, the pastor who was convinced that I was a liberal heretic but who apologized for his role in having me fired, sent upon my request his file of letters and summaries of phone conversations between himself and SWBC administrators. Second, Dudley previously began to call and write administrators at Southwest, especially after attending a "School of the Prophets" sponsored by Criswell Baptist Institute. The school began in 1971

---

[28] Paul Simon, "The Boxer," Columbia Records, released 21 March 1969, vs. 1.

and was renamed Criswell College in 1985. Dr. Paige Patterson became president in 1975.[29]

As previously related, Bill told H. K. that during one of the "School of the Prophets" sessions, Patterson basically told the participants to "write, call, call, write until you get something done" about liberal teachers. Bill, who was already attacking me, was inspired to increase his attacks. He now practiced what Patterson preached, as evidenced by the letters and phone descriptions he sent me. The presentation under Patterson probably took place between 1974 and 1977, based upon the installation of him as president and the first of Dudley's letters to SWBC administrators. It certainly fits the time framework of rising developments in the Southern Baptist Convention leading up to the Controversy.

The earliest letter from Dudley to SWBC President James Sells was dated December 15, 1976.[30] He was following up on a conversation which he had with Sells on December 13, 1976, in Jefferson City, Missouri. It presumably was held at the headquarters of the Missouri Baptist Convention in the state capitol. The topic of the letter to Sells was my "liberal positions" which various students had reported to their pastors. Let me reiterate that young students were impressionable and easily influenced to engage in a campaign to root out perceived liberalism in a conservative institution of higher education. Most college students lack the knowledge and experience to properly evaluate a professor's theological orthodoxy. This is an important reason to pursue an education and to gain critical thinking skills.

I recall that my fellow students and I spent time discussing the positions of religion professors during our own educational pursuits. It contributed to our developing positions in the educational process. But we never became participants in a strategy to have our professors fired.

Dudley attributed my liberal views as being revealed primarily in my Old and New Testament history classes. He added that "most of the people in our Missouri Baptist Churches would not appreciate some of the teachings that have been credited to him." No specific examples were given. Dudley concluded his letter affirming his and his church's love for SWBC, adding

---

[29] See https://www.criswell.edu.about/history-and-heritage/.
[30] Rev. Bill Dudley, letter to Dr. James Sells, President, SWBC, December 15, 1976.

that "we do not expect we could all ever agree on everything but a man who teaches the Bible ought to believe it is so."[31]

In defense of my "teaching," I would point out that during my seven years at SWBC, I served as interim pastor of more than a dozen churches, served as pulpit supply at many more congregations, and spoke at numerous associational and other Missouri Baptist organizations. I was aware of no complaints at any time from any of my positions taken at these gatherings. Furthermore, after the news of my release at SWBC came out, both members and pastors from such churches came to my defense and support. At the same time, the strategy recommended at the "School of the Prophets" by Patterson, and reflected in Dudley's first letter, was now aggressively being practiced, and eventually would prove successful.

In a January 19, 1977, letter to Sells, Dudley expressed appreciation for the way that my situation was being handled. He referenced two discussions with H. K. Neely, in which he stated his position that I "be not hurt but guided away from my 'liberalism' into a firmer position." H. K. was genuinely appreciated by Baptist pastors in Southwest Missouri. He was also very supportive of me and diplomatically and professionally balanced his relationship with churches and pastors. At the same time, he worked hard at encouraging and supporting me.[32]

Sells forwarded a copy of Dudley's January 19, 1977, letter to me. At the top he addressed a handwritten note to me. It stated: "Dear Slayden! All kinds of things hit my desk— I have not wanted to hurt anyone in this rather - I believe it is important that we know where we are – thanx to you & others for dealing with this so forthfully [sic]."

On February 14, Dudley visited me in my office on campus. H. K. had recommended that he do so. In a later note he recalled that we had an honest discussion about our different views. He sent a personal letter to me dated February 10, 1977. While being cordial, he also wrote that "To be truthful. Our differences are quite wide, but I want to do what is right for you and for the students as well as for the college—a college that I dearly love." He added, "I am sorry that you cannot accept, as historical fact, these early chapters of Genesis." These comments indicated that he accepted a literal and historical

---

[31] Dudley to Sells, December 15, 1976.
[32] Rev. Bill Dudley, letter to Dr. James Sells, January 19. 1977.

interpretation of the Genesis creation material, and that he recognized no other possible interpretations of the stories.[33] I replied in a letter dated March 2, 1977, pointing out that I considered non-biblical material in providing background, not only to Genesis but in the same way as I sought "to understand what Paul was saying, or James, or Luke, or the prophets, etc."[34]

In a letter to Sells on May 3, 1977, Dudley wrote a long letter commending by name current and past professors who taught Old Testament courses at SWBC. He began by stating that "I would especially like to say a word of appreciation in relation to the Bible or Christianity Department (I only know of one weak link in it)." It is obvious who that "weak link" happened to be. He went on to commend my colleagues, starting with Dr. Surrette, who had been professor of Old Testament prior to his appointment as academic dean. He had been my Old Testament professor when I was a student at Southwest; Dr. Tom Pratt, a fellow graduate of the Ph.D. religion program at BU; Dr. Harry Hunt, one of my very best friends at Southwest and one of the most conservative teachers on the faculty; and Dr. Gary Galeotti, the current Old Testament professor at that time of Dudley's letter to Sells. As he often did with his other letters, Dudley sent copies to Surrette and Neely.[35]

Over the years I have received testimonies from some of my students. They told me that my views during the Old Testament class opened their eyes to other possibilities. They often changed the direction of their interpretations of not only the Genesis material but the rest of the Bible itself. None of them said that I destroyed their faith. On the contrary, they confirmed that I enhanced it.

Included in the Dudley file was a copy of a letter dated February 2, 1977, from another pastor and SWBC student, Dave Williams of Finey Baptist Church of Deepwater, Missouri. He wrote to Sells of his and his church's concern of "reports of a few faculty members." His accusation stated that "there is the liberal teaching concerning Biblical error, anti-supernaturalism, and the historicity of Genesis, of Dr. Yarbrough in his Old and New Testament classes (Fall/76)."

---

[33] Rev. Bill Dudley, letter to Dr. Slayden Yarbrough, February 10, 1977.
[34] Slayden Yarbrough, letter to Rev. Bill Dudley, March 2, 1977.
[35] Rev. Bill Dudley, letter to Dr. James Sells, May 3, 1977.

He also criticized Dr. Carl Huser of the science department for evolutionary teaching. Once again science and religion were being pitted against each other as a test of faith. Williams described the accusations against me and my colleague as "dangerous teachings." He stated that "it is the confusion and spiritual damage that could be caused in the lives of students that disturbs us." He concluded that he hoped the college would "continue to uphold the tradition of Baptist beliefs and principles, as you have in the past."[36]

My defense is that by now I was teaching the course in the Baptist denomination regularly. During my tenure at SWBC, I also developed a sermon entitled "Southern Baptists: Who Are We?" This presentation primarily included detailed information on Southern Baptist history, theology, and mission and ministry organizations and their contributions. The sermon was widely accepted when I spoke in the churches in Missouri, and later in Oklahoma.

The sermon also became the foundation for a series of lectures on the denomination delivered in Baptist meetings, a series of articles in the *Oklahoma Baptist Chronicle*, and a book resulting from these articles entitled *Southern Baptists: Who Are We?* My variety of presentations were built upon an appreciation for Southern Baptists, which I developed in Neely's class on the Baptist denomination taken during my senior year at SWBC. My service while at OBU as a board member and then later as interim executive director of the SBC Historical Commission, followed by my role as executive director of the SBHS, affirmed my recognized credentials as a teacher and advocate of the historic role and interpretation of Baptist history.

Issues over my teachings continued into the fall semester of 1977. On November 8, Dudley sent a letter to Surrette. He referenced a call with Rev. Roy Jerrell, pastor of First Baptist Church in Mt. Vernon, Missouri, and a trustee of the college. Jerrell had met with me and Neely and discussed the accusations against me.[37] The decision was made for me to stop teaching Old Testament history in the future. My recollection is that I was not a part of that decision, but when the next semester's schedule came out, I observed that I was not listed to teach the class. I asked Neely if that was a decision that had been made to resolve Dudley's concerns. He confirmed my analysis,

---

[36] Rev. Dave Williams, letter to Dr. James Sells, February 2, 1977.
[37] Rev. Bill Dudley, letter to Dr. G H Surrette, November 8, 1977.

and that decision was okay with me, although it was one of my favorite courses.

However, Dudley's complaints soon moved beyond my Old Testament class to my courses in Baptist history and church and state. He even mentioned a lecture in an anthropology class (which I did not teach, and a class in which I never recalled having served as a guest professor from the religion faculty). Apparently, students from his church were now looking for heresy in all my classes, and then reporting back to him.

Dudley did not mention any specific issues. At the same time, he asked Surrette if it would be best to "just call the matter to the attention of the Board of Trustees?" He indicated that he had promised Jerrell that he would not talk to any other trustees until he talked with him again. He also referenced the attacks on Dr. David Moore, church history professor at William Jewell College, who was openly being condemned in the press. Dudley simply referred to "a professor at William Jewell."[38] It was now apparent to me that I could not avoid further scrutiny of my classes, and that a generation of future heresy hunters was in the making.

In a letter dated November 27, 1978, to Jerrell, Dudley expressed his concern that "the problem with Dr. Yarbrough" was not resolved. He cited the introduction to a class I was teaching on missions on February 14. He stated that I told students that I "could not teach what I believed because it differed from the administration. I suppose this means Dr. Surrette."[39] In a handwritten note on the side of the letter, I had written "I did not say this. I talked with the student (who was the source of Dudley's accusation.) I said that another faculty member (one of my best friends) and I disagreed on the concept of foreknowledge. I was lecturing on the concept of election or chosen-ness as related to missions." I am sure that the friend was Harry Hunt. Once again, a student looking for heresy in my teachings either was not paying attention or misunderstood what I was saying, and reported back to Dudley.

Matters began to accelerate both from Dudley's efforts to force the administration to act aggressively and remove me from the faculty, and in terms of my own initiatives to be supported by the administration. On

---

[38] Dudley to Surrette, November 8, 1977.
[39] Rev. Bill Dudley, letter to Rev. Roy Jerrell, November 27, 1978.

February 28, Dudley wrote to Surrette and copied to Jerrell, following up with the charges from my missions' class, which he had addressed with Jerrell.[40]

Dudley's passion against my teachings was evident in the letter. He wrote that "It is a terrible thing to teach or not to teach a certain thing to keep a man's job." He added that "we are entitled to have a good Bible believing and Bible teaching college in Missouri and I do not know one better than SWBC."[41] He was comparing the school with William Jewell College in Liberty, which is evident in a later statement in this letter.

Dudley then included a statement that confirmed my belief when a few years later he called me while I was at OBU. I would ask him for his file on me, and he sent it. In his letter of February 28, he stated that "I have kept a file of my correspondence with Dr. Sells, Dr. Yarbrough, you and Rev. Roy Jerrell from December 15, 1977 through February 28, 1978."[42]

At this time, he took the communication with Surrette to a new level, the proverbial "line-in-the-sand" position. He asked "What do you think about my making copies of this file and sending them to each member of the Board of Trustees and a set to Bob Terry?" Bob Terry was the highly-respected editor of the Missouri Baptist Convention newspaper, the *Word & Way*. If Dudley took this action and if Terry published an article related to my story, then the accusations against me would go public. This was already happening in relation to David Moore at William Jewell College. Dudley continued "All efforts have been kept within the SWBC administration to this point and this would still keep it there with the exception of Bob, and would give the trustees an opportunity to know what has transpired."[43]

In his concluding paragraph, Dudley clearly framed the matter. He wrote "I do not believe there is any point in waiting any longer. Dr. Yarbrough does not agree with the views, as I see it, of Southwest supporters and should not teach any further after this term." The ball was now in the court of the administration of SWBC. Dudley was backing them into a corner.[44]

---

[40] Rev. Bill Dudley, letter to Dr. G H Surrette, February 28, 1978.
[41] Dudley to Surrette, February 28, 1978.
[42] Dudley to Surrette, February 28, 1978.
[43] Dudley to Surrette, February 28, 1978.
[44] Dudley to Surrette, February 28, 1978.

In Dudley's files he included a note written from memory on November 20, 1979. Surrette called him on March 2, 1978, in response to the February 28 letter. He requested a personal conversation with Bill before he sent his file on me. Surrette then called him on March 7 or 8. He asked Dudley to make no further comments on me or my teachings until after the end of May, 1978. If he was not satisfied, then he could do as he pleased. Dudley agreed. He was also asked to reply to any questions about my situation by saying that "Dr. Surrette is taking care of it and let it go with no additional comment."[45]

**Tenure and Action of the Board of Trustees**

I was now convinced that a decision about my future had been made and would be recommended to the board of trustees at their meeting during the graduation period in the spring of 1978. What is ironic is that the solution for administrative and trustee action was initiated by me because I also would pressure them to render a decision. Whether a decision had been made on me by March 2 is not clear. It was obvious, however, that by March 7 or 8, Dr. Surrette was promising Dudley that his concerns were being addressed in a satisfactory manner.

On March 3, in between Surrette's two calls, I sent a memo to Neely, which he in turn forwarded to Surrette, the academic vice-president. I carefully laid out my case that according to the faculty handbook, tenure should have been automatic with my seventh contract with the school. The handbook stated that a faculty member in an administrative position who had faculty rank would automatically receive tenure unless the contract said that he or she would not be eligible. This was my case.[46]

An article in the *Bolivar Herald-Free Press*, dated February 16, 1978, entitled "Garrett out at SWBC" described a situation I considered to be equivalent to my circumstances. Howard Garrett was the men's basketball coach. The article citing information from the SWBC public relations office stated "Had Garrett been offered a contract for the coming year he would have gone on tenure at the college." He received three years credit when he began coaching. The article stated the school policy that "Tenure is granted after six years if

---

[45] Personal note of November 20, 1978, of Bill Dudley recalling a phone conversation with Dr. G H Surrette on March 2, 1978.
[46] Slayden Yarbrough, memo to Dr. H. K. Neely, March 3, 1978, which he forwarded to Dr. G H Surrette.

faculty members meet all criteria."[47] The rationale for firing the basketball coach was consistent with my assertion that according to the faculty handbook, tenure was automatic once a faculty member received a seventh contract.

I had been offered my seventh contract, signed it, and returned it to the academic vice-president's office. The article in the *Bolivar Herald-Free Press* appeared before I sent the memo requesting tenure to Neely, which he forwarded to Surrette. In my memo to Neely, I pointed out that two faculty members who came during the same year that I was employed received tenure. I also pointed out that I was required to teach courses in the religion department, and that I had the rank of assistant professor of religion. I quoted the faculty handbook, which was provided to me when I began my appointment at Southwest, by including the statement on tenure in my memo, which read:

Staff members whose duties are primarily administrative, not teaching or research, may be granted faculty rank and faculty standing. Where appropriate to their duties, these persons shall have academic freedom, but they are not necessarily eligible for academic tenure as defined above. If a staff member appointed to one of these positions is not to be considered eligible for academic tenure, this judgment is to be communicated to the person at the time of his appointment and clearly communicated in his contract.[48]

I added that I assumed my failure to receive tenure was an oversight. I requested an examination of my circumstance, with the assumption that they would correct the error and grant my tenure. After all, I had a signed contract for my seventh year at the school. Looking back, I should have been more direct, although I am now certain that this assertion would have made no difference in the eventual outcome. I was naïve in thinking that the administration and trustees would honor my request and award me tenure. After all, I quoted the faculty handbook by chapter and verse. I was convinced that the defense of my case was valid. I still am, of course.

---

[47] "Garrett out at SWBC," *Bolivar Herald-Free Press*, 19 February 1978, 1-C.
[48] Yarbrough, memo to Neely, March 3, 1978, containing direct quote from the Faculty Handbook on tenure.

Furthermore, my accusers should have appreciated my proof-texting of my assertions.

On March 7, 1978, I received a memo from Surrette indicating that he had received my memo to Neely. He replied that he would investigate the matter.[49] This is the same day or the day before that he called Dudley a second time, and asked him to hold off on any further action until the end of May, promising action that he assumed would please him. My memo provided the administration with the strategy to withhold tenure from me. I had bought my own rope to my hanging.

I find it interesting that the first real clue to my being fired at SWBC came not from the administration but from a student. Late during the spring semester of 1978 before my class in the Baptist Denomination began, a student raised a question. He asked "Is it true that you are not coming back?" I laughed it off, and rightly so. I had a signed contract for the 1978-79 school year. I had received no communication from the administration that this would not be honored. After all, it was a legal, binding contract.

But I soon found out that the student's information, which he said came from his pastor, in the end was accurate. I do not know who that pastor was, and did not pursue it. My contract for the upcoming year was set and would be honored. However, I would not be granted tenure, and this would be my final contract. Call it what you may, but the bottom line is that I would not be returning after the spring of 1979. I would not receive tenure, regardless of what the faculty handbook said about my request. In other words, in my understanding of the trustees' and the administration's action, I would be fired. The firing was simply delayed until my contract expired.

A sequence of events took place which led up to tenure being denied. On April 19 I sent Surrette another memo, inquiring about the status of my request for tenure. However, since I had heard nothing back, I asked that the matter be pursued before the next board meeting, so that my concerns would be addressed rather than waiting until the following board meeting scheduled for November.[50] This was a misguided request on my part.

---

[49] G H Surrette, memo on tenure to Slayden Yarbrough, March 7, 1978.
[50] Slayden Yarbrough, memo to G H Surrette, April 19, 1978.

On May 22, 1978, I received a reply from Surrette. He affirmed that a motion was formulated and adopted by the board of trustees. It stated "That the Board of Trustees of SWBC considered and discussed tenure consideration for Dr. Yarbrough and determined, 1) Not to grant tenure, and 2) that Dr. Yarbrough be notified, and 3) that it be understood that the college will fulfill its obligations for 1978-1979." Surrette then pledged to be as helpful as he could during the summer and in the year 1978-1979.[51]

Often when a person is fired, they change the lock on your office door. They give you a deadline to move everything out of your office. And, you exit in shame, or at least anger. In my case, I not only was allowed to finish the semester, and my contract to teach the next school year, 1978-79, was honored. But the bottom line was still that I was being let go, even with a soft landing.

It might be argued that I was not fired. I simply was not given tenure by the trustees. I would argue that Rev. Bill Dudley was convinced that I was fired. His phone call to me in Oklahoma, and the evidence he forwarded to me in his file on me containing letters and phone conversations affirm that the action taken by the administration and trustees was a result of Dudley and other pastors demands that I be fired, and that my request for tenure provided them with the rationale to take action that pleased my attackers.

Furthermore, Dudley's initial conversation with me when I was at OBU clearly revealed that he believed that he was asked to lie about the reason for my dismissal. He was convinced that I was fired for heretical teachings, but the tenure issue provided the institution with a rationale that would allow the school to avoid a messy public conflict in the rising division in the Southern Baptist Convention. It had already begun when I began my career at Southwest.

On a more positive note, I was not without my defenders. Rev. Lewis Krause, a former Mennonite, and at the time pastor of First Baptist Church of Camdenton, Missouri, and Rev. Glen Pence, pastor of First Baptist Church of Buffalo, Missouri, met with Sells, and defended me. John Duncan, Minister of Music at First Baptist Church of Mountain View, Missouri, plus several other Southern Baptists in the state sent letters affirming my

---

[51] Dr. G H Surrette, memo to Dr. Slayden Yarbrough, May 28, 1978.

contributions to their churches in service of pulpit supply, interim pastor, and the education of their students.[52]

Perhaps my most affirming show of support came from Doyl Shepherd, chairman of the deacons at First Baptist Church of Monett, Missouri. I served as interim pastor there during my first year at Southwest, and as I neared the end of my days at Southwest, I was completing a second service as interim at the church in the same capacity. Doyl was a Baptist layman. He was a quiet and effective leader in the church and among the deacons. He was a pig farmer by vocation. In other words, in my mind he was in the "salt of the earth" category for followers of Jesus.

After he found out about my situation at Southwest, he on behalf of the deacons, wrote Sells, and copied his letter to Surrette, Neely, and three pastors and trustees of the college. He portrayed my work with the church. He described my efforts at recruiting students from the congregation to the college, leading the church to include Southwest in its annual budget, how I had led one couple to include the institution significantly in their estate plans, and how I encouraged the church to contribute $3,000 to its chapel construction campaign. He then asked why the action had been taken against me. He affirmed that I was more than capable in serving First Baptist, and that surely the same could be said in terms of my contributions to the school. He asked for a written response to share with the church.[53]

Sells replied with a glowing account of my relationship to Southwest, but that I had pressed for tenure, and that the board had decided that it was not yet time.[54] Doyl related to me that he responded back, telling Sells that "You did not answer my question." The question was, of course, "Why was this action taken?" Again, Sells said nothing negative, but simply restated that I had made the decision to press the issue. Nothing was going to change, but my respect for Doyl, and friends and pastors who came to my defense continue to be appreciated by me.

The official reason for my not receiving a contract after the 1978-79 school year was that I had demanded tenure. The trustees did not accept my request, voted not to grant tenure, and therefore no further contracts were offered.

---

[52] I have several copies of letters of support sent by friends and ministers to administrators and trustees of Southwest Baptist College.
[53] Doyl Shepherd, letter to Dr. James Sells, April 10, 1979.
[54] Dr. James Sells, letter to Doyl Shepherd, April 12, 1979.

Correspondence provided to me by Dudley, and transcribed recollections of his phone conversations and meetings with administrators and trustees of Southwest, confirmed time and again a "great emphasis" upon the position that the question was tenure. Dudley, however, felt guilt over being asked to affirm the official rationale that the issue was tenure. He was convinced that it was not, but rather I was fired over my heretical opinions about the Bible. I would add that his threat to directly take the matter to the trustees put the administration in an untenable position.

My request for board review of my tenure status gave administrators a way out. They were between the proverbial rock and a hard place. They asked questions, informed me of accusations, but never accused me of being a heretic. At the same time, standing up to a pastor and other pastors was a part of a new environment, where the accusers would not be satisfied.

Dudley's phone call to me during my first semester at OBU, his sending to me copies of communications with Southwest administrators and trustees to back up his efforts against me, and his desire to clear his conscience and set the record straight provided me with the opportunity to make my case. I can without hesitation state that I was fired because of the charges made against me, not necessarily because I was considered guilty by the school officials. My request for tenure does not change that dynamic. Dudley was pleased with the action. He was not pleased with the insistence to make sure that he stated that tenure was the issue.

On November 19, 1979, I received a follow-up letter from Dudley. He was sending me his file on my situation and requested that I be cautious in how I used it. He believed that it could be harmful to the college, but that I had the right to see it. He pleaded with me not to bring harm to the college. I read the documents, then filed them away. I returned to them for the first time over forty-five years later, as I began to research material for this book. One sentence stands out from his letter. He wrote that "You should have been dismissed from the school but the grounds used were less than honest, in my opinion. You can be assured that I am willing to state to anyone, if needed, the facts as I see them."[55] In a follow-up letter the next day, he once again

---

[55] Rev. Bill Dudley, letter to Dr. Slayden Yarbrough, November 19, 1979.

stated his belief that I should have been fired, and again expressed that he rejected the rationale for the action as being a question of tenure.[56]

The story, however, did not end at this point. On October 25, 1980, Dudley wrote me once more. He expressed regret that Dr. Neely had left Southwest for a position at Hardin-Simmons University in Abilene, Texas. He confessed that his actions in relation to me contributed to H. K.'s departure. He then added the following statement. "Dr. Yarbrough, you still should be at SWBC."[57] I will describe this letter in greater detail in the next chapter.

## Evaluating my Future as a Baptist

During my last contract year, I candidly questioned whether I should remain a Southern Baptist. My entire spiritual journey traveled through the local church, three educational institutions, and seven years on the faculty and staff of my alma mater. But now in my mind and the mind of my accuser, I had been dismissed for heresy, and the question was whether I should move on. During the months ahead, and while I remained on the faculty until the completion of my final contract, I kept asking the question on whether I had rejected my denominational roots, and whether being Baptist was no longer a consideration. It was an extremely important and personal question.

By now I was a good Baptist historian. I had moved a long way from when Rev. Belcher, my home church pastor in Washington Park, gave me a copy of J. M. Carroll's *Trail of Blood*, the small pamphlet that claimed Baptists could trace their history back to the baptism of Jesus by John the Baptist in the Jordan River. I now understood that Baptists appeared out of English Separatism in the early seventeenth century. I examined the historical, theological, and practical advances and changes of the movement over almost four centuries. I had been taught well by Neely in the course on the Baptist denomination at SWBC during my senior year.

Furthermore, upon my return to teach at the college in 1972, Dr. Neely assigned me to teach the course on a regular basis. In so doing, I found myself committed to the rich heritage of the movement. Moreover, during my years at SWBC I wrote and presented my sermon entitled "Southern Baptists: Who Are We?" As mentioned previously, I gave a thorough overview of the

---

[56] Rev. Bill Dudley, letter to Dr. Slayden Yarbrough, November 20, 1979.
[57] Rev. Bill Dudley, letter to Dr. Slayden Yarbrough, October 25, 1980.

movement historically, theologically, and practically (in terms of the denominational organizations and institutions that arose). After moving to OBU, this sermon became the basis for an early book by the same title. It also became the foundation for another book on Southern Baptists in 2000, and then an edited treatment and expansion in 2021 by myself and Mike Kuykendall.

These experiences and preparations strengthened my commitment to the essential characteristics and contributions of the denomination. In my self-examination I never wavered on the biblical and Baptist principle of justification by faith alone. I deepened my commitment to the most significant beliefs and principles of Baptists. They included justification by faith in Jesus, commitment to the Scriptures, or written Word, as the written guide for faith and practice; freedom though faith in Christ; confessional, not creedal theology; the autonomy and freedom of the local church under the Lordship of Jesus, as well as voluntary cooperation with like-minded congregations; separation of church and state, rooted in religious liberty; and the freedom to organize and develop organizations and institutions as needed, committed to carrying out the command to be "witnesses both in Jerusalem and in all Judea, and Samaria, and as far as the remotest part of the earth" (Acts 1:8 NASB). Remarkably, my interpretations and understanding of these principles resulted in my being considered a liberal in the eyes of those committed to orthodoxy and the pursuit of heresy. I plead guilty on all counts.

## Where have you come from, and where are you going?

I find comfort in the question of the angel of the Lord to Hagar in Genesis 16:7-8, "Hagar, Sarai's slave woman, from where have you come, and where are you going?" (NASB). As she was fleeing an oppressive situation with Sarah, pregnant with a child who we would know as Ishmael, and confused about her identity, she was asked this important question or, is it two questions? She was requested to look at her past, where she had been, and its effect upon where she was now. Then she was directed to look to the future and determine what direction she should travel in the days ahead. Interestingly, she went back home to Abraham and Sarah.

I can identify with her dilemma in a lot of ways. After a period of self-evaluation, I accepted the conclusion that I liked being a Baptist despite all its shortcomings. I determined to stay the course as long as I could. I honestly believed that I had a lot to offer the Baptist movement. That would, however, necessitate finding a new opportunity to teach. I approached that task aggressively, even as one opportunity after another proved futile. The odds of finding a new position were not good, especially if word of my circumstances in Missouri became well known.

My service at the university ended in May, 1979. One month later, in June, the Controversy in the Southern Baptist Convention officially burst onto the scene during the annual convention. In my case, it had already arrived during my time at SWBC. Furthermore, I still was looking for a teaching position as the fall semester rapidly approached. My future as a college professor was uncertain, and certainly not promising. In fact, I had traveled many times in the past year, following clues to potential possibilities. None worked out. The window for finding a teaching position for the fall semester in 1979 was rapidly closing. My future as a religion and Baptist history professor lacked any certainty.

# Chapter Four

# In Search Of A Teaching Position

George W. Truett On Baptist Education

"The time has come as never before; our beloved denomination should worthily go out to its world task as a teaching denomination."58

## Introduction: Failed Efforts to Find a Job Anywhere

Beginning in 1978 and into 1979, the year of my final contract at SWBC, I began an aggressive search for a new teaching position. I contacted friends at other institutions, registered with the Education Commission of the Southern Baptist Convention, searched professional listings for possible openings, sent letters of inquiry to many Southern Baptist institutions, and even visited several schools hoping that a position might be available. Much of the following information is from memory, so its detailed accuracy cannot be documented. But the basics of my search are correct.

I took a trip south and contacted William Carey College in Hattiesburg, Mississippi, which had an opening in the religion department. George Williams, a good friend who worked in the financial aid department for students, came along and helped me drive. It would be filled with an alumnus of the institution. I went from there to New Orleans Baptist Theological Seminary, but again no opening was available. Interestingly, the school would play an important, if unintended, role in my next teaching position.

I also made a trip to California and contacted Dr. Morgan Patterson, the academic vice president at Golden Gate Baptist Theological Seminary in Mill Valley, California. Dr. Patterson previously served as church history professor at Southern Seminary in Louisville, Kentucky. He later would be appointed as president of Georgetown College in Kentucky. I consider him

---

58 George W. Truett, pastor of First Baptist Church, Dallas, TX, from a sermon preached on the steps of the U.S. Capital in 1920.

a good friend, especially after he taught as guest professor at OBU during a summer school session.

I scheduled an interview with Dr. Patterson, and drove to the seminary for a mid-morning appointment. When I arrived around 10 a.m., he was in an unscheduled meeting with the president and others. One may have been the chair of the board of trustees. I waited until almost noon when the party finally emerged from the meeting room. They all looked like they had been through an extremely rough meeting.

A short time later, I concluded that they were dealing with the firing of their church history professor. A major issue related to ethical impropriety had arisen. Somewhere during this time, my sister informed me about the details, although they had not been made public. My assumption was that her source was my brother-in-law, Rev. John L. Hall. John was a Navy chaplain and a graduate of Golden Gate Seminary. He apparently learned through the proverbial grapevine what had happened at the seminary.

The timing of my interview fit perfectly with the timeline, as I understood it, and of the action taken by the seminary against the accused professor. My interpretation is that the emergency meeting held just prior to my interview may well have been to address the crisis surrounding the church history professor. I cannot document that, but it certainly is consistent with the timeframe of the events at the seminary and my visit.

I, of course, was optimistic. I had a Ph.D. from BU in the history of Christianity, had teaching experience in a Baptist college, and was available. But I did not get the job. A short time later I had coffee with Dr. Patterson during a professional meeting in San Francisco. He politely told me that the seminary policy was to hire only seminary-trained professors for the faculty. Somewhere in our discussion, I am not certain of the actual context, I informed him that I was aware of the situation with the previous professor, and assumed that the meeting on the morning of my interview concerned the matter. He was surprised at my observation. But all the pieces fit for my interpretation of the event. He did not confirm nor deny, as I remember our conversation.

## My Last Hope to Find a Teaching Position

I made at least one other visit to a school, where I had learned of an opening in the religion department. In late spring of 1979, I attended a professional meeting in the Dallas-Fort Worth area. While visiting some fellow faculty friends, one mentioned that Dr. Dan Holcomb was leaving OBU to take a position as church history professor at New Orleans Baptist Theological Seminary. The spring semester would soon be over. I quickly planned an uninvited trip to Shawnee, Oklahoma, to pursue the possibility. The term "desperate" was applicable to my situation.

The Shawnee, Oklahoma, campus was quiet since the spring semester had ended. I was able to visit Dr. Gerry Gunnin, acting provost. He was cordial and took the time to interview this unexpected visitor. He also arranged for me to meet with a couple of faculty members in the religion department. Since summer school had not begun, few were on campus. Dr. Warren McWilliams, who later became my best friend at OBU, came from his home, where he had been writing a book, to take part in the interview. Long-time professor Dr. James Timberlake was also among the small faculty gathering for the interview. It went well, and I returned to Bolivar, Missouri, with my hopes high. However, I was soon informed that an offer was not forthcoming. I learned later from Warren that the school was pursuing another candidate, I believe from Florida.

My prospects for a position for the upcoming school year plummeted. I found myself with no job, no hope, and no teaching prospects. The fall semester was rapidly approaching, and my final check from my last contract at SWBC had been received. I began to consider other possibilities outside the teaching community, but a university setting was where I wanted to be.

A few weeks later I received a surprise phone call from Dr. Gunnin. Although he did not tell me, the preferred candidate decided not to consider OBU. Because of the late date the university decided to fill the position for one year only, and determined to begin a more active search for a permanent professor during the upcoming school year. OBU offered me a one-year only contract with no promise of a second. It clearly was not a tenure track position. The offer came near the end of July, and with only a month to go before fall classes began, I was really desperate (as I had been in 1972 after graduation from BU), when it came to finding a job.

OBU was also desperate. Since Dr. Holcomb had suddenly resigned to take the position at New Orleans Baptist Theological Seminary, OBU needed a religion professor who could teach church history courses, plus other religion offerings as well. I was an experienced church history professor who could teach a variety of religion courses. Most importantly, I was immediately available. It was a match made in heaven, or at least in Shawnee, Oklahoma. I accepted the one-year-only contract from the institution just before the fall semester started in August. Although it was not a tenure-track position, I was now a seasoned veteran in these one-year-only contracts.

I began the fall semester at OBU, delighted to have a teaching position and as always, optimistic that I could convince my new colleagues and the administration that there would be no need to search any further for a church history professor. In fact, Dr. Neely assured me that I would be hired long term. He proved to be correct. As things would have it, I retired from this position twenty-two years later, in 2001. At the same time, upon arriving in Shawnee, I continued to keep an eye open for possible positions the following fall. Fortunately, in the spring of 1980, I was offered a tenure track position as religion professor at OBU.

Others who lost their positions at Southern Baptist entities during the Controversy found new positions. Often, they were in new organizations established by moderates. Some found openings in local churches. Some found positions in religious-oriented institutions, though not necessarily Baptist. And, some found opportunities beyond denominational and religious organizations in the secular community. Their journeys need documentation, such as I am doing in this book.

## The Unexpected Phone Call and the "Heresy" file on Me

I have related some of the following information in the previous chapter, to document the developing charges against me for my "heretical teachings." At the same time, certain events are worth repeating to frame a greater picture of the rising denominational conflict. My access to the accusing documents that led to my release from Southwest Baptist developed within a few months after arriving in Oklahoma. It was in the fall semester during my first year at OBU that Rev. Bill Dudley, who led the charge against me at SWBC, unexpectedly phoned me early one morning. The call came in mid-November, 1979. He "confessed" that he was wrong in his actions for attacking me. Then he demonstrated his sincerity in asking for my forgiveness. He also invited me to teach a study of Baptist history at his church. That was a major concession on his part considering his successful campaign to get me fired for teaching heresy at SWBC.

As our call ended, he asked if there was anything that he could do to make it right. I responded that I assumed that he was the kind of person who would keep a file of his communications with the school authorities. I asked him to send the file to me. A short time later I received a large, manila envelope. Inside was almost forty pages of letters and records of several telephone

*Fired for Heresy*

conversations. All detailed the account of his role that led to my firing. He aggressively sought to have me fired, and he eventually was successful.

The reading of the letters and transcripts in the file is most enlightening and sometimes entertaining in places. The communications also represent an actual case study of the strategy proposed by the right-wing element in the convention, which by the time I finished my service at SWBC had begun to initiate its quest to reshape the Southern Baptist Convention. The Controversy, as it quickly was termed, officially began at the annual meeting of the Southern Baptist Convention in June of 1979. Ironically, this paralleled the conclusion of my time at Southwest, and a few months before I found my new position at OBU.

Dudley and I had additional communication during the next few years that is worth noting. On November 19, 1979, his letter that stated "You should have been dismissed from the school but the grounds used were less than honest, in my opinion" arrived. Then on November 20, Dudley sent me more documents from his file. These documents provided much of the information described in the previous chapter, and contributed additional insights that not only reflected my journey, but also included background to the developing Controversy in the convention. At the same time, the letters and phone call summaries provided invaluable evidence concerning my conflict with ministers in Missouri and the administration of SWBC.

My personal case study reveals important background information to frame the radical developments arising in the late 1970s within the Southern Baptist Convention. Few people are presented with the opportunity to obtain primary source material in a situation such as I encountered. Therefore, this book makes a distinctive contribution to the understanding of the bigger picture of the denominational conflict. The Controversy was denominational and centered around its agencies and institutions. But it also was a struggle for many, many individuals, including myself, and therefore was extremely personal in nature for us.

Almost a year later, Dudley sent another letter to me, dated October 25, 1980. Dr. Neely left SWBC to accept the dean's position in the theology school at Hardin-Simmons University. Again, Dudley asked for forgiveness for his part in my "removal" from Southwest. He confessed "I was wrong." He also stated that his actions contributed to the "great loss to the Redford School of Theology." That was a reference to the departure of Neely from SWBC.

It is worth repeating that in the final paragraph, he wrote "Dr. Yarbrough, you should still be at Southwest Baptist College." He added "Debate is good and in place but purge is wrong."[59] He stated a position that I had long held, based on what I had learned as a Baptist. On his view that I should still be at SWBC, I would venture to say that in the long run, being fired was the best thing that happened to me for my future. I was indeed fortunate that my career took a major turn for the better following the conflict in Missouri. However, this understanding of this development certainly was not a given in the summer of 1979.

## Historical Precedents in the Southern Baptist Convention

Dudley was part of a new trend to seek out and call for the removal of heretics in Southern Baptist institutions and agencies. Heretic hunting appeared several times in the history of the denomination. In the 1920s there was a debate over Genesis and creation, or science and religion. This controversy resulted in the adoption by the Southern Baptist Convention of the first *Baptist Faith and Message* in 1925.

In the 1960s, Ralph Elliott lost his position as Old Testament professor at Midwestern Seminary in Kansas City. As related in a previous chapter, Broadman Press, the publishing arm of the Sunday School Board, produced his commentary, *The Message of Genesis*.[60] The book was attacked at the annual meeting of the convention in 1962 and withdrawn from circulation. Midwestern Seminary instructed Elliott not to seek a new publisher. However, a paperback version was published by Beacon Press. Elliott was fired not for heresy but for insubordination. Elliot's dismissal resulted in a pattern where the real reasons behind firings were hidden behind administrative rationale. I can certainly document that in my case at SWBC.

I am convinced that I was the first professor to be fired in the new wave of attacks beginning in the 1970s that culminated in what would be called the Controversy. My removal set the stage for what followed in the next two decades. New fundamentalist and radical conservative leadership in the Southern Baptist Convention eventually drove out most of those Baptists in the denomination who were considered "moderates," including me.

---

[59] Rev. Bill Dudley, letter to Dr. Slayden Yarbrough, October 25, 1980.
[60] Elliott, *Message of Genesis*.

*Fired for Heresy*

In my case, like the Phoenix bird, I rose from the ashes, and eventually took early retirement from OBU in 2001. And, unique to most moderates who lost their positions or chose to leave the SBC, somehow, I not only found a university teaching position but I also transitioned to leadership roles in the SBC Historical Commission and then the SBHS. Few, if any others, found themselves in denominational roles, where they could actually stand for and defend historic Baptist principles, after being removed from their jobs.

I was fortunate in that I survived professionally for more than two decades. At the last minute I was hired at OBU on a one-year only contract. Twenty-two years later I retired from the institution, and Janis retired from her public-school position. We moved to Denver and became American Baptists.

In 2000, as I was finishing my teaching career, I published *Southern Baptists: An Historical, Ecclesiological and Theological People*. With the help of my good friend, Mike Kuykendall, we edited and updated this earlier volume in *Southern Baptists: A History of a Confessional People*. Although I consider myself a disenfranchised Southern Baptist, I believe that my treatment of the Controversy and the restructuring of the agencies of the convention is an objective, valuable and important contribution to the history of the denomination. Written from the perspective of a dedicated researcher, while at the same time framed in an environment of one who was an active participant in the conflict and organizational restructuring, the published narration of events over two decades significantly adds to the record when seeking to understand denominational developments taking place at the end of the first quarter of the twenty-first century. The chapters on the Controversy and the restructuring are not simply a historical record. They narrate the context of my career, which shaped who I was in the later decades of the twentieth century.

The publication of the history of Southern Baptists by Mike and me also provided the incentive to write a personal and humorous book on growing up and beyond. I mentioned it earlier because it included a brief chapter on my Baptist journey. I titled it *We Coulda Been Killed: Two Brothers and Others Growing Up*. I should have called the chapter on Baptists "I Coulda Been Fired." At the time, I considered it to be my last book. Instead, coffee on a regular basis with Mike provided the incentive for one more project, this book. Hopefully, my career shaped by the historic Controversy in the largest Protestant denomination in the United States provides an example of the effect on one person in this conflict, as I responded to a unique battle that not only redefined the convention but also my career, my character, and my contributions.

Slayden A. Yarbrough

## A Preview of a Career at Oklahoma Baptist University

I went on to have a productive and rewarding career at OBU as a teacher. But my career also developed as a writer of several books, numerous articles, and a variety of other publications. Many of these related directly to the history of Baptists and Southern Baptists. Other writings indirectly were influenced by all that was happening in the Southern Baptist Convention.

Importantly, I became a pretty good Baptist historian. I also realized that being fired is not so bad after all. Not being fired would have been even worse. I maintained my integrity, and affirmed what Baptists taught me. Gaining an education and learning to think are among the highest ideals of the people called Baptists. In fact, I feel fortunate to have experienced the turmoil that shaped my identity for the rest of my career and beyond. I consider myself as both a student and a professor to be a fortunate product of the Baptist ideal of emphasizing the pursuit of a quality education. My story also was an example of how controversy in Baptist history was a source of life and growth individually and denominationally.

Besides becoming a writer, especially in the field of Baptist history, one other very important professional development took place during my time at OBU. In 1987 during the period of theological turmoil and restructuring in the denomination, I became very active as a commissioner of the SBC Historical Commission, almost by accident. Eight years later on June 1, 1995, I took a leave of absence from OBU. I served two years as interim executive director of the Historical Commission. The term "interim" was removed by the trustee chair, Dr. Ron Martin, after the convention voted to dissolve the agency. How I slipped by the enforcers of orthodoxy to receive these appointments is a mystery to many. But I did. My interpretation is that I was qualified as a Baptist historian with a proven track record of service, and that once again I was available at the right time.

Following the dissolution of the Historical Commission, I was chosen as executive director of the SBHS, which began a process in 1995 to continue its existence as a voluntary, historical organization independent of the convention. The Society changed its name to the Baptist History & Heritage Society in 2001. Not a bad resume for a convicted heretic in a conservative denomination. More than a quarter of a century later the Baptist History & Heritage Society continues to champion the cause of Baptist history.

In *We Coulda Been Killed!* I included many insights and observations throughout the volume, which I called *Lessons Learned*. In a chapter on my journey as a Baptist, I stated tongue-in-cheek that "There are worse things than being fired for heresy. One is not being fired." A second conclusion is that when you are fired, it is better when they do not use actual fire. My final conclusion was that "when someone accuses you of heresy, you must be doing something right."[61] Reflecting upon this transforming event in my life, I believe that my conclusions accurately characterize my career and contributions during my time at OBU. I had risen from the ashes, and many good things would come my way during my years in Shawnee.

---

[61] Yarbrough, *We Coulda Been Killed!* 190.

Chapter Five

# Oklahoma Baptist University and the Rise Of the "Controversy"

## A Living Faith

"A living faith must experience a growing understanding of truth and must be continually interpreted and related to the needs of each new generation. Throughout their history Baptist bodies, both large and small, have issued statements of faith which comprise a consensus of their beliefs. Such statements have never been regarded as complete, infallible statements of faith, nor as official creeds carrying mandatory authority."[62]

**Introduction: Reflections**

Reflecting back on a twenty-nine-year career as a religion professor at two Baptist colleges, my development as a participant in the discipline of Baptist history, and my removal from one institution rooted in charges of heresy, I have reached definite conclusions. First, faith is the beginning of a journey, not the end of a quest. Paul in Galatians 5:1, tells us that faith in Christ sets us free. For me, that freedom in the lordship of Jesus is to learn, change, and consistently evaluate one's views and positions in the context of the Scriptures, Baptist principles, and the need to be relevant in a changing world. Theology clearly fits into these parameters.

Second, based upon my foundations in Baptist history, the movement at its best results in the freedom to continually evaluate one's positions in the discovery of new knowledge and understanding, to be relevant in a constantly changing world. A careful review of Baptist history reveals a movement that has cautiously but continually changed and adjusted its principles and practices. I cannot underestimate the importance of a quality education at three diverse Baptist institutions in shaping my life, where I developed the tools to reach these conclusions.

---

[62] *Baptist Faith and Message* (Nashville, TN: Sunday School Board, 1963), Preface.

My growth, development, and changes were consistent with my Baptist heritage. They also resulted in coming under attack for not following the narrow orthodox beliefs of others, whose faith had not resulted in the change that I experienced as a believer and a Baptist. I posit that because I sought to be a good Christian and a good Baptist, I wound up being fired as a heretic. To me that is a positive result, not a negative one. I am proud to be considered a heretic. It means that I must have been doing something right to upset others locked in to old ways.

Based on these arguments, I conclude that a believer should at least have risked being labeled a heretic in one's personal theological pilgrimage. Faith should lead a person to push the boundaries, not build walls to shelter the individual from growth. If you wind up where you started in your commitment of faith in God and your dedication to the Baptist heritage (or whatever group with which you identify), then you have traveled nowhere but in circles, and quite possibly retreated backwards.

## Oklahoma Baptist University: A Brewing Storm on the Plains and Beyond

Beginning in the fall semester of 1979 up until my retirement at the end of the spring semester 2001, I served in an environment continually shaped by the "Controversy" and the resultant radical "Restructuring of the Southern Baptist Convention." My career during these years was framed in the denominational battle that took place between the fundamentalist and conservative forces and the so-called "moderates" in the Southern Baptist Convention. I, of course, identified as a moderate. In a very real sense, there was no time during my professional career when conflict in the Southern Baptist Convention was not occurring.

I arrived in Shawnee with a new job, and once more breathing the fresh air of Baptist freedom. OBU had a premier reputation among the small, Baptist colleges and universities in the Midwest and Southwest. The events at SWBC seemed like a small blip on the radar in trying to detect a brewing storm in the Southern Baptist Convention. However, dark clouds would soon appear on the horizon, or should I say in Oklahoma "where the winds come sweeping down the plain."[63] The storm would sweep like an Oklahoma

---

[63] Richard Rogers and Oscar Hammerstein II, *Oklahoma!* 1943.

tornado roaring across the landscape, seeking to devastate anything that got in its way.

During my seven years at SWBC, the first rumblings of a new or at least a revitalized conflict appeared. It quickly and effectively organized, led by Paul Pressler, an appellate judge from Houston, to enlist pastors and workers from churches across the convention. The generals came from mega churches in Texas, Tennessee, Georgia, Florida, and beyond. The foot soldiers were drafted from small and medium-sized churches eager to fight for the power in the Southern Baptist Convention, and the truth as they perceived it.

But in the fall of 1979, my own battle with the heresy hunters was becoming a fading memory. I had fought the battle in Missouri and lost. Or, looking back, I could say that actually I won. Dr. Dan Cochran, a good friend who taught philosophy at Southwest, commented to me as I was preparing to head for Oklahoma. He smiled and said "Slayden, you are the lucky one. We have to stay!" He was accurately interpreting the future for me, and for himself and his colleagues at the Missouri school.

Fortunately, at the last minute, even if only for a year, I had gained the high ground and achieved victory with a contract from OBU. Add to that the joy of being a fulltime professor with no administrative duties, and I felt vindicated. All was peaceful on Bison Hill. Moreover, as in the description of the Union position by an officer to Gen. George Meade at Gettysburg, the high ground of Bison Hill for me was indeed "very good ground."

Or so I thought. A few months after I arrived at OBU, charges were made against some of my new faculty members in terms of perceived heretical teachings. I was too new to have my name included on the list in a document soon to be called the "Heresy Paper." Besides, as I jokingly told my best friend, Dr. Warren McWilliams during later times when we discussed the developing turmoil at OBU, I was 100 percent orthodox on all my theological positions. We always had a good laugh on this comment that came from a guy who had already been fired for heretical teaching at another Baptist school. Yet in a few years I would face another battle concerning tenure at OBU. Not once, but twice more. This time, however, the administration stood with me.

I taught Baptist history annually at the university, a course required of students preparing for careers in church vocational ministry. I believe that I helped my students understand the history and heritage of Baptists and Southern Baptists. Some of them took active roles in moderate churches after their time at OBU, and often following seminary studies. I frequently served as a speaker and resource in a variety of Oklahoma Baptist churches, especially those affirming the moderate position of their Baptist heritage. I was establishing a reputation as a good Baptist historian, and a good religion professor at OBU. Pastors in the state were becoming aware of the rising Controversy in the convention, and many looked to me for help for their churches in understanding what was taking place.

At OBU I began to actively write for publication, especially on subjects on Baptist history in terms of denominational history. I produced numerous articles in academic journals, and books on Baptist history at the local church level, the history of Oklahoma Baptists, Southern Baptists, and Baptists in general. Such writings contributed to a surge of published articles and books defining and defending the Baptist tradition from both conservatives and moderates in the denominational battle.

During my early years at OBU, the hunt for heretics, and the quest to seize the political, organizational, and institution control in the convention was expanding to all corners of the denomination. Although, for the most part I initially was not a major player in the battle in the denomination, I would play an important role at OBU and in the response to the rising conflict at different levels.

I also was active in the local churches and in the state convention environment, thanks to the influence of one person, Dr. J. M. Gaskin. I became involved in the work of Baptist history at the national level especially because of the efforts of Dr. Gaskin, who served as executive director of the Oklahoma Baptist Historical Commission, and the administrator of Oklahoma Baptist Historical Society. He opened doors of opportunity for me to be involved in Baptist history work at both the state and national level.

Through Dr. Gaskin's efforts I became actively involved in Baptist history organizations, which included the Oklahoma Baptist Historical Society (OBHS), the Oklahoma Baptist Historical Commission (OBHC), the SBHS, and the SBC Historical Commission. I became an important contributor to the Southern Baptist Convention organizations as both a trustee of the SBC Historical Commission, including election twice as chair of the organization. I also served two years as the last executive director of the Commission, when the convention decided to dissolve the agency. The SBHS also elected me as executive director of the voluntary organization after it underwent significant changes because of the restructuring of the Southern Baptist Convention. The SBHS moved to Shawnee for about three years under my leadership.

Slayden A. Yarbrough

The SBHS was now an independent organization. As mentioned, in 2001 the name was changed to the Baptist History & Heritage Society. I will expand on this topic later in the book.

## Teaching Baptist History

My twenty-two-year tenure at OBU was overall a genuinely positive experience. I enjoyed the opportunity to teach on a fulltime basis. I taught courses in my discipline in church history and Baptist history, as well as in church and state studies. I also taught courses in Old Testament History and Literature, New Testament History and Literature, Biblical Ethics, and a variety of specialty courses as needed.

I need to add that the OBU religion department provided a small printed resource for the freshman level Old Testament and New Testament classes. It was entitled "Understanding the Bible." Dr. Warren McWilliams, my colleague and best friend, told me that he understood that Dr. Dan Holcomb, who I succeeded, prepared the original version of this booklet. I loved using the document.

The religion department required it for the students in the Bible survey classes, regardless of the textbook being used. It provided several articles which contained essential background material for studying the two testaments. The resource included brief but substantive articles about revelation, inspiration, canon, text, translations, biblical criticism, archaeology, political background, and maps of the Bible land. Most students for the first time discovered how the Bible came into being and developed over the centuries. In 1990, based upon new discoveries and information since the handbook's original version, I revised "Understanding the Bible," by adding updated information about new discoveries and translations. I am convinced that the Baptist battles over the Bible would have been lessened in intensity if participants in the conflicts would have recognized and understood all the information available in this document.

With the conflict at SWBC squarely behind me, the 1979 fall semester at OBU began on a very positive note. I taught two sections of Old Testament History and Literature, Church History: Early-Medieval, and Biblical Ethics. However, a major crisis arose on campus. My lengthy tenure at OBU was shaped immediately by the constant reality of conflict within the Southern Baptist Convention.

The campus was shaken by what became known as the "Heresy Paper." The issue of doctrinal orthodoxy openly influenced the period from 1979 and well into the last decade of the twentieth century in which the Southern Baptist Convention fought through and concluded with the major restructuring of the denominational agencies and institutions. My 22-year career at OBU would be framed in the context of the battle for control of the denomination.

I would play a contributing role as a teacher, researcher and writer, and a participant in a variety of denominational and historical Baptist organizations. Before I continue with my roles as a writer and a denominational contributor, I believe that it is important for me to frame the environment which dominated Southern Baptists from 1979, the year of my departure from SWBC and my arrival at OBU, until my retirement in 2021.

## An Introduction to the Controversy: The Context of a Career

In 1979, what became known as the "Controversy" officially began in the Southern Baptist Convention. In two books, I examined a detailed view of the events, issues, and personalities involved in the radical changes that took place. In 2000 I published a history of Southern Baptists, and included important chapters on the Controversy, the restructuring of the convention, and Southern Baptist theology. I provided particular attention to confessional theology and the *Baptist Faith and Message* and its major revisions.

With the assistance of Dr. Michael Kuykendall, in 2001 we edited and updated the earlier version under the title of *Southern Baptists: A History of a Confessional People*. Despite my own subjective positions, I attempted to provide an objective and historically based treatment of these topics and avoided polemical debate as much as possible. I honestly believe that my treatment of this challenging time provides an important presentation of the personalities, issues, and conflicts of the battle over theology and power.

There was no lack of articles and books on various challenges and defense of the divisive character of the denominational war, or simply the Controversy. In my two books on the convention, there are numerous references to contributions of leading researchers and participants in the unfolding events.

I encourage any reader who wants to understand what took place to check out either of these books.[64]

Baptists, especially Southern Baptists, have a history of controversy. For more than 400 years conflicts over the Bible, theology, worship, organization, and ethics demonstrated a movement where life and energy arose within its diversity. The Southern Baptist Convention in 1845 arose primarily over the slavery controversy in the appointment of both international and home missionaries. This occurred more than a decade and a half before the Civil War exploded on the scene and threatened the continued existence of a divided nation.

Other denominational controversies arose after the Civil War. Landmarkism and what was called anti-missions led to divisions within the convention and other Baptist groups in the late nineteenth century. Local church versus denominational authority characterized these conflicts. A pattern was set for the rise of the fundamentalist-modernist controversy in the early twentieth century.

In the following years national and international issues dominated the news. Southern Baptists focused attention on two world wars and the Great Depression, which resulted in a more unified nation and convention. The remarkable rise of science and technology in the twentieth century resulted in developing tensions within the denomination, as Southern Baptists grappled with a changing world, rapidly advancing knowledge in every important discipline, and the consequences of the challenge to be relevant in a continually developing world.

The battle over science, especially evolution, appeared in the 1920s. An effort to appease the diverse parties resulted in the adoption of the 1925 *Baptist Faith and Message*, the first doctrinal "confessional statement" of the convention. It proved effective for the immediate future, especially as the preface became the standard for the role of confessions of faith. The independency of local churches was affirmed over convention authority and

---

[64] A thorough treatment of the Controversy and the restructuring of the Southern Baptist Convention is found in Yarbrough and Kuykendall, *Southern Baptists*, 69-130. The book is an edited version and update of Yarbrough's 2000 book *Southern Baptists: An Historical, Ecclesiological, and Theological Heritage of a Confessional People*.

reflected the historical heritage of Baptists in affirming toleration and diversity within the denomination.

Eventually, Sunday School Board publications stirred the fires of theological controversy once more. Elliott's 1961 publication of *The Message of Genesis* ignited the flames of division in the convention. The long-held slogan of "unity in diversity" in the following decades gave way to "unity in conformity." Other publications by the Sunday School Board in the late 1960s, along with attacks upon seminary and university teachers, provided the battleground for the biggest theological conflict in the history of the denomination.

Control of the convention resources, agencies, and institutions resulted in intense and organized partisan division. The largest Protestant denomination in the United States waged a war over theology, which would radically reshape the direction of Southern Baptists in a new century. Individuals, churches, associations, state conventions, institutions, national boards and commissions, and voluntary societies and movements could not stay neutral in the struggle. A line was drawn in the "rope of sand," a term often used to describe Southern Baptist unity.

The unifying cause for both the conservatives and the moderates became the Bible. The strategy focused on the nomination process of trustees and boards of the convention agencies and institutions. The battleground became the annual meetings. Convention business meetings were conducted and characterized by angry debate and politicized maneuvering. "Messengers" as they were called arrived by the busloads to vote on numerous contentious issues to determine who would seize the reigns of authority in the agencies and institutions, as well as control the finances distributed through the Cooperative program. Feeble efforts at compromise were doomed to fail. Winners and losers were determined by majority vote under the guise of theological orthodoxy.

The Controversy brought about the most dramatic transformation in the Southern Baptist Convention. Initially, different names described the conflict, in the end it was soon known as the Controversy. Other titles were the Moderate-Conservative Controversy, or the Inerrancy Controversy. Terms like the Conservative Resurgence, Conservative Reformation, and Conservative Renaissance described the point of view of conservatives. Moderates labeled the battle simply as the Fundamentalist Takeover. The major public battles ended in the 1990s, as most moderates threw in the towel and left, usually joining other organizations which arose in the last two decades of the twentieth century. At the same time the fallout and consequences characterized the convention during the first quarter of the twenty-first century.

No other battle in the history of the denomination affected Southern Baptist life like the Controversy. In 1979, the convention elected Adrian Rogers as president. This action officially began a period of intense struggle over control of the denominational machinery. The conservatives kept winning the presidency and kept stacking the boards of agencies with individuals committed to the cause. The battle was fought over the Bible, theology, politics, and methodology. Trust disappeared and disunity replaced cooperation as the Southern Baptist Convention underwent radical transformation under the guise of biblical and theological orthodoxy.[65]

The next two decades witnessed the historic restructuring of the denomination. The rationale and the unified effort at doing ministry and missions resulted in upheaval for Southern Baptists from the national to the state and to the local levels. Cooperation was set aside as the relationships between the Southern Baptist Convention with state Baptist conventions, associations, churches, institutions, and individual Baptists were strained to the breaking point. National organizations were dissolved, including five commissions. Included among these was the Historical Commission, where I served as a trustee and then its last executive director. Some Southern Baptist Convention entities absorbed the work of dissolved commissions. On the other hand, the responsibilities of others discontinued and were not replaced. Often name changes reflected the new realities and new emphases.[66]

Moderates began to organize new associations and societies, and sought to continue the respective ministries and services of dissolved agencies. In some cases, they revitalized older organizations (such as the SBHS, in which I took on an active role), or created new ones. At the same time, there was not a monolithic approach. Moderates responded to the new reality differently. Some addressed national challenges whereas others established groups centered at the state level. Some groups, churches, and individuals sought to

---

[65] Yarbrough and Kuykendall, *Southern Baptists*, 69-97, describes in detail the personalities, events, and issues in the Controversy.

[66] Yarbrough and Kuykendall, *Southern Baptists*, 98-130, describes the major restructuring of the agencies and institutions following the takeover of the Convention leadership resulting from the Controversy.

remain within the Southern Baptist Convention but participated in viable options. I was one of those who remained a Southern Baptist, while at the same time identified with the moderate positions.

State conventions also faced challenges. Many examined and often redefined their relationship to the Southern Baptist Convention. Some identified with the new directions at the national convention, while others sought to remain open to the diversity of Southern Baptists. Moderate-leaning states moved away from cooperation with the national organization. New conservative conventions arose in Virginia and Texas. These were organized by those who failed to redirect their older state conventions upon the new conservative model.

Associations and churches were caught up in the battle for control the denomination. Associations often felt the tension of the struggle with their respective bodies. Churches faced a variety of options. Many churches left the Southern Baptist Convention and joined moderate organizations. Other churches sought new alliances but tried to remain Southern Baptist. Numerous churches experienced little change, while others openly welcomed the reshaped Southern Baptist Convention. Baptist churches have a history of splits, and the restructuring led to congregational divisions. First Baptist Church of Shawnee, my home church, was threatened with removal from the Pottawatomie-Lincoln Association over issues like women deacons and commitment to the 1963 *Baptist Faith and Message*. In one instance Rev. James Paul Maxwell, a good man and the associational minister, conveyed a threat from some ministers to have FBC voted out. Our pastor, Dr. Joe Brown, simply reminded him that our church provided most of the funding for the organization. Unsurprisingly, the issue disappeared.

The conflict reshaped the identity of Southern Baptists. After two decades of conflict, the national convention unquestionably was much more conservative. Most moderates were gone. Denominational leadership definitively became more authoritarian. State conventions often underwent their own restructuring. At the same time congregational polity became a greater issue as churches independently responded to the resulting changes.

The effect of the Controversy demanded an understanding of the historical modifications within the Southern Baptist Convention. Well-known moderate historians documented the battle.[67] Conservative Baptist historians published their views, as well.[68] Jesse Fletcher and Leo Garrett attempted brief, evenhanded studies.[69] Conservative histories began to appear from writers such as Jerry Sutton, James Hefley, Paige Patterson, Paul Pressler, Roger Richards, Anthony Chute, Nathan Finn, and Michael Haykin.[70] These writers and others, including myself, interpreted the effects of the Controversy on the traditional understanding of the identity of Southern Baptists. Many were written as immediate responses to address the rapidly developing conflicts and issues.

At OBU I joined the expanding group of Southern Baptist historians. I established my credentials as a professor of Baptist history, a participant in state and national Baptist historical organizations, and as a writer of numerous articles on Baptist and Southern Baptist topics. I recognized the need to present the facts related to the Controversy. Through all my roles, I was actively involved in efforts to preserve the study of and commitment to the heritage of the denomination. I certainly was not without my own subjective biases. At the same time, I attempted to be as objective as possible

---

[67] For example, Walter B. Shurden, ed., *The Struggle for the Soul of the Southern Baptist Convention: Moderate Responses to the Fundamentalist Movement* (Macon, GA: Mercer University Press, 1993); Walter B. Shurden and Randy Shepley, eds., *Going for the Jugular: A Documentary History of the Southern Baptist Convention Holy War* (Macon, GA: Mercer University Press, 1996); Bill J. Leonard, *God's Last and Only Hope: The Fragmentation of the Southern Baptist Convention* (Grand Rapids: Eerdmans, 1990); Grady C. Cothen, *What Happened to the Southern Baptist Convention?(Macon, GA: Smyth & Helwys, 1993);* also see David T. Morgan, *The New Crusades: Conflict in the Southern Baptist Convention, 1969-1991* (Tuscaloosa: University of Alabama Press, 1996).

[68] Robison B. James, *The Takeover in the Southern Baptist Convention* (Decatur, GA: Southern Baptist Convention Today, 1989); Barry Hankins, *Uneasy in Babylon: Southern Baptist Conservatives and American Culture* (Tuscaloosa, AL: University of Alabama Press, 2002).

[69] Jesse C. Fletcher, *The Southern Baptist Convention: A Sesquicentennial History* (Nashville TN: Broadman & Holman, 1994) 59-305; James Leo Garrett, Jr., *Baptist Theology, A Four Century Study* (Macon, GA: Mercer University Press, 2009), 491-513.

[70] Examples are: Jerry Sutton, *The Baptist Reformation: The Conservative Resurgence in the Southern Baptist Convention (Nashville: Broadman & Holman, 2000);* James C. Hefley, *The Truth in Crisis*, 5 vols. (Dallas: Criterion Publications; Hannibal, MO: Hannibal Books, 1986-1990); James C. Hefley, *The Conservative Resurgence in the Southern Baptist Convention* (Hannibal, MO: Hannibal Books, 1991); Paige Patterson, *Anatomy of a Reformation: The Southern Baptist Convention 1978-2004* (Fort Worth, TX: Seminary Hill Press, 2004); Paul Pressler, *A Hill on Which to Die: One Southern Baptist's Journey* (Nashville: Broadman & Holman, 1999); Roger C. Richards, *History of Southern Baptists*, Rev. ed. (Nashville: CrossBooks Publishing, 2015); and Anthony L. Chute, Nathan A. Finn, and Michael A. G. Haykin, *The Baptist Story: From English Sect to Global Movement* (Nashville: B & H, 2015).

in presenting the historical developments, which resulted in the major split within the convention. I was convinced that Baptists who were "immersed" (a good Baptist term) with the facts would properly interpret what was taking place.

## The Controversy: The Strategy

It is important to understand the strategy developed by the conservatives. Controversy over theology can be traced at least to the conflict of Texas Baptist J. Frank Norris, a fundamentalist pastor of First Baptist Church in Fort Worth. During the first half of the twentieth century, Norris aggressively attacked Baptist leaders and institutions. Eventually, he was banned for life from the Baptist General Convention of Texas. Fast forward to the 1960s. As discussed in other places in this book, the Sunday School Board's publications of Ralph Elliott's *Message of Genesis* (1961) and Volume 1 of the *Broadman Bible Commentary* (1969)[71] ignited a major debate over views found in these two volumes.

Although the Controversy ended as restructuring of the convention was completed, in 2004 I published an article entitled "Academic Freedom and Southern Baptist History" in *Baptist History & Heritage*. I discussed Crawford Howard Toy and the liberal tradition in the convention. Gregory Wills, a conservative Baptist historian, had traced theological problems back to what he called the Toy Controversy of 1879. Professor Toy taught Old Testament at Southern Seminary. He held to what is called "modernist views." Although Toy resigned, his theological positions remained among the Southern Baptist ranks. According to Wills, this incipient progressive thought was evident in all convention agencies by the 1950s.[72]

I also examined the firing of William H. Whitsitt over his position on Baptist beginnings. As previously mentioned, Whitsitt, president, and church historian at Southern Seminary, rejected the Landmark successionist theory, which traced the beginnings of Baptists back to the New Testament period. He traced the origin of Baptists back to the English Separatist movement of

---

[71] Hefley, *Conservative Resurgence*, twenty-nine-35; Garrett, *Baptist Theology*, 457-73, 486-88.
[72] Gregory A. Wills, "Progressive Theology and Southern Baptist Controversies of the 1950s and 1960s," *Southern Baptist Journal of Theology* 7, no. 1 (2003): 12-31. See also Paige Patterson, "Theological Drift—World War II-1979," *Southwestern Journal of Theology* 54, no. 2 (2012): 150-64; and Chute, Finn, and Haykin, *Baptist Story*, 278-79.

the seventeenth century. No reputable contemporary Baptist historian defends the Landmark interpretation.

The Toy and Whitsitt controversies provide evidence of the debate concerning the seminaries over scholarship and defective historical interpretation.[73] As noted in another place in this book, I initially held to the efforts to trace Baptist beginnings back to John the Baptist and his baptism of Jesus in the Jordan River. I adopted this view after my pastor gave me a copy of J. M. Carroll's *Trail of Blood*.[74] This small pamphlet was based upon a series of lectures or sermons, in which Carroll attempted to trace the origin of Baptists from the New Testament period to the present. It inspired many pastors to teach this view based upon denominational pride rather than historical accuracy. Eventually, Baptist scholars overwhelmingly rejected Carroll's view.

My article on academic freedom among Southern Baptists also discussed the conflicts arising from Ralph Elliott's *The Message of Genesis*, G. Henton Davies and *The Broadman Bible Commentary*, Dale Moody and his teachings on apostasy, H. Leon McBeth's centennial history of the Sunday School Board, scholarly controversies over seminary journals, the rise of new divinity and graduate schools originating from the Controversy, and the withdrawal of a Historical Commission pamphlet. In other words, Southern Baptists engaged in polemical controversies over academics throughout much of their history. They demonstrated the continual struggle to define whether institutions and their professors existed to educate or indoctrinate.

In Houston, Texas, during the 1979 Pastors' Conference held prior to the convention's sessions, a strategy appeared of electing the president of the convention who would commit to carrying out the agenda of the developing conservative movement. Leaders of the movement were Paige Patterson, president of Criswell College, and Paul Pressler, an appellate court judge from Houston. This initiated the official beginning of the Controversy.[75]

Conservatives openly attacked doctrinal deviations they perceived to be present in the convention institutions and agencies. They attacked the

---

[73] Slayden Yarbrough, "Academic Freedom and Southern Baptist History," *Baptist History & Heritage* 39 (Winter 2004), 45-47.
[74] J. M. Carroll, *The Trail of Blood* (n.c.: n.p., January 1, 1931).
[75] Fletcher (*Southern Baptist Convention*, 243-44) and Sutton (*Baptist Reformation*, 68-84) discuss the background of both Pressler and Patterson.

seminaries for teaching progressive and liberal theological views. They warned of a division in the convention if their concerns were not addressed.[76]

One of the early issues raised by the conservatives was the demand for "parity" in trustee appointments. Conservatives claimed that all they wanted was balance in trustee appointments to the various agencies of the convention. However, once they were successful in their strategy, parity was no longer the goal. Total control was. Conservatives also defended "designated giving."[77] Churches were justified in contributing only to causes and organizations which they supported.

The conservative strategy was successful beyond imagination. The annual strategy of electing the president of the convention would enable them to control the Committee on Committees. Changing the convention was simple: control the presidency and its appointive powers and the control of the convention is eventually assured. Paul Pressler had studied the convention's constitution. The president in conference with the vice presidents of the convention appoints the Committee on Committees, which in turn appoints the Committee on Boards (known during the early years of the Controversy as the Committee on Nominations).

During the annual meeting of the convention, the Committee on Boards nominated trustees for the agencies and institutions. The messengers from the churches usually elected the trustees without dissension, although additional nominations could be made from the floor. Elected trustees served as the legal authority for their respective agencies. They approved (and could remove) the chief executive officer of the agency to which they were appointed.

The executive, often referred to as the president, executive secretary, or executive director, administers the agency. Each agency head follows the charter and implements the policies approved by the trustees. It is important to know that each agency or institution is a separate, legal entity controlled by its trustees and not by the convention. Pressler developed the strategy, which concluded that "if the president appointed to the Committee on Committees only persons committed to the agenda of the conservatives, and

---

[76] Sutton (*Baptist Reformation*, 18-30) and Wills ("Progressive Theology," 14-25) listed several examples of "continued theological drift."
[77] Morgan, *New Crusades*, 191.

that this committee in turn appointed only the same kind of persons to the Committee on Boards, who then would nominate for trustees only those committed to the cause, then control of the convention and its agencies could be achieved."[78]

"Southern Baptist trustees are elected by convention messengers to four-year terms. A trustee can be reelected for a second term, and usually is. Most trustees therefore serve for eight years. If a trustee completes an unexpired term of a trustee of no more than two years, that trustee can serve up to a total of ten consecutive years before being required to rotate off a particular board. The conservative strategy was to control the presidency for a ten-year period. During this time the entire body of trustees of the agencies would be replaced only by those committed to the agenda of the group. The successful implementation of the conservative strategy resulted in the Controversy."[79]

When Richard McCartney moved from Oklahoma to Texas to work at the Radio-Television Commission of the Southern Baptist Convention, I was nominated to replace him on the Historical Commission board. Dr. J. M. Gaskin, the executive director of both the Historical Commission of the Baptist General Convention of Oklahoma and the Oklahoma Baptist Historical Society, contacted Dr. Joe L. Ingram, the executive director-treasurer of the Baptist General Convention of Oklahoma. He recommended me to finish the remaining two years of McCartney's term. Dr. Ingram carefully maneuvered the Oklahoma member of the Southern Baptist Convention nominating committee to put my name before the messengers at the annual SBC meeting.

Although I was certainly qualified, I would also soon be identified as a moderate. I was elected to replace McCartney, and then elected successively to two additional four-year terms on the Historical Commission. However, when Dr. Lynn E. May Jr. retired because of health issues, I was chosen by the board of the Historical Commission to be the interim executive director. I resigned from the board and replaced May. Dr. May told me that he had tried to convince retired executives and retired seminary teachers to take the position, but when all refused, he and Charles Deweese agreed to ask me.

---

[78] Toby Druin, "Patterson Group Seeks Long Range Control of Southern Baptist Convention," *Baptist Press*, 21 April 1980, 1-5.
[79] Yarbrough and Kuykendall, *Southern Baptists*, 73.

After I returned from serving in Nashville as executive director of the Historical Commission, I met a pastor who had served on the nominating committee, when my name came up for a second term. At the time I did not pay much attention to my conversation with the individual. But I remember that he had become a moderate. Reflecting upon the meeting of the nominating committee, he told me that when my name came up for nomination, there was a long discussion on whether I should be re-nominated. Prior to the rise of the Controversy, this was a process that was usually automatic. By this time, it was evident that my home church in Shawnee was labeled moderate. The presumption (and correctly) was that I was as well. I need to point out once more that my initial nomination to replace McCartney was rooted in my credentials as a good Baptist historian, not my denominational political leanings.

Once more, it is important to note that the conservative strategy had identified the authority of the president of the convention in appointing (along with the vice-presidents) the members of the nominating committee. If the president determined to appoint only individuals who were not only theologically conservative but also committed to the agenda of the president and to the conservatives seeking to control nominations to the boards of the agencies and institutions, then over a ten-year nominating and election cycle, takeover of the boards could be completed. Election of the president became the strategy to assume power and remove theological liberalism in the convention.

A significant development was the expanding role of the Executive Committee. It exerted power that enabled it to exercise creedal and political authority over the agencies and institutions. The Executive Committee recommended budget allocations for all entities of the convention. This practical responsibility became a source of power to dictate to the agencies and institutions. During the time that I was a trustee, Paul Pressler threatened the Historical Commission with dissolution if it did not remove a pamphlet that mentioned that moderate organizations provided financial support for entities beyond the Cooperative Program. This event will be described later, but in the end even though the pamphlet was withdrawn, Pressler's threat was carried out.

The conflict over control of the convention began with the 1979 annual meeting. The conservatives gained final victory by the mid-1990s. Therefore, the Controversy provided the context of my entire career as a professor at OBU. It also contributed to my commitment to serve in my expanding roles

Slayden A. Yarbrough

as both a publisher of articles and books on Baptist history, and as an officer of Baptist history organizations.

# Chapter Six

# Teaching at Oklahoma Baptist University during the "Controversy"

Thomas Helwys Defining The Scope Of Liberty

"Let them be heretics, Turks, Jews, or whatsoever, it appertains not to the earthly power to punish them in the least measure. This is made evident to our lord the king by the scriptures." Quote from Thomas Helwys, *A Short Declaration of the Mystery of Iniquity*[80]

## Introduction

I served on the faculty of OBU from 1979 to 2001. During this time the Controversy in the Southern Baptist Convention was full-blown. It provided the context of my teaching and speaking in churches and Baptist organizations. It also contributed greatly to my publishing activities, which began at SWBC. I published my initial article there. While at OBU, I began to participate in Baptist historical organizations at the state and national level. Dr. J. M. Gaskin was the most significant influence in this regard. He opened doors for service both in Oklahoma and in the national convention.

Without question, all that was taking place in my career felt the impact of the Controversy. At the same time, when I arrived in Shawnee, I confidently felt that the major impact of denominational conflict was now behind me. Boy was I wrong. It seems that I had barely unpacked my books when the campus was rocked by charges of heresy, although at the time I was simply a bystander.

---

[80] Joe Early, Jr., *The Life and Writings of Thomas Helwys* (Macon, GA: Mercer University Press, 2009), 191.

Slayden A. Yarbrough

## The Heresy Paper at Oklahoma Baptist University – 1979

I was teaching at the university for two months. Then, during the Baptist General Convention of Oklahoma (BGCO) annual meeting, a document dated October 12, 1979, was distributed to the trustees of the university and the messengers attending the convention. This document became known as the "Heresy Paper." The exposé was reportedly written by a group of upperclassmen, led by David Eberhard and Stewart Bedillion, two future graduates of the university. The two seniors acknowledged their role in the preparation of the document, which was twenty-four pages long.[81]

The "Heresy Paper" charged nine professors, including three in the religion department and two in the philosophy department, with heretical teaching, liberalism, and Neo-orthodoxy. Similar charges were also leveled at a former professor of religion. The two chief administrators of OBU were accused of insensitivity and irresponsibility in relation to the issues. The document also leveled charges of prevalent drunkenness, immorality, and homosexuality on campus. Another section of the document criticized several textbooks used by the religion department, and included seven pages of sample material from these textbooks.

The students provided a copy of the paper to Jerry Sullaway, pastor of Emmanuel Southern Baptist Church of Edmond. He provided funding for the printing of the "Heresy Paper." Under his coordination was the distribution of the document to the Pastors' Conference, which was held in conjunction of the 74th annual meeting of the BGCO in Tulsa. Coordination between student charges of heretical teaching by the faculty and pastoral involvement in aggressive criticism of specific professors was a tactic I observed during the time of my controversy at SWBC. It appeared again at OBU to provide evidence of a growing and coordinated movement at targeted educational institutions across the Southern Baptist Convention.

Although church messengers to the BGCO affirmed confidence in OBU, they also recommended that a committee of trustees be appointed by the

---

[81] Information on the "Heresy Paper" is thoroughly discussed in Slayden Yarbrough, *The View from Bison Hill, 1961-1985*, in the section entitled "The Hall Years: Construction, Curriculum and Controversy (1977-1983)." Yarbrough wrote his history as a part of the 75th anniversary of OBU published in 1985, and entitled *The View from Bison Hill: 75 Years of Remembrance*. The book was produced and published by the university, and written by four authors: Dr. J, M. Gaskin, Eunice Short, Helen Thames Raley, and Yarbrough in 1985.

chair of the board of trustees to review "textbooks, teaching assignments, doctrinal stance, and all other matters pertinent to the instruction and teaching at OBU."[82] During the early days of this controversy, active and overwhelming student support of the faculty was evident. This contributed to a close bond between the two groups on the campus in the future months.

On December 4, 1979, trustee chair Dr. Larry Adams appointed the academic affairs committee to commence the study. Dr. Charles Graves, former chair of the trustees and pastor of Nichols Hills Baptist Church in Oklahoma City, was added to the committee. Dr. Adams and Dr. Joe L. Ingram, executive director of the BGCO, served as *ex officio* members.[83] The committee over the next year did interviews with students (including the authors of the paper), faculty (including those named in the document), administrators, pastors and other ministers and laymen. On September 11, 1980, the committee report was presented to the board of trustees and adopted unanimously.[84] The OBU board presented it to the BGCO messengers on November 12, 1980, at the annual meeting in Del City. The report was accepted without protest and a motion to require all faculty members to be a member of a Southern Baptist church was defeated.[85]

Basically, the report affirmed that OBU was effectively discharging its academic obligations. It also described a deep dedication to the Christian faith but also stressed the need for greater sensitivity to the Baptist constituency in Oklahoma. The report asserted that the moral climate at OBU was substantially above what was found in society.[86]

Changes were made at the university in response to the report. The 1963 *Baptist Faith and Message* as the theological base for the school was affirmed.[87] The School of Christian Service was established, and included the religion and philosophy departments.[88] The office of provost was terminated and the deans of the colleges and/or schools reported directly to the university

---

[82] "A Report from the Board of Trustees of Oklahoma Baptist University to the Baptist General Convention of Oklahoma," 12 November 1980.
[83] "Report from the Board."
[84] "Report from the Board."
[85] "Report from the Board."
[86] "Report from the Board."
[87] "Report from the Board."
[88] "Report from the Board."

president.⁸⁹ Other changes resulted from updated policies and procedures resulting from the "Heresy Paper."

In the end OBU and its faculty were commended for carrying out the responsibilities relating to the churches of Oklahoma. No faculty members were dismissed because of the charges. One of the accusing students left Southern Baptist life. The other attended a non-Southern Baptist seminary following graduation from OBU.⁹⁰

Meanwhile, in the Southern Baptist Convention, the Controversy was just beginning. Turmoil would engulf the denomination in the next decade and beyond. Charges of heretical teaching and unbiblical stances developed and grew rapidly. Control of the boards and agencies underwent great change as the nomination and election of trustees sympathetic to the right wing of the convention resulted in the removal or the resignation of denominational leaders. A significant number of Southern Baptists and Southern Baptist churches felt disenfranchised from the denomination and chose new directions.

On a more personal note, the one-year only, last-minute replacement faculty member at OBU, actively engaged the new environment affecting Southern Baptists. As one who lost his teaching position at SWBC, during the next twenty-two years at OBU, I would assume an important role in teaching Baptists their history at church, university, and denominational levels. I discovered the motivation and need to write articles and books about Baptist history and heritage. And, I became an active participant and leader in Southern Baptist historical organizations at the state and national levels of the denomination, which would help shape the future for Baptist historians into the twenty-first century.

**The Advancing Controversy**

The Heresy Paper and my challenge at SWBC were events which signaled the advancing controversy in the Southern Baptist Convention. A major battle during the Controversy focused on the mind. The issued affected two major arenas: educational institutions and news services publications. In fact, prior to 1979, three conservative institutions were established: Criswell Bible

---

[89] "Report from the Board."
[90] Yarbrough, "The View from Bison Hill, 1961-1985," 181.

Institute (now Criswell College) in Dallas, Texas; Mid-America Baptist Theological Seminary, which began in Little Rock, Arkansas, and later moved to Memphis, Tennessee; and Luther Rice Seminary, a correspondence school in Jacksonville, Florida. These schools became training grounds for ministers to become conservative participants in the Controversy.

Focus upon the theological teachings at Southern Baptist institutions had been around since the Elliott and *Broadman Bible Commentary* controversies. Accusations and suspicions against seminary teachers, their views, and their publications increased. I am certain that during these days, a growing number of students participated in the effort to uncover heresy in the classrooms. In fact, at the seminary level, many students were also pastoring in churches and commuting to the campuses. A result of the quest to uncover heresy resulted in the establishment of a convention committee to examine seminary professors and their publications, as well as agency personnel who came under suspicion.

Dr. Harry B. Hunt Jr. was one of my closest colleagues at SWBC. Harry had a doctorate from Southwestern Baptist Theological Seminary in Old Testament studies. He was hired as In-Service Training Director at Southwest Baptist. Like me, he wore a second hat as a professor of religion courses. Harry without question was the most conservative professor in the religion department during my time at Southwest. Our families lived in the same subdivision, and we were quite close. Harry and I would debate issues of disagreement, especially related to the Old Testament, and depart laughing and appreciating each other. I often said that if I found myself in a theological battle, I wanted Harry on my side. His integrity and his friendship were unquestioned. Harry's greatest passion was to teach on the faculty of Southwestern Baptist Theological Seminary in Fort Worth. After a few years at SWBC, his dream came true.

In one of the most shocking developments related to the Controversy, Harry came under investigation because of an article published in *Biblical Illustrator*. I do not recall the content of the article, but it was used as an example of liberal teaching found at the Southwestern. The appointed committee to examine charges of heresy in the convention met and discussed Harry's writing, along with other examples of theological heresy at the seminaries.

In Harry's case, someone had accused Harry of heretical teaching on a subject from an Old Testament book. I was informed by an inside source that the committee carefully examined in detail Harry's article in *Biblical Illustrator*. As reported to me, their conclusion was that they could not find anything in the article which fit into the category of unacceptable teachings. But just the charge caused my very conservative friend great anguish. If Harry Hunt was considered a closet heretic, polluting the minds of our youth, something was dreadfully wrong in the convention.

For the record, I also had a sermon entitled "Religious Freedom: Right and Responsibility," which *Report from the Capitol* published in July-August 1986. It too was used as an example of liberalism in the Baptist Joint Committee on Public Affairs. I defended it as a superb example of the traditional Baptist views on religious liberty and separation of church and state, along with examples of both Baptist and faith freedom.

The roots of the public search for heretics in denominationally affiliated educational institutions can be traced to the Pastors' Conference, which met prior to the 1979 convention in Houston, Texas. Evangelist James Robison issued the call to root out heresy in Baptist schools. In a sermon which rallied the troops to meet the challenge of liberalism in colleges and seminaries, Robison called on the participants "to elect a president who is totally committed to the removal from this denomination of any teacher or any educator who does not believe the Bible is the inerrant, infallible Word of the living God."[91] Robison allowed no room for compromise, diversity, or discussions over the issue. The battle cry was issued in the war against Southern Baptist seminaries and professors. The conservatives call for "parity" was quickly disappearing.

In the subsequent years, attacks, conflict, and the struggle for control occurred at Southeastern Seminary in Wake Forest, North Carolina, Southern Seminary in Louisville, Kentucky, and Southwestern Seminary in Fort Worth, Texas. Once again, the strategy to control the appointment of trustees provided the incentive to make significant changes at these schools to prepare future ministers as defenders of the orthodox faith demanded in the Controversy.

At the university and college level, numerous battles also were fought. The challenge for the Conservatives was greater, because these institutions were affiliated with state conventions rather than the Southern Baptist

---

[91] Sutton, *Baptist Reformation*, 98. Sutton added that Robison was "perhaps the most caustic speaker during the Pastors' Conference" and "a man of deep passion." Robison declared concerning teachers who cast doubt on God's literal truth that "I would not tolerate a rattlesnake in my house... And I would not tolerate a cancer in my body..."

Convention. Furthermore, the relationships between the educational and state conventions varied from institution to institution.

One example took place in Missouri at the same time I was being attacked at Southwest Baptist. Dr. David Moore, a church history professor at William Jewell College in the early 1970s, came under attack. Accusations appeared in the public press. At the same time, William Jewell College was dually aligned with both Southern Baptists and American Baptists, and Moore was able to survive the assaults. The conflict in Missouri signaled what was to come. The issues related to Moore and to me foreshadowed a constant assault upon college and university professors of religion. The conservative base fervently began to root out heresy in the quest for denominational theological purity. Soon, other schools felt the assaults and the accusations from the right, with professors of religion being the most visible targets. [92]

Baylor took the most aggressive response to the attacks of the conservatives upon colleges and universities. In 1990, BU trustees surprisingly changed the charter of the institution to prevent a conservative takeover. Dr. Joel Gregory, who would soon become pastor of historic First Baptist Church of Dallas, Texas, led the opposition to BU. Other schools soon followed BU's lead.[93] They included Furman University, Greenville, South Carolina; Samford University in Birmingham, Alabama; and Carson-Newman College in Jefferson City, Tennessee. Each school risked defunding by their respective state conventions. At the same time, in late 1999, Jerry Falwell's Liberty University announced that it had become a Southern Baptist school. Of course, the reactions to the news were mixed.[94]

New seminaries and divinity schools were established in response to the Controversy. Baptist Theological Seminary in Richmond (Virginia) was an example of moderate initiatives. Traditional universities established seminaries and theological schools. They included Truett Seminary at BU, Logsdon School of Theology at Hardin-Simmons University, Campbell

---

[92] Several professors are named in Bill Leonard, *God's Last Hope*, 155-60; Sutton, *Baptist Reformation*, 6-30; Wills, "Progressive Theology," 12-31.
[93] Fletcher, *Southern Baptist Convention*, 413-14.
[94] Yarbrough and Kuykendall, *Southern Baptists*, 91.

University Divinity School, Gardner-Webb Divinity School, Wake Forest Divinity School, and McAfee School of Theology of Mercer University.[95]

The Controversy spread to Baptist state newspapers, which faced the task of reporting on the continuous battles within the denomination. A constant supply of stories, issues, and personalities resulted in a barrage of letters to editors, accusations of favoritism, and challenges to the journalists' responsibility to inform readers. Influencing the press became part of the conservative strategy to stir the passions of its adherents. Charges of favoritism flowed freely to provide evidence of the threat of liberalism in the denomination. Conservatives understood the power of the press and became experts at using the media to enhance their positions. They charged that Baptist news media sided with the moderates.[96]

The dismissal of two of writers for *Baptist Press*, the official news agency of the convention, was most controversial. The Executive Committee fired Dan Martin and Al Shackleford. The presence of armed security guards in the Southern Baptist Convention Building in Nashville shocked many Southern Baptists. Especially surprising was the fact that Shackleford was theologically conservative. Moderate editors responded by organizing *Associated Baptist Press*, which began receiving support from the new organization of the Cooperative Baptist Fellowship.[97]

## Tenure: Rounds Two and Three and a New President at Oklahoma Baptist University

My quest to receive tenure as a professor at a Baptist institution did not end with my termination at SWBC. When OBU renewed my "one-year only contract," I now became eligible according to university policy for future consideration as a tenured professor in my seventh year. Furthermore, OBU

---

[95] See William H. Brackney, *A Genetic History of Baptist Thought* (Macon, GA: Mercer University Press, 2004), 385-429, for a brief history of Baptist schools; and Yarbrough and Kuykendall, *Southern Baptists*, 91.
[96] Fletcher, *Southern Baptist Convention*, 309-10.
[97] For the conservative understanding of *Baptist Press* reporting and the firings, see Pressler, *Hill to Die*, 207-24; and Sutton, *Baptist Reformation*, 392-400. For the moderate take on these events, see Cothen, *What Happened to the Southern Baptist Convention?* 232-45; and Morgan, *The New Crusades*, 157-61.

credited me with three years from my faculty service at SWBC. As I approached my fourth year, the possibility of tenure at OBU became a reality.

However, two events took place which redirected my pursuit of tenure. First, Dr. Eugene Hall resigned as president of the university. Second, he was replaced by Dr. Bob Agee who had been serving at Union University in Jackson, Tennessee. Dr. Agee in my opinion was a superb choice for OBU. He had excellent credentials and a vision for what a Baptist university should be. He understood the importance of excellence in the classroom. He respected the contributions of faculty members not only in teaching but in professional commitment, including publishing by the faculty in their respective disciplines.

At the same Dr. Agee understood Oklahoma Baptists and worked effectively with the Oklahoma Baptist Convention, whose executive director was Dr. Joe L. Ingram. They were a good team. I often remarked that a strength of Dr. Agee was that while he was committed to the academic goals of the institution, he also "spoke the language of Zion." In other words, he communicated effectively with the pastors in Oklahoma. In my case I felt that he always supported me, even during times when I was vocal about the struggle taking place in the convention. OBU thrived under his leadership, as he made the university a safe place and a learning environment for the students from the Baptist churches throughout the state and beyond.

Shortly after becoming president, Dr. Agee made an important decision related to tenure at the university. It affected me greatly. Three faculty members were eligible for consideration of tenure during his first year, as the board of trustees made decisions for contracts for the upcoming school year. Dr. Agee decided to postpone all decisions on tenure for one year until he settled in as president. He spoke with me personally, as I am sure he did with the other two faculty members. He assured me that if I kept on doing what I was doing, that I would be recommended for and receive tenure in the next go-around of contracts. I also suspected that concerns had been expressed to him about one other faculty member who was eligible for consideration, and possibly about me as rumors of my experience at SWBC had by now surely spread to Oklahoma.

Dr. Agee's decision was very emotional for me. I had battled through the tenure issue at Southwest and felt like I had proven myself at OBU. I had several discussions with Dr. Shirley Jones, the provost. I pleaded my case passionately and had become very anxious about the outcome of waiting an additional year. My pleas were to no avail. I had to wait.

Slayden A. Yarbrough

When the next year rolled around, I was assured by colleagues and administrators that I soon would be tenured by action of the board. There seemed to be no red flags on my record. I had been successful in the classroom. I was active in professional organizations. And, I had been contributing articles, which were published in academic journals. I had the credentials respected by a Baptist university, and my circumstance at SWBC did not appear to be an issue.

Once again, however, another obstacle unexpectedly appeared which threatened my goal of becoming a tenured professor. When I arrived at OBU, Bob and Joy Burgess served on the staff and ministered to church vocation students. They planned many activities for students preparing for church service in a variety of positions. Although we did not have a lot of interaction, I observed them to be caring and passionate in their positions. My conversations with them were always positive, and I felt them to be a part of the same team that I was on in terms of caring for our students.

A few years later Bob resigned to take a position as pastor of a church in Bartlesville, Oklahoma. He soon was elected to the board of trustees. He was on the board when I was recommended to receive tenure. After the board meeting, Dr. Shirley Jones, Academic Vice President, met with me and took me through the process. When my name came up for a vote in the Academic Committee of the board, Bob expressed that he felt like I should not be tenured.

Dr. Jones was caught off guard and defended me. Bob continued to resist. Dr. Jones then called Dr. Agee into the meeting. This was a committee meeting on academics rather than the full board. Dr. Agee defended me and when Bob continued to express his reservation about me, the president asked that he explain why he was opposed. Bob would not make any specific charge. Dr. Agee basically insisted that Bob either explain his concerns or that the committee move forward on the question of my tenure. Bob reluctantly agreed not to oppose the administration's recommendation. The committee voted to accept the recommendation, and I was approved by the full board. I also remember that one of the other candidates from the previous year did not receive tenure.

In the end, my quest for tenure was stretched out over several years. I failed my goal at SWBC. My quest at OBU was delayed one year with the arrival of a new president since a tenure vote was postponed one year. And, when I finally came up for a vote, an unexpected obstacle almost derailed me once more. I credit Dr. Agee and Dr. Jones for standing with me. I also credit Dr.

Agee's leadership and the respect that he had already attained in the Oklahoma Baptist Convention as a major factor that finally resulted in my becoming tenured at OBU. Finally, I suppose, the old saying that "Three's a charm" applied to my quest for tenure, although "barely" might be added to the old adage. The quest for tenure tested my emotions and resolve more than any other issue in my academic career.

## The Battle of Atlanta

Another event took place which involved Dr. Agee and his Baptist history professor. During the annual meeting of the Southern Baptist Convention in Atlanta in 1995, Dr. Agee served as chair of the Credentials Committee. I was at the time serving as interim executive director of the Historical Commission.

Dr. Agee had approved of my taking a year's leave of absence to serve in this capacity and to close this Southern Baptist Convention agency, should the messengers to the convention approve the recommended restructuring of agencies. A committee had been appointed by the Executive Committee to study the structure of the convention agencies. The plan to merge or close several entities, including the Historical commission, was to be voted upon.

I tried to enlist individuals to present an amendment to the motion to preserve the Commission, but no one was willing to do so. So, I determined to make a motion myself. I consulted with Jim Henry, pastor of First Baptist Church of Orlando, Florida, and president of the Southern Baptist Convention. The popular pastor surprisingly had been elected to this position, defeating a candidate of the right-wing conservative group.

I asked Dr. Henry for advice on how to make my motion at the convention. A class of students from Southwestern Seminary were assigned to various microphones throughout the convention floor. When the call came for motions, the student would hit a button which switched on a light and notified the moderator of a messenger who wanted to speak. Dr. Henry advised me to sit next to a student monitor, tell him that I wished to make a motion, and ask him to immediately hit the switch. This was good advice, and I followed his instructions. As soon as the floor was open for motions, my student monitor instantly hit the switch. I was the first messenger recognized.

I had carefully prepared my diplomatic motion to save the Historical Commission. I even included my intention to present instructions for changes to the restructuring motion, if my amendment passed. Unfortunately, by voice vote my motion failed. The chair ruled a call for a written ballot to be out of order, based upon his experience in determining voice votes over many years in business meeting.

Dr. Agee, in his role as chair of the Credentials Committee, was on the platform. He surely must have gasped in surprise when one of his faculty members went to microphone to oppose the recommendation of the Restructuring Committee. However, my effort at providing a diplomatic rather than hostile approach must have pleased, maybe even surprised, him. A few weeks later I returned from my office in Nashville to the OBU campus. Several administrators told me how pleased Dr. Agee was with my effort and the professionalism which I displayed making my motion. I had taken my stand in defending the need for preserving the Historical Commission and had not embarrassed my university nor president in the process. Unfortunately, I lost the vote.

## A New President at Oklahoma Baptist University

One final event took place related to my determination to defend the importance of Baptist history involved Dr. Agee and Dr. Mark Brister, who chaired the Restructuring Committee. Dr. Brister was pastor of First Baptist Church of Shreveport, Louisiana, and the son of Dr. C. W. Brister, a distinguished and highly respected faculty member at Southwestern Baptist Theological Seminary.

When Dr. Agee resigned from Oklahoma Baptist to become the executive director of the now independent Education Committee (which also had been dissolved in the restructuring), Dr. Brister was selected to replace him as president of OBU. When word filtered around campus that Dr. Brister was chosen as president, several colleagues stopped by my office to inquire what I knew about him, since I had been actively involved in convention matters. He had served as chair of the Restructuring Committee and presented the report at the Atlanta convention. My pat answer to my colleagues was tongue-in-cheek "Other than standing before 10,000 messengers at the Southern Baptist Convention meeting in Atlanta and telling him as chair of the Restructuring Committee that he was wrong, not much." I always made this statement with a smile on my face.

When word became public about Dr. Brister becoming our next president, Dr. Agee made a special visit to me to assure me that Dr. Brister was a good choice. I assured him that I intended to support him, as I had supported Dr.

Agee. I appreciated the fact that he took the time and had the sensitivity to come to my office and converse with me on the appointment. It ended up that Mark and I got along well. As with Dr. Agee, I felt the freedom to share my concerns as a Baptist historian about convention life and politics. When Betty, my sister, passed away from cancer in 1999, Mark received word of her death while he was on a business trip out of state. He immediately called me to express his condolences, and his experience as a pastor made a positive impression upon me.

**Reflections on a Career in Teachings**

Beginning college in 1963, I soon concluded that I was not to be a pastor or evangelist. I developed an affinity for the college life, and defined my goal to be a college professor of religion. Interestingly, while a senior at SWBC, Dr. G H Surette recommended that I consider the new Ph.D. program in religion at Baylor instead of attending seminary. As a rather naive graduate from a conservative college, I was accepted into the program, and received my Ph.D. in Religion with an emphasis in the History of Christianity in 1972. I returned to Southwest that fall to begin my academic career. Dr. Surette as academic vice president hired me. Later, he would be involved with issues related to my teachings and the question of tenure, which resulted in my failure to receive a contract beyond my seventh year at the institution.

In late summer, 1979, with my back to the wall professionally and no possibilities on the horizon, and mere weeks before the opening of the fall semester, OBU opened the door to a one-year only teaching position. My career was salvaged at the last moment. Without question, I had a most rewarding career at OBU. Although the context of my entire teaching experience was in the Southern Baptist Convention, I would have it no other way. Twenty-nine years as an academician were certainly not boring. I look back on my time there with a sense of great pride and appreciation.

## Chapter Seven

# Publishing During The "Controversy" Part 1: Baptists And Books

### ECCLESIASTES 12:12 (NASB 1995)

"As to more than these, my son, beware. Of the making of many books there is no end, and in much study, there is weariness for the flesh."

### Introduction

In Chapters 7, 8, and 9, I will examine my publications during my career and the Controversy in the Southern Baptist Convention. A reader might ask the legitimate question, "Why should I be interested in reading three chapters on one person's published writings?" I would answer that these writings are significant in the ongoing presentation of material related both directly and indirectly to the understanding and interpretation of the most divisive period in the history of the denomination. They provide historical insights, an understanding of Baptist principles and practices, and the ongoing dialogue to inform the adherents to the churches and organizations affected by the ongoing changes in the convention. The writings are much more than simply the academic pursuit of respective topics. They are framed in the life and struggle for the very soul of Southern Baptists, and in the greater context Baptists in all of their diverse expressions and movements.

Therefore, I encourage the reader to understand the foundation that these writings are a reflection and a result of the conflict over theology and authority in the Southern Baptist Convention. They provide a contemporary commentary on all that was going on. Although personal in one sense, they contributed to the understanding and defining of what it means to be Baptist. They are much more than a collection of titles and paragraphs about my publications.

Also, they form a significant part of the Baptist emphasis on higher education, and the contributions of professors, academicians, and denominationalists to provide with integrity resources for all who wish to better understand topics and issues of research. When properly used, such writings are tools for teachers, historians, professionals, and lay persons, who desire not only to know but also to apply good scholarship to all areas of Baptist life. They are a major part of the pursuit of knowledge in the application of faith. They provide evidence that Baptist educational institutions are not simply schools for indoctrination. They are places where students receive an education in order to think, evaluate, change and contribute to the world about them.

In describing and discussing my publications, I encourage the reader to be aware that I intentionally seek to frame them in wider terms. They often flow directly from the tensions and struggles evident in the ongoing conflict in the denomination. Even practical articles, sermons, and lessons for church classes, have an underlying context that displays the importance of the Baptist emphasis that encourages study, interpretation, and application of the resources available. These are lessons which I remembered as I prepared these chapters. I believe that they will elevate those principles instilled in me in my personal journey of faith by influential Baptists, especially those in the world of academics. Therefore, be cognizant of the bigger picture of my publications. It is an important part of the story in these three chapters.

**Initial Publishing Goals**

Dr. Rosalee Beck, a good friend and president of the SBHS during the most critical period following the dissolution of the Historical Commission, once humorously introduced me at a meeting. She discussed my credentials in a paraphrase that went something like this. "Slayden published his doctrinal dissertation on Henry Jacob."[98] She paused and then said "one article at time—in several scholarly journals." Her comment brought a good laugh from my friends, and certainly from me. Rosalee was correct. I bled my dissertation for all it was worth. I used my doctoral research to write several articles on a variety of topics, which often contributed to an understanding of Baptist church polity and organization. They reflected goals for publishing that I established at the beginning of my academic career.

**Goal # 1:** When I started teaching at SWBC, I prepared a list of several publishing goals. The first was to publish an article in any professional

---

[98] Slayden A. Yarbrough, "Henry Jacob, A Moderate Separatist, and His Influence on Early English Congregationalism" unpublished PhD dissertation (BU University, Waco, Texas, August, 1972).

journal. Anything to get my name in print. I succeeded when my first article entitled "The Ecclesiastical Development in Theory and Practice of John Robinson and Henry Jacob" appeared in *Perspectives in Religious Studies* in the fall of 1978. It was the initial article based upon my dissertation, and examined the parallel views of two English Separatists. Robinson, pastor of the Pilgrim church in New England, called for complete separation from the Church of England, which he determined to be a false church. Jacob wanted to separate from the corruptions, and reform the national established church to adopt congregational polity. Both Englich Separatists presented similar views on congregational church government, which helped me in defining and refining my own views on Baptist polity.

While at SWBC I also submitted a subsequent article on Henry Jacob, who I labelled a moderate English Separatist. "The Ecclesiology of Henry Jacob" appeared in *The Quarterly Review*, which is described as "A Survey of Southern Baptist Progress."[99] The article discussed detailed Jacob's developing views on congregational church polity. Jacob's understanding of the local church contributed to my own understanding of congregational polity in Baptist life. I was especially impressed by his tolerance and respect for other viewpoints.

Jacob organized a nonconformist congregation in 1616 in Southwark, England, across the Thames River from London. From this church arose an English Particular Baptist congregation led by John Lathrop, and then Henry Jessey. Jacob's congregational polity, including the freedom of church members to discuss openly any issues of disagreement, led to the discussion of baptism and the movement toward the formation of this early Particular (Calvinistic) Baptist Church under the leadership of Henry Jessey in 1645.

**Goal # 2:** A second goal was to publish an article in *Church History*, a quarterly published by the American Society of Church History, and the standard publication for church historians in the United States. I wrote "The Influence of Plymouth Colony Separatism on Salem: An Interpretation of John Cotton's Letter of 1630 to Samuel Skelton." The article examined the influence of John Robinson, pastor of the Pilgrim Fathers, and the influence of the Plymouth Church in New England. The article was published in 1980.

---

[99] Slayden A. Yarbrough, "The Ecclesiology of Henry Jacob" *The Quarterly Review* 40:2 (January-March 1980): 66-78.

**Goal # 3:** A third goal was to publish an article in *The Journal of Church and State*, published by the J. M. Dawson Institute of Church-State Studies at BU. During my first year in graduate studies at BU, I served as graduate assistant to Dr. James E. Woods, professor of church and state studies. Beginning in 1972, Dr. Woods became executive director for eight years of the Baptist Joint Committee for Religious Liberty. I developed a deep interest in the history and issues related to the topic. I added a course in the subject at both SWBC and OBU.

I never wrote an article for the journal. I did, however, contribute several book reviews on the subject. So, in this regard, I did publish in a more limited way in the journal. I suppose an asterisk could be added to this goal, explaining that I partially reached it. In addition, I published book reviews in several professional journals throughout my career.

**Goal # 4:** My fourth and final goal was to publish a book related to Baptist history. With the first edition of *Southern Baptists: Who Are We?* in 1984, and with updated revisions in 1985 and 1990, I achieved this final goal. In 2000 I published *Southern Baptists: A Historical, Ecclesiological and Theological Heritage of a Confessional People*. Finally, in 2021, Dr. Michael Kuykendall and I edited and updated this volume with a new title: *Southern Baptists; A History of a Confessional People*. Before my career ended, I achieved my goals, and actually expanded upon my contributions even in retirement.

## Publishing Initiatives During "The Controversy"

As a university professor I was in an appropriate environment to research and write articles for professional and topical publications. Preparing lectures and teaching as a fulltime professor, the availability of a good library, interaction with colleagues in my discipline and department, and the opportunity to attend professional meetings assisted in efforts to contribute to the study and application of Christianity and Baptist history. I also became a member in state and national Baptist history organizations of the denomination, and in organizations for religion professors and teachers at Baptist, denominational, and secular educational institutions. While initially entering the field of publishing articles at Southwest, I became even more active in these organizations committed to Baptist history after arriving at OBU.

At the Shawnee university I began to contribute regularly as a writer. Of course, a major impetus in my activity was the appearance of the Controversy in the Southern Baptist Convention. As a professor and a participant in the developing events, I began to publish several articles in *Baptist History & Heritage*, the journal produced jointly by the Historical Commission and the SBHS. I provided articles on Baptist history in a few seminary journals, and other publications. I also became a regular contributor of articles in the *Oklahoma Baptist Chronicle*, edited by Dr. J. M. Gaskin.

Even articles and sermons which appeared in several practical denominational publications were prepared in the context of Baptist principles, which I learned and practiced over my years as a student and professor. The importance of study, research, and application of these principles was essential to affirming the relevancy of the Baptist tradition to the contemporary challenges of a constantly changing world. I contributed to a variety of categories in the publishing world.

For example, one publication was *Biblical Illustrator*, a Southern Baptist journal aimed at Sunday School teachers that provided the necessary background for upcoming lessons. I wrote nine articles that appeared in this quarterly resource. Countless Sunday School teachers benefited from the important background material provided by biblical scholars. I also published a few articles and sermons in a pastor's magazine entitled *Proclaim*. And, I wrote lessons related to Baptist and Christian history for church training classes. Through these publications I expressed my commitment to helping pastors and lay leaders communicate the Baptist message and its influence on scholarship in other disciplines on solid, well-researched information. I will discuss more thoroughly these contributions in a later chapter.

## A Professor and Publisher of Baptist History

During my twenty-nine years as a college professor, I taught both Bible Survey courses, as well as a variety of other subjects. Included in the category of church history, I taught Baptist History (with a special emphasis upon Southern Baptist history, organizational life, theology, and missions and ministries), Early-Medieval Christianity; Reformation and Modern Christianity, and Religion and the State or Church and State. I also taught courses in missions and evangelism, and pastoral ministry.

During my early career, I read the early histories of Southern Baptists and Baptists, including those of W. W. Barnes (*The Southern Baptist Convention: 1845-1953*); and Robert A. Baker (*The Southern Baptist Convention and Its People, 1607-1972*). I assigned Robert G. Torbet (*A History of Baptists*) as a textbook for several years. Afterwards, I used as a text H. Leon McBeth's extensive *The Baptist Heritage: Four Centuries of Baptist Witness*. I also studied several resource books during my teaching years, including Baker's *A Baptist Source Book* and McBeth's invaluable companion volume *A Sourcebook for Baptist Heritage*.[100] Throughout my career I continued to read contemporary histories of Baptists, which were published by my generation of scholars. They are listed here in a footnote.[101]

## Influences on Becoming a Writer

Several important factors opened the door to publish, especially in the discipline of Baptist history, and to reach my initial and developing publishing goals that arose out of the denominational conflict arising in the late 1970s. Researching and writing so many papers on a variety of topics in graduate school contributed to my development as a writer to publish, once I became a university professor. During my academic years, especially as a student at BU, I anticipated producing scholarly writings. But I also felt anxiety over my writing and research skills. Writing publishable material was challenging work for me.

After a few years at Southwest, I concluded that future advancement as a professor required that I publish in academic journals to enhance my credentials. The statement "publish or perish" circulated in academic circles. But I naively never thought it applied to teaching at a Baptist institution. At the same time, there were teachers who appeared to subscribe to the

---

[100] Robert A. Baker, ed., *A Baptist Source Book* (Nashville: Broadman Press, 1966); H. Leon McBeth, *A Sourcebook for Baptist Heritage* (Nashville: Broadman Press, 1991).

[101] A plethora of contributions by outstanding Baptist scholars, who described and defined Southern Baptists, was available for the study of Baptists and Southern Baptists. Among those which I read during my teaching years, and especially during and beyond the Controversy, included: Robert G. Torbet, *A History of Baptists,* 3rd ed. (Valley Forge, PA: Judson Press, 1973), and Bill J. Leonard, *Baptist Ways: A History* (Valley Forge: Judson, 2003). Studies centered more on Baptists in America included William H. Brackney, *Baptists in North America: An Historical Perspective* (Malden, MA: Blackwell, 2006), Smaller and more popular works of significant value include Pamela R. Durso and Keith E. Durso, *The Story of Baptists in the United States* (Brentwood, TN: Baptist History & Heritage Society, 2006). Moreover, The Baptist History & Heritage Society (baptisthistory.org) published several pamphlet and video series. Studies emphasizing Southern Baptists include W. W. Barnes, *The Southern Baptist Convention: 1845-1953* (Nashville: Broadman Press, 1954); Robert A. Baker, *The Southern Baptist Convention and Its People, 1607-1972* (Nashville: Broadman Press, 1974); Albert McClellan, *Meet Southern Baptists* (Nashville: Broadman Press, 1978); and Fletcher, *Southern Baptist Convention*. I might add that my Southern Baptist histories published in 2000 and 2021 also contributed to the books on the denomination, especially with the chapters on the Controversy, the Restructuring of the Convention, and theology.

possibility of "publish and perish." This seemed especially true of seminary professors that I knew. They often experienced anxiety over the dangers of being accused of promoting "heretical" opinions, at least in the eyes of very conservative ministers. Therefore, many avoided addressing controversial topics when publishing.

As previously discussed, I published my first article based on my dissertation in *Perspectives in Religious Studies*, the journal of the Association of Baptist Professors of Religion. I discussed the ecclesiological development of John Robinson, pastor of the Pilgrim Fathers, and Henry Jacob, founder in 1616 of a non-Separatist congregation in the Southwark, England.[102] I also submitted the article entitled "The Ecclesiology of Henry Jacob," which appeared in *The Quarterly Review*. This article was the second one based upon my dissertation. These early efforts at publishing on congregational polity provided the foundation for understanding the issues that faced Southern Baptists during the long conflict in the late twentieth century. Importantly, as an historian, I unequivocally assert that the foundational Baptist commitment to the autonomy of the local church has eroded in the twenty-first-century distorted version of the Southern Baptist Convention, giving way to the pastoral authority of leaders and especially, the dominating power of the Executive Committee of the convention.

At OBU, Dr. Warren McWilliams became my best friend and colleague. Warren was a few years younger than me. I soon realized that he was a prolific scholar who had already established a reputation in writing not only books, but academic articles for professional journals, and a wide range of denominational publications to assist pastors and laymen in the ministries of the local churches. Not only was I impressed by the scope of publications by Warren, I also dedicated myself to contribute on a regular basis in the publishing world. Over the rest of my career, I constantly sought the advice and assistance of my good friend. Even today, as I exercise by walking in an area mall, I call Warren and discuss writing projects, including this one.

Warren not only gave me helpful direction in writing, he also recommended me to publishers of Baptist academic journals and denominational publications, which opened doors to opportunities to write and publish. Even in the writing of my last four books, I have turned to Warren for

---

[102] Slayden A. Yarbrough, "The Ecclesiastical Development in Theory and Practice of John Robinson and Henry Jacob," in *Perspectives in Religious Studies* 5, no. 3 (1978): 196-210.

critique, information, and recommendations, especially on matters of theology and biblical resources. If there is one person who influenced me more than others in my publishing pursuits, it is my former fellow religion professor at OBU.

As I developed as a writer, I recognized that I was not the original thinker that I envisioned. In fact, I often say that I have come up with only one original thought in my numerous publications. When writing my book on Southern Baptists in 2000, in the chapter on theology, I concluded that for Baptists theology is not a test of faith, but rather the result of faith. To me, this is a crucial and extremely relevant insight. It may be that I came across this principle from some other writer. If so, I have absolutely no recollection. To me, I believe that my position was a commonsense conclusion based on extensive research into the subject of the Baptist confessional approach to theology. So, I will claim originality until someone else redirects me to an earlier source.

At the same time, I also concluded that I developed a skill of being a good synthesizer of the thoughts of others. I developed as an organizer, summarizer, and digester of the contributions of Baptist scholars, and of primary resources. In so doing, I used the contributions of established Baptist historians often in my research and writings on subjects from Baptist history and thought.

I find value in this approach. Good scholarship includes the ability to communicate clearly detailed research. I developed this skill as a graduate student at BU. Most of my classes required research papers, and the assignment deadlines came fast and furious at times. One semester I had fourteen papers assigned. That worked out to be one paper every week. I organized my personal schedule based upon deadlines. I then outlined each paper. This approach works well and I utilized it when I became a professor who assigned papers.

I often told my students that when they wrote a paper, tell the reader what they intended to do in the paper, why they were examining the topic, and how they would present it. Then they needed to do what they said they would do in the main text of the paper. Finally, I advised them to write a conclusion telling what they had done and why it was relevant. This was a rather simplistic approach, but it provided structure for gathering, organizing, and presenting material.

Slayden A. Yarbrough

When it came to personal publications, my ability to gather, organize, and present material proved to be effective. The end products usually enabled the reader to understand important information in a well-organized document. As a byproduct, this approach also enabled me to provide important information while staying within the pagination and other guidelines of the editor of the periodicals.

A good example of this approach was when Dr. H. Leon McBeth, professor of Baptist history at Southwestern Baptist Theological Seminary, who was serving as an editor for the fourth volume of the *Encyclopedia of Southern Baptists* asked me to write an article. The topic was on "Premillennialism" in the denomination since the updated publication of Volume III, written a decade earlier. Leon gave me a limit of two-typewritten, double-spaced pages, which included a set number of words.

When I write, I produce my first draft as aggressively and as fast as possible. Then, I carefully review the document, and edit according to the guidelines. My initial draft was eight pages, four times the allowable requirement by Leon. I begin to edit the draft (on my Smith-Corona portable typewriter), initially reducing it to six pages, then four, and finally finishing it at the two-page limit. In so doing, I somehow did not sacrifice the important content in the article. I then forwarded it to him.

Later, during a meeting of the SBHS, Leon told a group of people the challenges of editing the encyclopedia, especially since he had to edit all articles that exceeded the word/page requirements. He then turned to me and said that "Slayden was the only writer who stayed within the required wording and pagination." And, as stated I did not sacrifice the quality of the assigned subject. Over the years, Leon and I became good friends. I even took a course in Baptist history under him at Southwestern Seminary's summer program at Regent's Park College in Oxford, which further enhanced our friendship.

Another influence on my writing (and speaking) came from several leading scholars in Baptist history. I was so impressed by the warm, kind spirit of these teachers and writers. They had the ability to tell stories in such a positive yet constructive manner. Leon was one of those who displayed this quality. His love of Baptist history was contagious, and I simply followed his example.

Dr. Bill Leonard and Dr. Walter "Buddy" Shurden are also great storytellers, whose passions for the rich heritage of the denomination were infectious.

Their commitment to the history and principles of Baptists is unquestioned. They practiced what they preached—and published—in accord with this conviction.

I joined Bill on a tour of Baptist history which he led to the British Isles in the 1990s. On a train trip from Edinburgh to London two Oxford students sat across from us. They were from Japan and were engaged in a conversation in their native language. Bill surprised them and me as he soon engaged them, communicating with them in fluent Japanese. Bill spent time in Japan doing mission work in his younger days. He was simply comfortable with people, respectful of who they were, and so pleasant in his conversational style. The two students were delighted to meet someone who had learned to use their language so easily.

I vividly remember a meeting in Nashville of the SBHS, when Bill was delivering a paper related to Calvinism in the Baptist tradition. Bill told a story of his grandmother, who was a Primitive Baptist. She was uncertain about whether she was one of the "elect" or "chosen" from the foundations of the earth. She had a dream one night where she saw Jesus signaling to her to "come to me." She told her friends, who assured her that she was certainly one of the chosen of Jesus. Her doubts vanished. Bill told this story with such sensitivity for his grandmother, and such warmth and appreciation for her and her tradition of this group of hyper-Calvinistic Baptists. He always displayed this spirit in every story that he told, as he made Baptist teachings simple and clear in such an easygoing way, while expressing a genuine respect for the diversity of the people called Baptist.

Buddy Shurden is a similarly wonderful storyteller. He too is able to simplify the Baptist message in such a positive manner, while never sacrificing the depths of its principles and contributions. I remember a presentation at an SBHS meeting in Nashville, as the Controversy was dividing the denomination. Of course, the conservative group had made one's view of the Scriptures a test of faith. Buddy presented a monologue on the Bible, which was superb. He addressed the issues over the Scriptures in the first person in a way that clarified the challenges in such a conversational approach.

For several years, I tried to figure out a way to teach my listeners among other topics about the history of the canon, text, and translations of the Bible. These topics were so important in my own journey in understanding and interpreting the Bible. I do not remember much of Buddy's address, but I seized upon the idea of a monologue, which I initially wrote during the early 1980s. I have presented throughout my career and beyond my version of "I

Slayden A. Yarbrough

Am the Bible" in over sixty congregations, as well as other Baptist organizations. I continue to edit the presentation to incorporate new material, especially in the ongoing publications of newer translations. An early version on my presentation was published in 1986 in *Proclaim,* a minister's magazine of the Sunday School Board.

I also included an edited version of the monologue in a book that I published in 2020 during the COVID crisis. The volume is *I Am: Storytelling in Worship,*[103] and includes nine monologues and dramatic readings in the first person. I credit Buddy with the inspiration to develop the technique of first-person presentations as an effective means of a conversational style in engaging listeners (who often love to tell their own stories). Like Leon and Bill, Buddy's warm spirit impacted my attitude and approach not only in speaking, but also in writing.

Dr. Michael Kuykendall has certainly been an influence in my writing during my retirement years in Vancouver, Washington. Mike, a recently retired professor at Gateway Seminary (formerly Golden Gate Baptist Theological Seminary), used as a textbook my *Southern Baptists: A Historical, Ecclesiological, and Theological Heritage of a Confessional People.* When Janis and I moved from Denver to Vancouver in 2009, I looked up Mike and we quickly became friends. When I decided to edit and update this book, I enlisted Mike's help. He has been an invaluable help in critiquing a few other writing projects in recent years, and simply has been a good friend and a great sounding board on my publishing efforts.

As mentioned throughout this book, one of the most significant motivations on my publishing contributions was the rise and appearance of the "Controversy" in the Southern Baptist Convention. My entire academic career was framed by the battle among Southern Baptists. Most of my writings resulted from my commitment to address topics related to Baptist history, Baptist principles, Baptist theology, and Baptist interpretations of the Baptist heritage and the biblical tradition of the Baptists. Looking back on my career as a professor, almost everything I published was in some fashion related to the dominant struggle in the Southern Baptist Convention.

---

[103] Slayden A. Yarbrough, *I Am: Storytelling in Worship* (Rapid City, SD: New Harbor Press, 2020).

## Publications: Books From My Career Years

Introduction: I published several books while at OBU. They ranged in subject matter from Southern Baptist history to local church history to Baptist institutional history. All of them resulted from my role as a Baptist historian. In one way or another they also reflect the influence of defining and defending the Southern Baptist heritage in a denomination infected by controversy.

### *Southern Baptists: Who Are We?* [104]

While at Southwest Baptist, I developed a sermon on "Southern Baptists: Who Are We?" which was jam-packed with Southern Baptist history, theology, and mission and ministry organizations and their contributions. The sermon was widely accepted in the churches in Missouri, and later in Oklahoma. The sermon also became the foundation for a series of lectures on the topics discussed in Baptist meetings, a series of articles in the *Oklahoma Baptist Chronicle*, and a book resulting from these articles entitled *Southern Baptists: Who Are We?* All these accomplishments were built upon an appreciation for Southern Baptists developed in Dr. H. K. Neely's class on the Baptist denomination taken during my senior year at Southwest.

Soon after arriving at OBU, I met and became good friends with Dr. J. M. Gaskin, the executive director of the Oklahoma Baptist Historical Commission and the Oklahoma Baptist Historical Society. He encouraged and assisted me in becoming active in Baptist history organizations at both the state and national levels. He intentionally provided me with many opportunities to speak, write, and serve as a Baptist historian.

Dr. Gaskin served as editor of the *Oklahoma Baptist Chronicle*. In this capacity he presented initial and numerous opportunities for me to contribute articles on Baptists. One summer in the early 1980s I was invited to speak to an annual program for seniors on the OBU campus. I presented my lecture on Southern Baptists entitled "Southern Baptists: Who Are We?" Dr. Gaskin attended, and after hearing my presentation invited me to prepare an article

---

[104] Slayden Yarbrough, *Southern Baptists: Who Are We?* 3rd ed. (Oklahoma City: Historical Commission of the Baptist General Convention of Oklahoma and the Oklahoma Baptist Historical Society, 1990). Although complete information has previously been footnoted for most of my books, since this chapter discusses each book, I am including the full reference for each one.

for the *Oklahoma Baptist Chronicle*. I began to revise my material for publication. By the time I finished writing, the project had expanded to three articles on the three sections of my presentation.

The articles were published in successive issues of the *Oklahoma Baptist Chronicle*. Dr. Gaskin saved the copy, and approached me about combining the articles into a small book to be published by the Oklahoma Baptist Historical Commission. With a little further editing, the first edition of *Southern Baptists: Who Are We?* was published in 1984. In the years that followed, the denomination which was now engaged in the Controversy, was constantly changing in terms of leadership of the organizations, and new emphases and programs. New editions of my book were published in 1985 and 1990.

In summary, I am thoroughly indebted to Dr. H. K. Neely, my professor in "The Baptist Denomination" class at Southwest, and his assignment for me to teach the class after I became a professor at the institution. A second significant influence was Dr. Gaskin, who provided me the opportunity to publish my initial volume on the history of the denomination. This small publication *Southern Baptists: Who Are We?* became the foundation for an expanded book in 2000.

**Southern Baptists: A Historical, Ecclesiological, and Theological Heritage of a Confessional People**: During the decade of the 1980s and into the 1990s, Southern Baptists were aggressively engaged in the "Controversy," which would radically reshape the convention, replace the leaders of almost every agency, and result in numerous state organizations, churches, and members leaving the denomination. I would be among those, taking early retirement from OBU in 2001, moving with Janis to Denver, and becoming active in the American Baptist Churches of the USA.

During the last two decades of the twentieth century, I continued to chronicle and edit my material on the denomination. I collected, researched, organized, and prepared historical information on the "Controversy" and the "Restructuring" of the convention as these movements developed. I drew material from contemporaneous events, publications of other Baptist historians, and contemporary accounts about the Southern Baptist struggle for authority in both Baptist and secular newspapers and publications.

During the process I also became actively involved in the institutional life of the denomination. In 2000, using my previous book on the denomination, editing it thoroughly, and adding significant chapters chronicling the

Controversy and the restructuring, I self-published *Southern Baptists: A Historical, Ecclesiological, and Theological Heritage of a Confessional People*.[105]

As I made plans to publish this book, I decided to complete it after the annual meeting in June of 2000 of the Southern Baptist Convention. The convention planned to vote on the updated version of the *Baptist Faith and Message*. This document included controversial changes to the preface. It also included the 1998 revision, which added the section on "The Family."

I knew what the outcome would be in terms of the vote. So, I wrote about the 2000 *Baptist Faith and Message* with the anticipated changes. Not being a prophet, but also being a pretty good Southern Baptist historian, my predictions came true. The day after the action by the convention messengers to approve the newly edited *Baptist Faith and Message*, I mailed my manuscript to Fields Publishing in Nashville to be printed in my book, which I considered the very latest and the first history of the denomination in the twenty-first century (although I am among those who believe that the new century would not officially begin until January 1, 2001).

To this day, I believe that the chapters on the Controversy and the restructuring of convention agencies are my most significant contributions to this critical period in Southern Baptist life. The convention would never be the same. And, I not only chronicled it, I was an active participant.

**The Lengthening Shadow: A Centennial History, Heritage, and Hope of First Baptist Church, Shawnee, Oklahoma 1892-1992**. Local church histories are important in understanding Southern Baptists. In 1992, First Baptist Church of Shawnee, Oklahoma, was preparing to celebrate its centennial anniversary. As a member of the congregation and a Baptist historian, I was asked to write the centennial history. The experience was enjoyable. I did most of my writing by arriving at my office on the campus of OBU around 6 a.m., and working until my first class, usually at 8 a.m.

Reading the early minutes of the church was delightful, and in many ways entertaining. The church clerk left nothing out when it came to controversy or "de-churching" members for ethical or theological issues. The minutes also told of members coming from all over the United States into the Indian

---

[105] Slayden A. Yarbrough, *Southern Baptists: A Historical, Ecclesiological, and Theological Heritage of a Confessional People* (Nashville: Fields Publishing, 2000).

Slayden A. Yarbrough

Territory, which began in 1834, and the Oklahoma Territory, which began in 1890. The boundary between the two territories prior to statehood ran north and south through the middle of Shawnee.

Like most of the churches organized in the 1890s, First Baptist Church of Shawnee reflected the major influences of war, social challenges, and denominational conflict. Initially, First Baptist Church was dually aligned with the Northern Baptists and Southern Baptists, but soon affiliated solely with the Southern Baptist Convention. Its history closely intertwined with that of OBU. The church aligned with the moderate element of the convention during the Controversy.

One of the early issues in the conflict was the ordination of women deacons, which First Baptist Church affirmed. Some pastors in the Pottawatomie-Lincoln Association wanted to boot the church from the organization. Rev. James Paul Maxwell, the association's missionary, met with the pastor of First Baptist Church, Dr. Joe Brown, to discuss the concerns. Joe quickly pointed out that the church provided the most financial support for the association among all the affiliated churches. The protest over women deacons against First Baptist quietly disappeared.

A second issue with the association was the adoption of the 1963 *Baptist Faith and Message*. First Baptist, along with thousands of churches, had affirmed this revision of the original *Baptist Faith and Message* (1925). The revision came under criticism of the conservative leaders of the Southern Baptist Convention in the early 1970s, and the association voted to criticize the document. As I remember, First Baptist simply referred to the preface, reaffirmed its acceptance of the confessional statement, and basically ignored the association's stand.

The history of First Baptist during these years reflected the challenges faced by churches across the wide spectrum of the Southern Baptist Convention. In the end many churches would eventually disassociate with the convention. First Baptist Church of Shawnee, however, was one of those congregations which was closely connected with a Baptist educational institution, and continued to remain connected to the state and national Southern Baptist Convention organizations, while seeking to express its independent nature on matters of faith and practice.

**The View from Bison Hill: 75 Years of Remembrance:** In 1985 I contributed to the 75th anniversary history of OBU. I joined Dr. J. M. Gaskin, Eunice Short, and Helen Thames Raley in authoring the volume. I was responsible for the section entitled "The View from Bison Hill, 1961-1985." During the latter part of this period the Controversy was in its earliest stages and affected not only individuals and churches, but also educational institutions. As previously mentioned, I arrived as a professor in 1979, just as the conflict was initially beginning.

A major challenge of my assignment was to record the story of the "Heresy Paper." I discussed this crisis earlier in Chapter 4 of this book. So, I will not repeat the details. It is important to note that the Controversy officially began in June of 1979 at the annual meeting of the Southern Baptist Convention, the same year as the "Heresy Paper." The university, however, survived this attack. No faculty were dismissed. And the relationship of the churches in Oklahoma and the university in Shawnee were strengthened. OBU and its faculty were affirmed for carrying out the responsibilities relating to the churches of Oklahoma.[106]

But the "Controversy" in the Southern Baptist Convention was just beginning. The strategy proposed by Paige Patterson of enlisting pastors to seek out heretics in denominational agencies and institutions would continue to be implemented throughout the convention. Anxiety on college and university campuses would continue to rise, and turmoil would engulf the convention in the next two decades. Charges of heretical teaching would go unabated. Control of the boards and agencies was seized by the conservatives. A major restructuring was the result for the denomination, which authoritatively chose new directions.

## Books: The "COVID Collection"

COVID 19 radically changed the twilight years of my retirement when it came to publishing. In 2020, after several months of practicing stay-in-place policies, binge-watching numerous documentaries, new and old movies and TV programs, and with Janis working numerous, 1,000-piece jigsaw puzzles (we have completed over 200 puzzles), I decided to spend time putting together a few writing projects that I contemplated during my retirement years.

For many years, I considered publishing a book of monologue presentations, updating my 2000 history of Southern Baptists, and writing a book of

---

[106] Yarbrough, "The View from Bison Hill, 1961-1985," 181.

growing up for my grandson. I kept putting all the projects aside for a later time, which in all honesty probably was not going to come. Then COVID arrived in radical force, upending daily lives throughout the world. I suddenly had a lot of time on my hands. Renewing my goals of books to publish became a challenge and an opportunity, and the pandemic provided the circumstances in which to write.

***I Am: Storytelling in Worship***: I initially presented my first monologue, while serving as interim pastor of First Baptist Church of Pawnee, Oklahoma. The town was the home of the wild west entertainer known as Pawnee Bill. The church had an evening service, and I was going over a sermon on Peter. I decided to set my notes aside, and present the story of the apostle in the first-person format. I without notes told the apostle's story, and it apparently went very well. Out of this positive experience I would venture forth with other characters in the years ahead. However, I never put the Peter monologue into a written form, and never presented it again.

As previously mentioned, I prepared, presented, and published in *Proclaim* my monologue "I Am the Bible." I began to write other monologues and dramatic readings in the first person. These conversations were addressed to the person in the pew. They conveyed old stories for a contemporary generation. I continue to present this monologue in churches. My most recent delivery came in early 2024 at Grace Baptist Church in Portland, Oregon. I have surpassed sixty presentations of "I Am the Bible" in congregations and other Baptist venues.

All my monologues reflected my role as a teacher and researcher as I prepared and delivered them. One of the most important characteristics of these presentations was the provision of the background material to the stories. Historical, political, and social contexts were woven into the narratives of each character. I also blended into my stories the context of the biblical information and interpretation to enhance the contributions of scholarly research in the presentations.

For my "I Am the Bible" monologue, I even wrote the words to a hymn, which I titled "Eternal Word, O Word of God." The tune for the song was "O God, Our Help, in Ages Past." It highlighted the creative word, and the written, proclaimed, and incarnate word of God through the ages.

Without following a particular order, I wrote a monologue on the prodigal son, telling his story from Luke 15. I followed up with a monologue of the older brother, and even added the character of the father who had to balance his love for both of his very different sons. I concluded that a lot of Baptists could identify with one of the two brothers. Presenting their stories in worship was very enjoyable for me. The challenge of a retired religion professor portraying a couple of young men telling their stories did not deter me. And, I successfully triggered the creative imaginations of my hearers to set aside my few gray hairs and accumulated wrinkles over many years to take them on a journey of an earlier age.

While teaching at OBU, I was invited by the pastor of University Baptist Church to do a presentation for Reformation Sunday, which of course is connected to October 31, Halloween (the eve of All-Saints Day), and the beginning of the Protestant Reformation. I decided to present a monologue, which I called "A Visit with Martin Luther." The service was held in an old church building, Stubblefield Chapel, which originally was the home of the First Baptist Church of Shawnee, Oklahoma. The BGCO Historical Society moved the building to the campus of OBU, and it was named Stubblefield Chapel. Wearing an old choir robe, I shared the pilgrimage of the sixteenth-century Augustinian monk who radically changed Christianity, and whose views influenced the people called Baptists when they appeared in the early 1600s. I continue to show up as Luther on Reformation Sunday, when an opportunity in a local church presents itself. My most recent presentation was in Grace Baptist Church, Portland, Oregon, in October of 2023.

I also decided to interpret the book of Revelation from the amillennial viewpoint in a narrative, which I titled "John and the Apocalypse." I have presented this monologue much less than others, but still enjoy doing it. When I began to compile my monologues into a book, I realized that I needed one more. So, I wrote "Mark and the First Gospel." For years I have loved the story of Mark, the influences on his life, and the record of Papias in the early second century. Papias related how Mark used the preaching of Peter to provide content for what is often interpreted as the earliest written Synoptic Gospel.

I also prepared three dramatic readings, which I included in my first "COVID" book project. My favorite is "I Am Christmas." It too involved editing and adding characters to the story. I now have around ten figures who tell their roles in the Christmas narrative. I continue to invite members of the congregation to participate, and it is always a delightful celebration of the advent season. This reading initially was published in *Proclaim* in 1986. The most recent performance of this reading was on Christmas Eve in 2023, again at Grace Baptist in Portland.

Slayden A. Yarbrough

I prepared a manuscript entitled "Voices from the Passion Week," which includes several characters from the entry of Jesus into Jerusalem up through the resurrection. I even created a few non-biblical characters, including a boy named "Zac" who observed the entry of Jesus into Jerusalem on Palm Sunday, and a moneychanger who I named "Simeon." Finally, I prepared a reading with four historical characters, and titled it "My Name Is Baptist, but My Friends Call Me Liberty." I usually present this reading around Independence Day, stressing the contributions of Baptists to the principles of religious liberty and separation of church and state. Historical figures include John Smyth, Thomas Helwys, Roger Williams, and John Leland.

**Southern Baptists: A History of a Confessional People:** My second COVID 19 project was an update of my 2000 book *Southern Baptists: A Historical, Ecclesiological, and Theological Heritage of a Confessional People*. As previously stated, I am convinced that my treatment of the Controversy and the restructuring of the Southern Baptist Convention is an important contribution to the history of this significant era. I was a contemporary observer, a participant, and a researcher of the radical changes taking place in the movement. I determined to be as objective as possible, although I confess that my biased views crept into the narrative in a few places. I was without question one who was a moderate. I realized that after two decades a revision was needed, and I continued to believe that my narrative of the Controversy and restructuring was still relevant, especially in the continuing conflicts in the Southern Baptist Convention.

I recognized that I had not kept up with recent developments in the denomination, since I retired in 2001. I needed a fellow historian to bring the work up-to-date, and to assist in editing the previous volume. Enter Dr. Michael Kuykendall. He had become a good friend after Janis and I moved from Denver to Vancouver in 2009. Mike primarily taught New Testament classes. But he also regularly taught Baptist history. He used my 2000 book on *Southern Baptists* as a supplementary text in his Baptist history class until it went out of print. We began to meet for coffee on a regular basis. I set him up at one of these sessions. I told him of my desire to update my earlier volume, but that I needed someone who had kept up with the convention in the past two decades. He readily volunteered, as I had hoped he would do.

Mike helped edit the earlier volume, including the expansion of bibliographical resources from the conservative movement. This would add to the credibility of the book. He also made excellent suggestions to improve the content of the 2000 book. He added additional historical information on the seminaries, which was lacking in my earlier volume. Finally, he wrote a section on specific challenges facing the denomination in the twenty-first century.

In 2021, McFarland Press published the new version. Mike and I also agreed upon a new title, *Southern Baptists: A History of a Confessional People*. For me, an important incentive in bringing this work up to date was my naïve belief that should any Southern Baptists who wants to understand how the denomination moved away from its historical and theological roots, this volume would be an excellent beginning resource. I was certain that the book would be my final contribution to the study of both Southern Baptists and Baptists in general. At the time I did not believe that I would write my own story of a career shaped primarily by the context of the Controversy. I proved to be wrong with the publication of this current volume.

**We Coulda Been Killed! Two Brothers and Others Growing Up:**[107] *We Coulda Been Killed!* is the most fun book I have ever written. I have always been a storyteller. I told and retold to family and friends the many tales of my adventures growing up and beyond. Numerous times my friends and relatives suggested that I write them down. Of course, I am not the only one who has ever been encouraged to provide a written record of my many adventures. Autobiography is a historical and personal approach which results in innumerable publications.

Up until COVID my last effort at this project came during my time at OBU. Somewhere along the way, I discontinued my narrative, and my 3½ inch floppy disk disappeared into cyberspace. After many starts and stops, I finally decided to attempt a serious effort at telling my stories to preserve them for relatives and friends.

In September of 2022, Scott, my son, and Kellan, my grandson, were visiting Janis and me at our home in Vancouver. I was telling Kellan some of my stories. Scott once again suggested that I write them down. So, in October I kicked it into gear. I started writing. Having published two books after COVID changed our lives and routines, I was determined to complete the process this time.

---

[107] Slayden A. Yarbrough, *We Coulda Been Killed! Two Brothers and Others Growing Up* (Vancouver, WA: Slayden A. Yarbrough, 2022).

Slayden A. Yarbrough

I developed a flexible schedule, which I followed rather consistently, if not religiously. Most mornings I arose around 6 a.m., ate breakfast, and then wrote for an hour or two until heading to the local mall to get my walking in. Restrictions were being lifted, although I wore a mask while walking. Not having to document too much, I recalled events and people on my journey, especially stories about my brother Steve and me, my love of sports, and my pilgrimage toward attaining an education. I always told the truth as I remembered it, while at the same time embellishing my narrative to make the stories entertaining and humorous.

The title of the book arose thirty years earlier. Janis and I were visiting Steve and his wife Shirley at their home in Collinsville, Illinois. Also present was Scott, who arrived from New York. Steve and I began telling the old stories. Steve, like so many others before, suggested that I write them down. Scott chimed in with "I know what you should call it: *"We Coulda Been Killed!"* We all laughed at the appropriateness of this suggestion. When I finished my manuscript, the title was a given. In February of 2023 I self-published the book through Amazon's KDP (Kindle Direct Publishing), fulfilling a decades long dream.

One of the special touches to the book is the cover. It is a compilation of several figures and scenes related to events which Steve and I engaged in which shaped our lives growing up in Washington Park, Illinois, in the 1950s. My grandson Kellan was in high school and developing skills in sketching scenes. I asked him to produce the cover and he agreed, even adding a few twists to my recommendations.

You may be asking why I included this book in my list of writings about my career as a Baptist. I included a chapter in the book about becoming a Baptist, the many positives that resulted from my pilgrimage, and my dismissal from SWBC. The events of my career at two Baptist educational institutions provided so much context in this volume that you are reading. I am sure that many of my friends and colleagues experienced their own journeys during the troubled and challenging years of personal growth of the Controversy. I am confident that many of these people will relate to my journey, as they evaluate their own participation in all that was going on in the late twentieth century.

***Fired for Heresy: A Baptist History Professor's Career During the SBC Controversy.*** This book really is my last book (as I thought were the first three volumes in my COVID collection). In fact, I like to say that it is my "fourth final book." I received Bill Dudley's correspondence and transcripts

1979. I began to consider the possibility of writing the story of losing my job at my alma mater. After retiring I reflected on my teaching career. I recognized that it was in the context of the background and the progression of the Controversy. After publishing my most recent volumes, I found myself once more with time to write in the mornings before walking. This final volume was waiting to be written. I finally began this project over forty years after its original inception. And, I assure you that this will be my final book. I hope.

The Controversy is known for its imprint upon agencies and institutions of the Southern Baptist Convention. At the same time, it had a profound effect upon so many individuals. I am one of those. Although I was not one of the most visible participants in the struggle, in terms of the effect on of Baptist history, I still played an important role. I taught, I published, and above all I participated in the struggle to maintain the work and the witness of the heritage of Baptists. I affirm that I was the one person who served as a trustee on the Historical Commission, including time as chair of the board, and who also led the agency as the final executive of the organization as it was being dissolved. I was the one messenger who made a motion to save his agency at the annual convention meeting in Atlanta in 1995.

I was also one of several leaders in the move to preserve the SBHS as a completely independent organization following the restructuring of denominational agencies. I was the first executive director of the Society elected following the dissolution of the Historical Commission in 1997. I led the effort to recruit the institutional and financial support of Baptist colleges and universities of the Society. In addition, I envisioned and in 2000 succeeded in the establishment of the Fellowship of Baptist Historians in Savannah, Georgia. Dr. John Finley, pastor of First Baptist Church, hosted the annual meeting of the Society. He recently served as the executive director of the BHHS. He retired in June 2024. I believe that this fellowship is now the most significant group to support the continuing work of the Society. On July 12, 2024, the BHHS announced the hiring of Dr. Aaron Weaver as the part-time Executive Director of the voluntary organization.

The bottom line is that I was one individual who had the passion, the experience, and several unique opportunities to work with so many other Baptist historians who refused to let the work die. It was a challenging task during and beyond the years of the Controversy and restructuring. But it was essential. That work is still important today. That this is still challenging is a given, of course. But it continues to be important and relevant. In this regard, it is still personal, while at the same time a collective effort. I was privileged

Slayden A. Yarbrough

to be a one of the many who were passionately committed to the significance of Baptist history. My published books, especially *Fired for Heresy*, are a relevant part of the record of this tumultuous period of Baptist history.

# Chapter Eight

# Publishing During The "Controversy" Part 2: Encyclopedias, Dictionaries, And Editorials

## *Baptist History & Heritage: A Journal In Pursuit Of History*

*Baptist History & Heritage* is "dedicated to the pursuit of historical information that will enable Baptists to understand themselves, to appreciate their past, and to discover historical perspective for the future. If an occasional article helps Baptists to avoid mistakes of the past and enunciate more positively the cherished truths that have made and sustained them across the years, the journal will have served a worthwhile purpose." Quote from Davis C. Woolley. [108]

## Introduction

During my career I had numerous opportunities to write and publish not only books but also articles for reference works. I also served as editor of *Baptist History & Heritage* during my tenure as executive director of both the Commission and the Society for three years. I thoroughly enjoyed my role as editor, and often addressed contemporary issues and challenges.

## Publications: Baptist Encyclopedia and Dictionary Articles

***Encyclopedia of Southern Baptists*:** Early in my teaching career at OBU, I was invited to prepare an article for inclusion in the *Encyclopedia of Southern Baptists*, volume IV. Dr. J. M. Gaskin recommended me as a writer to the Historical Commission, which was preparing the update of the original two-volume set (1959), and the updated volume III (1971). He proposed that I write an article on premillennialism in Baptist groups. His recommendation was forwarded to Dr. H. Leon McBeth, professor of Baptist history at

---

[108] Davis C. Woolley was the first editor of *Baptist History & Heritage*. This quote comes from the first volume of the journal: https//thebhhs.org/resources/baptist-history-heritage-journal/.

Slayden A. Yarbrough

Southwestern Baptist Theological Seminary, who was on the editorial committee for volume IV. Leon officially invited me to write an article on "Premillennialism Among Baptists."[109] I previously described my effort at reducing the size of the article from eight pages before finally reaching the required two pages.

As the Controversy was heating up in the Southern Baptist Convention, the Historical Commission was considering an updated version of the *Encyclopedia of Southern Baptists*. The project was brought before the commissioners, or trustees, of the organization. After thorough discussion, the members recommended that it was not a good time to engage in such a project. Finding qualified historians to treat topics and personalities engaged in both sides of the Controversy could result in unwanted criticism of the Commission. On the one hand, this was a good decision. One the other hand, it did not make a difference in the end since the agency was among those dissolved in the restructuring of the convention.

One final development on the *Encyclopedia of Southern Baptists* occurred during my tenure as interim executive of the Commission following the retirement of Dr. May. After the messengers voted to restructure the convention agencies, among the publications that the Sunday School Board (SSB) decided to no longer publish was the four-volume *ESB*. I contacted Dr. James "Jimmy" Draper, who was the president of the SSB. I asked that the copyright be transferred to the SBHS. After consultation with its lawyers, the SSB granted my request. At OBU, I asked the Mabee Learning Center to copy the four-volume set, which they did. The library produced a CD version and preserved the reference work in a format that was electronically available. Although the set has not been updated since 1982, it remains a valuable source for the history of the Southern Baptist Convention for the first 140 years of the convention.

***Dictionary of Baptists in America*:** Dr. Bill Leonard served as editor of this important reference source, published in 1994. This almost 300-page book contains a wealth of historical information on Baptists. The back cover states that "this dictionary covers the ideas, events, people, movements, practices, institutions, and denominations that have made up the Baptist tradition in

---

[109] Slayden Yarbrough, "Premillennialism Among Baptist Groups" *Encyclopedia of Southern Baptists*, vol. IV (Nashville: Broadman Press, 1982), 2424.

North America from the earliest days to the present."[110] The selection of topics demonstrates clearly the diversity and influence of the tradition of the people called "Baptist."

The contributors comprised a wide range of Baptist historians identified with many Baptist denominations. I was fortunate to be included among the writers, and was honored to have my name appear with so many Baptist historian friends that I had made during my career. I contributed five articles to the dictionary: "Jones, Samuel, 1735-1814," "Landrum, William Warren, 1853-1926," "New Connection Baptists," "Oklahoma Baptist University," and "Orthodox Baptist Movement."

## Editor of *Baptist History & Heritage* and Thematic Issues

Introduction: On June 1, 1995, I began my service as interim executive director of the Southern Baptist Historical Commission. My major responsibility was to lead the organization in the dissolution recommended by the Executive Committee of the convention. That task would take two years. It would require adoption of "Covenant for a New Century" by messengers to the annual Southern Baptist Convention, followed by two years of implementation.

Dr. Ron Martin was chairman of the board of the Historical Commission during this time. Following the vote of messengers to the convention in June of 1996 to dissolve the agency, Dr. Martin removed the title of "Interim." He concluded that since there would be no new executive director with the dissolution of the Commission, the term "Interim" was no longer relevant. I therefore became the last executive director in the final months of the Commission's existence.

In addition, the SBHS selected me to serve as executive director. I would serve in this capacity from 1996-1999. As executive director of the Society, one on my responsibilities was being the editor of *Baptist History & Heritage*, the journal of the Commission and Society, and then the Society only following the dissolution of the Commission. I served in this capacity

---

[110] Bill J. Leonard, ed., *Dictionary of Baptists in America* (Downers Grove, IL: InterVarsity Press, 1994), back cover.

through the fall issue of 1998. Beginning with the winter 1999 issue, Dr. Merrill M. Hawkins Jr. assumed editorship of the journal.

My role as editor proved to be one of the most enjoyable experiences of my academic and denominational career. As a longtime professor of Baptist history, I was able to draw from my experience and training in the subject to develop thematic issues on important and relevant topics for the journal. Jim Taulman, managing editor of *Baptist History & Heritage* during these years, and I enjoyed many hours in brainstorming and selecting the topics for what I consider to be the most important journal devoted to the subject of Baptist history.

During my time as editor, I enjoyed the privilege of writing many editorials on a variety of themes. In this capacity I tried to serve as a voice for Baptist historians on the importance of the past and the issues of the present day. As I reviewed my editorials for this book, I once more realized that my writings reflected the challenges that resulted from the Controversy and the restructuring of the Southern Baptist Convention. The paragraphs that follow will highlight some of the relevant editorials during my tenure.

I also concluded that my personal journey through the Controversy and restructuring influenced my contributions as editor of *Baptist History & Heritage*. This renewed my passion for Baptist history and my commitment to sharing that dedication in teaching, publishing, and serving. I am confident that many of my fellow Baptist historians shared this feeling as well. Together, we recommitted our dedication to the discipline and in a variety of ways provided energy and commitment in interpreting to the wider Baptist community how our history defined the issues of the convention conflict. When it came time to work together, some of the very best Baptist historians devoted their energy and insights to this noble cause. Our Baptist heritage resulted in a fellowship defined by the dedication to our diverse, and yet united cause.

**Guest Editorial: Dr. Lynn E. May, Jr.:**[111] The first editorial I wrote appeared in the final issue of *Baptist History & Heritage* edited by Dr. May prior to his retirement on August 1, 1995. At the time, I was serving as a trustee and chair of the board. I had relocated to Nashville to work with Dr.

---

[111]Slayden A. Yarbrough, "Guest Editorial: Dr. Lynn E. May, Jr." in "The Spirit of Baptists, 1845-1995," *Baptist History & Heritage* 30, no. 3 (October 1995): 4.

May for a few months in the transition of executive leadership of the Commission. The editorial was a great opportunity to pay tribute to almost forty years of service to the agency by this humble, but effective leader. I recognized that as a member of the Society, a trustee of the organization, and a Baptist historian that I had learned much from him and his staff. The Historical Commission was dear to Lynn and his wife, Alta. As I prepared this writing, I realized once again how we all stand on the shoulders of those who come before us.

**Editorial: Atlanta 95, Celebration and Sorrow**: My first editorial as interim executive director of the Commission appeared in the October 1995 issue of *Baptist History & Heritage*. The Southern Baptist Convention met in June in Atlanta and celebrated the sesquicentennial anniversary of the denomination. Normally, this would be a moment of great celebration, and it was. But it also was a time of genuine sorrow.

The recommendation of the Program and Structure Study Committee (PSCC), which the Executive Committee of the Southern Baptist committee had appointed, called for the dissolution of numerous convention agencies. The report entitled "Covenant for a New Century" was presented to the Executive Committee on February 19, 1995, and accepted the following day. Previously, as chair of the Commission's trustees, I asked Dr. May if he wanted me to attend. He saw no need until a few days prior to the Executive Committee meeting, when he was informed of the recommendation as related to the Commission. It was to be dissolved. He was pledged not to tell anyone. He did not inform me what the Executive Committee was planning to propose, although some other agency heads did share the fate of their organizations with others.

Dr. May then contacted me to see whether I could attend. I quickly arranged a flight. I found out the recommendation to close the Commission as it was announced during the Executive Committee meeting. Final approval would be by vote of the convention messengers in June 1995, and during the 1996 annual meeting of the convention, although the second vote would not be held. The agency would end at the annual meeting in June, 1997.

I chronicled the opposition to the dissolution of the Historical Commission, including efforts by Dr. May, a unanimous vote of the agency board and past chairs, and numerous Baptist historians. During the Atlanta meeting, I made a motion to preserve the Historical Commission. It failed, but I was the only one able to speak for the agency that I represented.

Slayden A. Yarbrough

In my editorial I provided an informative overview of all the accomplishments of the agency as it provided a historical ministry to churches, associations, state conventions, and Baptist historians. This service was performed through programs, publications, other resources, like videos, and especially through operation of the Southern Baptist Historical Library & Archives. The library fortunately was able to continue.

The rest of the work of the Commission was assigned to the seminary presidents. I pointed out that of the $500,000 annual cooperative program distribution to the Commission, about $350,000 was available to the library, and only $150,000 was available to the rest of the agency. In closing the Commission, only a miniscule amount was saved in the overall budget of the convention.

I remain convinced that politics, not frugality, was the reason for the action against the Historical Commission. Of course, this opinion was obvious for anyone who was involved in denominational life for the previous two decades. I concluded by pointing out that while the future of Baptist history work was uncertain, the need for it would continue. The SBHS was already in the process of preparing to assume the responsibility as an independent organization. Over twenty-five years later, the Baptist History & Heritage Society, as it is now called, continues to meet the challenge that it was handed in 1997.[112]

**Editorial: Living According to God's Word**: The theme of the January 1996 issue of *Baptist History & Heritage* was "Living According to God's Word." My editorial addressed the topic and described the authors and articles in the issue. However, I also wrote on the subject "The SBHS."[113] The organization began in 1938 and was adopted into the Historical Commission in 1952. But it would soon have to revert back to a truly independent status in little over a year. The year 1996 and following required a refocus and the establishment of a new identity. One day the Society was a partner of the ministry of the Historical Commission. The next day the organization would be completely on its own for leadership, staff support,

---

[112]Slayden A. Yarbrough, Atlanta 95: Celebration and Sorrow in "Living According to God's Word," *Baptist History & Heritage* 30, no. 4 (October 1995): 4-6.
[113]Slayden A. Yarbrough, "Living God's Word," in "Living According to God's Word," *Baptist History & Heritage* 31, no. 1 (October January1996): 4-6.

finances, publications, services, offices—everything that an organization required to survive.

Several leaders emerged. Dr. Albert Wardin, with his longtime passion for the Society, assumed the role of executive director treasurer until a permanent one would be appointed. Dr. Rosalee Back was president of the Society and Dr. Alan Lefever was vice president. Dr. Charles Deweese served as secretary, Dr. Jesse Fletcher was development coordinator, and Dr. W. Morgan Patterson was membership coordinator. All were volunteers. Belmont University would house the offices of the Society until a new director was chosen. Dr. Wardin and Carolyn Patton, administrative assistant to the Commission, worked to obtain a new charter. Plans were made for the annual meeting in 1996.

I also described the challenge to solicit financial support. Dr. Wardin transferred the Alf-Wardin Fund, which was approximately $45,000, from oversight by the Commission to the control of the Society. The Society did have an additional endowment of about $10,000. Other smaller sources were available. I reviewed publications and plans. A new beginning for an old organization was taking place.

**Editorial: The Role of the Southern Baptist Convention President**: The theme for the April 1996 volume of *Baptist History & Heritage* focused on the president of the convention. As the position developed, the office of president began to focus on control of the Committee on Committees, or as it would later be called, the Nominating Committee. The conservative party began to elect candidates who would appoint only committee members committed to their agenda. The committee members would then nominate like-minded individuals to serve on boards, agencies, and institutions. Over a ten-year period, it was possible that all trustees would be committed to the conservative agenda. Therefore, the theme of the journal was most appropriate.

My editorial was on the subject of "The Role of the Southern Baptist Convention President."[114] This issue would be the final one before the last opportunity to reverse the restructuring of the convention, and the

---

[114]Slayden A. Yarbrough, "The Role of the Southern Baptist Convention President," in "Southern Baptist Convention Presidents: Credentials, Authority, Influence," *Baptist History & Heritage* 31, no. 2 (April 1996): 4.

Slayden A. Yarbrough

dissolution of the Commission among other agencies. Articles by Dr. Carolyn Blevins and Dr. H. Leon McBeth traced the history and the authority of the president. It was important for the journal to place in the record the changes made, and sadly the consequences of a more politicized and authoritarian presidency.

I candidly expressed my opposition to the changes and my concerns about the control of the leadership to prevent "all the time needed" to discuss the restructuring that was voted on in the previous convention in Atlanta. I used tapes in the library and archives to document that only five-and-a-half minutes were devoted to the actual proposal. I was the only messenger who was recognized at the microphone. Again, my energy focused on the challenges of the Controversy from the perspective of a Baptist historian.

**Editorial: Southern Baptists and Worship:** "Southern Baptist and Worship" was the theme of the July 1996 issue of *Baptist History & Heritage*. My editorial reflected on the diversity in local churches in terms of worship. Music, places of worship, the theology of worship, and the role of women in worship provided examples. In the years following the Controversy and the restructuring, the freedom of the local church as related to worship became more and more limited, as authority in the denominational leadership became more authoritative. The issue of women especially was limited in the developments because the view of "Complementarianism" dominated the direction of the convention and formed a litmus test for local churches. Basically, the view would prevent churches for having women as pastors in any position in a church.

I also included a section in my editorial, which I titled "The SBHS and Restructuring."[115] I reported on the good progress made toward increasing the endowment to almost $100,000. The Society had also selected me to be the new executive director of the Society. Initially, the position was volunteer. Dr. Jess Fletcher recommended a salary of $2,000 a month about a year later. Copyrights of the journal and other publications were transferred to the SBHS. I had also contacted state convention leaders in Baptist history work, as well as college and university presidents asking for support of the Society. The response was encouraging. Beginning with Dallas University pledging $1,000 annually, other schools soon followed. Two state conventions pledged

---

[115] Slayden A. Yarbrough, "Southern Baptists and Worship," in "Southern Baptists and Worship," *Baptist History & Heritage* 31, no. 3 (July 1996): 4-6.

annual support of $1,000, and others committed to helping. Churches and individuals responded, and financial stability was developing. The challenge was daunting for the Society, but the enthusiasm and commitment was never lacking.

**Editorial: Issues Shaping Baptist Identity**: As the October 1996 issue of *Baptist History & Heritage* was being prepared, Dr. Lynn E. May Jr. passed away on July 24, 1996.[116] He served as research director of the Historical Commission from 1956-1971, and as executive director from 1971-1995. He was a dedicated worker, committed to the ministry and promotion of Baptist history. And, of course, he was a friend of those who loved the history of Baptists.

In my editorial "Issues Shaping Baptist Identity,"[117] I pointed out that throughout my career the issues related to the Baptist identity were always present. A variety of writers were enlisted for the issue. James Leo Garrett wrote an excellent article which examined influences, distinctives, and principles. Thomas Nettles wrote on the Calvinistic influence in convention life while W. Wiley Richards traced a movement away from that theological position. Phil Roberts examined historical modifications to Calvinism. The theological issue has appeared again in the quarter century after the restructuring of the convention. A definitive increase in the number of pastors adopting Reformed theology has once more threatened the "unity" of the convention.

Karen Bullock wrote on the restructuring of the convention, and Mark Brister, chair of the restructuring committee, wrote an apologetic on the work of the committee. Bill Leonard prepared an article on the "Covenant for a New Century," the document which presented the restructuring recommendation. The Commission was in its last year of existence, and still addressing the history needs of the denomination. The issues of the journal during the last months of the agency were chronicled by the diversity of writers solicited to write on this most radical period of change in Southern Baptist life in its history.

---

[116] Slayden A. Yarbrough, "In Memoriam: Lynn E. May, Jr.," in "Southern Baptist Identity," *Baptist History & Heritage* 31, no. 4 (October 1996): 5.
[117] Slayden A. Yarbrough, "Issues Shaping Baptist Identity," in "Southern Baptist Identity," *Baptist History & Heritage* 31, no. 4 (October 1996): 4.

Slayden A. Yarbrough

**Guest Editorial by First Lady Rosalyn Carter: Shaped by Our Faith:** During the American presidential campaign of 1996, when Bill Clinton would be reelected, Jim Taulman and I planned the January 1997 issue on the theme "Baptists and the White House."[118] There have been four Baptists who served as president of the United States: Warren G. Harding, Harry S. Truman, James "Jimmy" Earl Carter, and William Jefferson Clinton. If you are looking for diversity, you need look no further than these four individuals who served in the highest office in the land, and the most powerful position in the world.

I wanted to find someone who would write a guest editorial. I could not ask Clinton or Carter, the two living presidents. I decided to invite Rosalyn Carter to accept the assignment. She turned me down. Southern Baptist leaders at the time were very negative toward the Carters. The Controversy in the Southern Baptist Convention had swung the denomination toward the political right.

I decided not to accept "no." So I wrote the former First Lady again, told her that many Southern Baptists like myself really appreciated the president and her, and asked that she reconsider. As soon as I dropped the letter in the mailbox, I had deep regrets. I felt that this was the most audacious thing I had ever done in my life. I assumed I would receive a second rejection to my request.

The Southern Baptist Convention annual meeting was in New Orleans in June 1996 (in which the restructuring was affirmed for the final time). As the executive director of the Historical Commission, I attended. While there, I received a call from the office in Nashville. Mrs. Carter's secretary had called. The former First Lady had agreed to grant my request. Her editorial was printed in the journal. Jim Taulman and I discussed who would receive the original copy of her editorial. I gave in and Jim had it framed. It hung on his wall for many years. Jim, who was such a vital help as managing editor of the journal, passed away in 2017. As I was preparing my manuscript for this book First Lady Rosalyn Carter, age 96, passed away on November 19, 2023.

---

[118] Rosalyn Carter, Guest Editorial, "Baptists and the White House: Strengthened by our Faith" in "Baptist and the White House," *Baptist History & Heritage* 32, no. 1 (January 1997): 4-5.

This issue was one of my favorite volumes of *Baptist History & Heritage*. I received a few negative calls from people who were opposed to including some of the recent presidents. The divisiveness of the country, both politically and religiously, was developing during the turmoil of the times, especially among Southern Baptists. The concerns look tame compared to what is taking place in the nation and among Southern Baptists at the time of this writing in 2024.

**Editorial: Baptist History & Heritage Publication Principles**: "Two Ways to Be Baptist" was the theme of the April 1997 issue of *Baptist History & Heritage*. Leon McBeth presented three papers at the annual meeting of the Society in 1996. He added an introduction for the journal, and the three articles were published. He compared George W. Truett, pastor of First Baptist Church of Dallas with J. Frank Norris, pastor of First Baptist Church of Fort Worth. The delightful issue contrasts the two men's personalities, their approach to pastoral ministry, and their influence upon Baptist life and history. In many ways, the conflict between these two Texans foreshadowed the conflict in the Southern Baptist Convention during the last quarter of the twentieth century.

After introducing McBeth's contributions, my editorial addressed the subject of "Baptist History & Heritage Publication Principles."[119] The restructuring of the convention already affected two other journals. *Review and Expositor*, which the faculty of Southern Seminary published, shifted control to a consortium of schools identified with the moderate position in the convention. The *Southwestern Journal of Theology* published by the seminary canceled an issue on the topic "The *Baptist Faith and Message*." Conflict had arisen over the selection of writers, and the political impact affected the freedom of the journal. Academic publications would feel the tension from the continuing influence of the recent conflict within the convention, and from the presence of political activity, resulting in a revision of publication principles.

I pointed out that *Baptist History & Heritage* never shied away from dealing with controversial issues, such as church and state, women in ministry, the Bible, ordination, and a variety of such topics. At the same time the publication enlisted writers from the theological spectrum ranging from

---

[119] Slayden A. Yarbrough, "*Baptist History & Heritage* Publication Principles," in "Two Ways to be Baptist," *Baptist History & Heritage* 32, no. 2 (April 1997): 4-6.

fundamentalist to conservative to moderate based upon experience and credentials, not politics. The approach was to present historical arguments from which the readers could determine their own positions. This was not always an easy task, but the integrity of the journal was never questioned. The same could said of the annual meetings of the Society, where diversity of speakers was the norm, not the exception. The integrity of legitimate theological and historical dialogue was the standard for the former Commission and the Society.

Following the restructuring, the Society assumed sole responsibility for *Baptist History & Heritage*. The Society at the time of my editorial was in the process of establishing an editorial board, which would direct the future of the publication. The board would establish publication principles to maintain the integrity of the journal. Established in 1958, *Baptist History & Heritage* has continued this tradition for over 65 years. It is without question the most constant and important ministry of the Society in terms of preserving the history of Baptists into the future.

**Editorial: War and Rumors of War**: The July/October issue of *Baptist History & Heritage* was the final one published jointly by the Commission and the Society. The theme was "Baptists and the Civil War."[120] I decided that it would be a double issue to complete the publication year. My decision was both a historical one and an economic one. This would be the last issue printed through the Commission budget. By printing a dual issue, I saved the Society money by not having to pay the cost of publication of the journal until the first volume in 1998.

Jim Taulman and I really enjoyed planning and preparing this issue. We plotted and planned a variety of articles, which would include both academic and personal material. We began to brainstorm over potential writers. In the end nine established researchers contributed to the issue. They covered a variety of topics on the Civil War ranging from nationalism and dissent to God in the camps to effects of the war on the churches to attitudes toward slavery to women to music to missions to presidents. The only regret I had was that we somehow failed to enlist American Baptist writers in the project.

---

[120] Jim Taulman, "Wars and Rumors of War: Guest Editorial," in "Baptist and the Civil War," *Baptist History & Heritage* 32, nos. 3-4 (July/October 1997): 4-5.

One of the most moving contributions to this issue was the insertion throughout by Jim of "Letters to Amanda from Sargent Major Marion Hill Fitzpatrick."[121] The letters of the Confederate soldier to his wife reveal the love and concern of a soldier in the field. He tells of the weather, the place of faith, the challenges of war, and a variety of ordinary events in the context of war. The passion and the loneliness were evident in the dozen or so letters. The last document is a letter from an officer of the regiment informing Amanda of the death of her husband in the battle of Gettysburg.

The letters should touch the hearts of all who read them. They reveal the sorrow brought by war. Amanda was the grandmother of Raymond Rigdon, former executive director of the Seminary Extension department of the Southern Baptist Convention from 1969-1988. Jim also included excerpts from the diary of G. W. Gwaltney of North Carolina, a colporteur and then a chaplain in the war. Both documents clearly demonstrate the very personal nature of war.

I asked Jim to write the editorial for this issue. He called it "War and Rumors of War: An Editorial." He pointed out that there was little material on the War and Baptists. Robert Gardner, along with his wife, Anne, were devoted members of the Society. He commented that in his own search there was such a dearth of material on Baptists and the War, that he was not sure there had even been a Civil War. This issue of the journal corrected that negligence. It filled a major void in the history of the conflict as related to Baptists. Jim also used his editorial to express his appreciation for the opportunity to serve as managing editor. Publication of the journal was in Jim's good hands during the crisis of dissolution.

I also contributed an article that I called "The Last Will and Testament of the Historical Commission of the Southern Baptist Convention: A Report and Observations on the Dissolution of the Historical Commission."[122] I described the actions of Dr. May, the board, and myself in criticizing the decision to dissolve the agency. The Commission was the only agency to openly challenge the action of the convention. I concluded with a positive

---

[121] Letters to Amanda from Sargent Major Marion Hill Fitzpatrick, Company K, 45th Georgia Regiment, Thomas' Brigade, Wilcox Division, Hill's Corps, CSA to his wife Amanda Olive White Fitzpatrick, 1882-1865.

[122] Slayden A. Yarbrough, "The Last Will and Testament of the Historical Commission of the Southern Baptist Convention: A Report and Observations on the Dissolution of the Historical Commission," *Baptist History & Heritage* 32, nos. 3-4 (July/October): 117-23.

note that the work of Baptist history would continue. And it has for almost three decades. And it must for the current and for future generations of the people called Baptists.

**Editorial: Church and State in Baptist History:** In the Winter 1998 issue of *Baptist History & Heritage* I wrote a short article. Or maybe it was a long editorial. The theme of the journal was "The Changing State of Church and State." The title of my editorial/article was "Church and State in Baptist History."[123] I was well indoctrinated from my teen years at the conservative and evangelistic First Baptist Church of Washington Park, Illinois. My home church was unquestionably committed to the Baptist principle of separation of church and state and religious liberty. Pastor Dick Belcher's opposition to the candidacy of John F. Kennedy for president was based on his Baptist understanding of these topics. Even after my college career and well into my teaching career, I never, ever envisioned a departure of Southern Baptists from the commitment to and defense of separation of church and state. I believed that if every other Baptist principle failed, church and state separation would remain. Boy, was I wrong. I am a good historian. Obviously, I was not a good prophet.

An assault began on this bedrock principle when the conservative party began to call for an "accommodationist" approach, where church and state worked closely together. The first erosion appeared when presidential candidate Ronald Reagan, during his first campaign, stated to a crowd of evangelicals in Dallas, that "You can't endorse me, but I can endorse you."[124] After he became president, Republicans began working behind the scenes to weaken the separationist principle. The Reagan Prayer Amendment proposed for allowing prayer in public schools was affirmed by the adoption of a resolution during the 1982 annual meeting of the convention in New Orleans. It was not the moderates who were undermining the Baptist tradition. It was the conservatives who were the "heretics." This action contributed greatly to the division among Southern Baptists, and resulted in many deciding to leave the convention.

Continuous efforts took place to defund the Baptist Joint Committee on Public Affairs (BJCPA). I attended the annual meeting in Las Vegas, where a

---

[123] Slayden A. Yarbrough, "Church and State in Baptist History," in "Changing State of Church and State," *Baptist History & Heritage* 33, no. 1 (Winter 1998): 4-11.
[124] Anthea Butler, "Faith Could Bring Us Together. But Too Often It Divides Us," CNN.com, 24 November 2019.

messenger made a motion to defund the BJCPA, emphasizing that we had to deal with this matter. Another messenger spoke in opposition by stating something to the effect that "We have decided on this at five different annual meetings." The speaker was James Dunn. He was reminding the messenger that the convention had voted down similar motions in recent conventions.

In the end, however, the conservative party kept stressing a move away from the historic principle of separation of church and state until they finally achieved it. I decided to tackle the subject in *Baptist History & Heritage*. The first writer I enlisted was James Dunn. He was as ardent apologist for separation of church and state as ever lived. I also enlisted a writer to present the accommodationist position. I was following the practice of providing balanced views, and allowing the readers to judge the arguments. The other writers reflected the moderate position on a variety of issues, but all were competent researchers and scholars.

In my editorial I traced the historical views of church and state theory of Erastianism (state over church), theocracy, and separation of church and state. I then described the Baptist defenders of separation of church and state in the colonial period and in the early years of the United States. The eventual adoption of the First Amendment to the Constitution affirmed the Baptist influence on politicians like presidents Thomas Jefferson and James Madison. I concluded my editorial with as strong a commitment to separation of church and state as I ever proclaimed.

James Dunn, however, was not happy with the inclusion of an accommodationist defender. I loved James, and unequivocally respected him as a mentor and a model. I appreciated his fervor always. Moreover, I agreed with his position. But I made the choice to have representatives of both positions. They reflected "the changing state of church and state." Whether I liked it or not, the landscape was changing with a second competing view. The journal addressed it with integrity, as I saw it. Interestingly, James Dunn passed away on July 4, 2015. He could not have planned a more appropriate day to leave this world.

**Editorial: The SBHS: 60 Years and Counting:** The theme of the Spring 1998 issue of *Baptist History & Heritage* was a forward looking "60 Years of Ministry/General Articles." My editorial was simply "60 Years and

Slayden A. Yarbrough

Counting."[125] The SBHS organized on May 13, 1938. The purpose of the organization was to raise historical consciousness before the centennial celebration of the beginning of the convention in 1845. Key figures among the twenty charter members were W. O. Carver, H. I. Hester, W. W. Barnes, Rufus Weaver, E. C. Routh, and Mrs. B. A. Compass. Baptist historians will be familiar with most, if not all, of these individuals committed to the cause of Baptist history.

I provided a brief overview of the Commission and Society, and the changes that resulted from the restructuring. I had been chosen as the executive director of the Society, and offices had moved to OBU, where I would resume teaching, and administering the Society. During a meeting of the officers and leaders of the organization, Charles Deweese asked me to prepare a list of priorities for the next few years as I saw them from my perspective as executive director of the now-dissolved Historical Commission, and in my new role as executive director of the Society.

I addressed his request in my editorial. I discussed location and leadership, including the future need of moving the offices to a more visible city, and the goal of providing a full-time director, an office manager, and a secretary. Funding these positions was a priority. I recommended a revenue goal of at least $200,000 to $250,000. Soliciting support was an essential and ongoing challenge for the group. It, of course, continues to be. Enlistment of new members was a significant challenge for the Society, which would be essential for the success of the voluntary effort to respond to the historical awareness of churches, and other entities.

Another challenge that I raised was the need to continue to develop quality and relevant resources. Charles Deweese brought outstanding experience in this regard, and would in a few years bring his talents as the first full-time director of the Society. Finally, I focused on the need to relate to other Baptist historical organizations, and to create a firm commitment to the changing world of technology. Keep in mind that the Society was seeking to traverse its way in a denominational world that had radically upended. Yet despite the challenges, I was optimistic about the future. We had on board the cream of the crop of Baptist historians, as well as a dedicated group of ministers and

---

[125] Slayden A. Yarbrough, "The SBHS: 60 Years and Counting," in "60 Years of Ministry / General Article," *Baptist History & Heritage* 33, no. 2 (Winter 1998): 4-11.

laypeople who recognized and committed themselves to preserving, protecting, and promoting the historical heritage of Baptists.

**Editorial: Is This Good Ground?** My final editorial appeared in the Autumn 1998 issue of the journal entitled "Texas Baptists and the Southern Baptist Convention." I titled it "Is This Good Ground?"[126] I referred to the book *The Killer Angels* by Michael Shaara, and the movie based upon it, *Gettysburg*. A key factor in the success of the Union forces was based on holding and defending the "good ground."

The Society had relinquished much of its leadership role in Baptist history to the Historical Commission, which was established in 1951. The Society became an auxiliary to the Commission with a charter change in 1952. With a full staff the Commission was able to address the needs of operation of the Southern Baptist Historical Library, providing quality publications, the preparation and distribution of useful resource materials, the publication in cooperation with the Society of *Baptist History & Heritage*, and planning the annual meeting of the SBHS. In 1995 this all changed. Now, the Society would face the challenge of assuming responsibility in all these ministries, except for the library and archives. The response to this challenge was the determination of whether the organization would even survive.

I subjectively suggest that when you stir up an angry group of Baptist historians, you will see a dogged aggressiveness that will not accept failure. We faced the battle, and seized the high ground, good ground, very good ground. Voluntarism was at the heart of our movement. Many had already stepped up. Baptist universities, like Dallas Baptist University, OBU, and Carson-Newman College immediately provided leaders, resources, and encouragement. Others soon followed. Churches, state conventions, and individuals stood with the Society on high ground. We looked to the future as we committed ourselves to preserving the past. The Society had a clear purpose and vision for affirming Baptist history for congregations, institutions, and amateur and institutional researchers and scholars. Challenges would not go away. Questions still needed answers, but the people and the commitment were there to find the answers. We were indeed on good ground. Carson-Newman College would host publication of the journal

---

[126] Slayden A. Yarbrough, "Is This Good Ground?" in "Texas Baptists and the Southern Baptist Convention," *Baptist History & Heritage* 33, no. 3 (Autumn 1998): 4-6.

under the guidance of Dr. Merrill M. Hawkins Jr., who assumed the role of editor of *Baptist History & Heritage*.

I also had notified the officers of my desire to step aside as executive director in May of 1998. To be candid, after almost two decades of involvement in the battle for Baptist history at the local, state, and national levels, and after returning to Oklahoma Baptist and wearing two hats as both professor and executive, I was worn down. I had devoted a lot of energy to the cause of Baptist history and had no reservations to the cause for which I had developed such a passion. But I was ready to hand over the leadership of the Society to others. The officers asked me to remain a year, and I agreed. In 1999 my good friend, Dr. Charles Deweese, became the executive director. He brought a unique set of credentials and was a superb choice. I was delighted to pass the mantle to him.

# Chapter Nine

# Publishing During The "Controversy" Part 3: Journal And Periodical Articles

Paul And The Importance Of His Writing Materials

"When you come, bring the cloak that I left with Carpus at Troas, and my scrolls, especially the parchments" (2 Timothy 4:13).

## Introduction

I wrote numerous articles in professional journals, reference works, and a variety of denominational publications. These articles were written in the context of the Controversy or in my personal commitment to contribute to the Baptist understanding of the movement's history, considering the challenges brought about by the Controversy. Combined with my fidelity to the historical ideals and principles that shaped the Baptist heritage, my writings on Baptist history, theology, biblical understanding, and practical application provide evidence that my contributions flowed out of a love for both biblical and Baptist freedom.

The dedication to such freedoms shaped a career that took seriously the foundation of liberty of conscience so cherished by Baptists. Of course, this commitment to liberty led to diversity, which time and again resulted in disagreements. If there is one word that resonates throughout Baptist history, it is "controversy."

Walter "Buddy" Shurden's wonderful book *Not a Silent People* clearly documented the contributions to the Baptist narrative, emphasizing the open and free discussions on a variety of topics. I like to use the phrase "meaningful dialogue" to describe the disagreements of Baptists over the many issues rooted in the heritage of freedom. Furthermore, Shurden's conclusion confirmed that controversy is a strength of Baptists, not a weakness. Controversy demonstrates life, not stagnation, which develops when freedom to disagree is removed. I must confess (another good Baptist term), I did enjoy the liberating controversy, as I personally and professionally defined and defended the Baptist tradition (at its best, I would assume).

Slayden A. Yarbrough

**Publications: Journal Articles**

The order of the articles in this section is not as easy as it might seem. While attempting to follow the chronological publication of these publications, I found I could not always do so. A thematic approach has value, but even then, determining categories is not always simple. Therefore, I will often explain why I include a particular article in the scheme of things. The big picture is that all my publishing endeavors—books, reference works, editorials, and both academic and denominational articles blended during my twenty-nine-year career as a professor and a denominationalist. Of course, so many of my fellow Baptist historians understand where I am coming from in my journey.

Finally, through the publication of articles directly related to the Southern Baptist Convention Controversy, I once again would expose myself to attacks from the right. However, I believed that I had the credentials as a Baptist historian to speak out. While I am not sure whether I always had the courage to muddy the waters, I did have the passion and commitment to the principles which defined the Baptist heritage on the one hand, and defended those principles on the other. Researching, writing, and publishing articles which flowed from the context of the Controversy was a very important way in which I contributed to the ongoing battle taking place in the Southern Baptist Convention. This effort, along with those of so many others, also preserved the historical principles and practices of the people called Baptist.

**Is Creedalism a Threat to Southern Baptists?** My initial and perhaps most important article on Baptist history and theology appeared in direct response to the developing Controversy in its early stage. The article appeared in two versions. Both resulted from a presentation I had delivered at the annual meeting of the Oklahoma Baptist Historical Society on October 23, 1981, at University Baptist Church in Shawnee, Oklahoma. Dr. J. M. Gaskin invited me to prepare the presentation, which addressed the developing crisis in the Southern Baptist Convention head-on.

I once told Dr. Gaskin that "You like a good hanging, just as long as your neck is not in the noose!" We both laughed heartedly. He told his wife Helen what I said, and she agreed with me completely. As the years of the Controversy developed, Gaskin and I discussed numerous times what was going on and the implications for the future of the denomination.

Dr. Gaskin published an abbreviated version of my presentation entitled "Is Creedalism a Threat to Oklahoma Baptists?" in *The Oklahoma Baptist Chronicle*.

He also recommended to the Historical Commission that the full article be edited and published in its journal. The article appeared as "Is Creedalism a Threat to Southern Baptists?" in *Baptist History & Heritage*.[127]

As previously stated, the "Creedalism" article may be my most significant publication that resulted from the Controversy. The content of my presentation and writing was drawn from personal experience, professional commitment, and adherence to traditional Baptist principles. First, my experience at Southwest Baptist University and subsequent dismissal made me acutely aware of the pending dangers of theological tests of faith in the Southern Baptist Convention. Second, my credentials as a professor of Baptist history enabled me to understand the significant principles of Southern Baptists, which I warned could be threatened by a major emphasis upon doctrinal orthodoxy in the denomination. And third, I early on recognized the dark cloud of divisiveness that publicly appeared during the Southern Baptist Convention annual convention in 1979, and which was growing with each passing day. The lecture and the article in *Baptist History & Heritage* were warnings of the dangers to the fabric of the Baptist heritage, which held a wide, diverse denomination together. I examined the issues of Baptist history, Baptist theology, and Baptist ministry and missions as a defense of confessional theology. I warned of the dangers of a creedal approach to theology to the denomination, whose unity was often called "a rope of sand." That rope was rapidly being erased in demands for orthodox opinions.

Although the article was based on historic principles in Southern Baptist life, it also proved to be prophetic. Maybe I had some prophetic credentials after all. Developments resulting from the Controversy confirmed my predictions. Interestingly, although the control of the convention was seized by narrow conservatives, subsequent events through the 2023 annual Southern Baptist Convention confirm that my warning continues to be relevant. Division rather than diversity currently characterizes the convention. Unity is based upon conformity, not freedom.

**Biblical Authority in Southern Baptist History, 1845-1945**: As the Controversy in the convention took shape, the conservative party framed the battle over the Bible. The movement presented the view that the

---

[127] Slayden Yarbrough, "Is Creedalism a Threat to Southern Baptists?" in *Baptist History & Heritage* 18, no. 2 (April 1983): 21-32.

conservatives were the only ones remaining true to the Scriptures, and that any diversion from an inerrant, infallible approach was considered heretical. The interpretation of what Scripture "is" was more important than valid, honest research of the biblical writings themselves, and narrowed what was acceptable Baptist belief. Remarkably, what was deemed acceptable continues to grow narrower and narrower with each passing year. That is the result of power to define orthodoxy and heresy in a previously freedom-loving denomination. Creedal orthodoxy becomes the test of faith. I rejected this creedalism in my earlier writings and I continued to reject it in subsequent publications and presentations.

Moderates were accused time and again with trying to undermine the integrity and the authority of the Scriptures. Of course, any accusation concerning the Scriptures raised an alarm among Southern Baptists, who often referred to themselves as the "people of the Book." Suspicion arose anytime a professor, denominational leader, or pastor was accused of undermining faith in the Bible. I can personally document that, based on my experience at Southwest. One interesting observation is that when moderate expansions of theological expression are advocated, they are rejected as unacceptable and heretical. However, more rigid, and narrower interpretations seem to have no restrictions, as long as one can proof-text them.

During the second decade of the Controversy, the Historical Commission decided to publish a thematic issue of *Baptist History & Heritage* entitled "Southern Baptists: Embracing God's Word." I was approached by Charles Deweese, managing editor of the journal at that time, to prepare an article entitled "Biblical Authority in Southern Baptist History, 1845-1945."[128] Dr. May and Dr. Deweese recognized the importance of choosing authors for the thematic issue in the context of the heated debate over the Scriptures. Charles told me that they felt that I would provide both an honest, historical, and diplomatic approach, rather than a polemical examination of the subject. Again, despite my personal pilgrimage of being charged with heretical teachings at Southwest, I had gained a reputation as a Baptist historian who would treat such an assignment with integrity and sensitivity.

My article documented the positions advocated by leading professors and Southern Baptist leaders during the first century of the convention. It

---

[128] Slayden A. Yarbrough, "Biblical Authority in Southern Baptist History,1845-1945," *Baptist History & Heritage* 27, no. 1 (January 1992): 4-12.

revealed a diversity of approaches and interpretations. That diversity expressed itself in examples related to controversial issues, such as slavery, women in the role of deaconesses, and the call to women to serve as missionaries. Time and again, the authority of the Scriptures was defined in matters of "faith and practice." I found no references to the Bible as a test for theological orthodoxy, but more consistently as a primary source of practical "orthopraxy."

**Academic Freedom and Southern Baptist History**: During my career I published numerous articles that may not have directly applied to the Controversy but nevertheless reflected issues related to it in the context of Baptist history. They included biblical interpretation of selected topics consistent with the Baptist approach to honest and critical examination of the Scriptures, and practical application of a variety of practices in the Baptist heritage of teaching and worship in denominational life.

In retirement I was asked to contribute to a thematic issue of *Baptist History & Heritage* (winter, 2004) that examined the subject of "Baptists and Academic Freedom."[129] The article surveyed numerous examples of conflict over academic freedom. Article XII of the 1963 *Baptist Faith and Message* addressed academic freedom as follows:

In Christian education there should be a proper balance between academic freedom and academic responsibility. Freedom in any orderly relationship of human life is always limited and never absolute. The freedom of a teacher in a Christian school, college, or seminary is limited by the pre-eminence of Jesus Christ, by the authoritative nature of the Scriptures, and by the distinct purpose for which the school exists.[130]

The article provided numerous case studies related to academic freedom in Southern Baptist history, which accelerated in the twentieth century. On an individual level, they included Crawford Howell Toy (1836-1919) and the liberal tradition, William H. Whitsitt (1841-1911) and Baptist origins, Ralph Elliott and *The Message of Genesis*, G. Henton Davies and the *Broadman Bible Commentary*, Dale Moody (1915-1990) and teachings on apostasy, and H.

---

[129] Slayden A. Yarbrough, "Baptists and Academic Freedom," in *Baptist History & Heritage*, 39 no. 1 (Winter 2004): 43-58.
[130] *Baptist Faith and Message* (Nashville: Sunday School Board, 1963), 16.

Leon McBeth (who died at age 81 in 2013) and his centennial history of the Sunday School Board.

Publications were subjected to criticism in the 1990s and as they were during the Controversy. Seminary journals were not immune to the conflict. They included Southern Seminary's *Review and Expositor*, *The Southwestern Journal of Theology*,[131] and New Orleans Baptist Theological Seminary's *Theological Educator*. Additionally, a Historical Commission pamphlet published in 1993 entitled *Understanding Southern Baptists* by Nolan P. Howington resulted in major pressure upon the agency to recall the pamphlet. All these personalities and publications provided case studies of the challenge of academic freedom in Southern Baptist educational institutions and denominational entities.[132]

The struggle related to academic freedom resulted in the establishment of new divinity and theological institutions. The challenges also moved the denomination away from confessional theology toward an orthodox creedalism, which resulted in a major revision of the *Baptist Faith and Message* in 2000. With a revised preface and a conservative article on "The Family" the new *Baptist Faith and Message* became a document that was applied as a test of faith rather than a confessional affirmation on unity through freedom and respect of congregational polity and diversity.

**The Believer's Church**: In 1986 I published upon request an article for the *Southwestern Journal of Theology*. The assigned title was "The Believer's Church." In one of the most academic articles that I wrote, I examined the historical development of the movement, which was rooted in both the Anabaptists and the Puritan English Separatists. The Separatists appeared in left-wing Puritanism in England. Both the English General Baptists and the English Particular Baptists arose out of Separatism. Many movements were characterized by congregational polity, voluntary church membership, believer's baptism, and freedom from state connections. Included among these in the broader free church movement were the Society of Friends (or Quakers), Moravians, Congregationalists, Church of the Brethren, and others. In relation to the history of the Baptists, the article provided an important historical connection with a variety of movements. This helped in understanding the important issues in the quest for the freedom to establish

---

[131] Among my journal articles was one that I published upon request on the subject "The Believer's Church," *Southwestern Journal of Theology* 28, no. 3 (Summer 1986): 33-44.
[132] Yarbrough, "Academic Freedom," 45-58.

voluntary-based churches rooted in biblical teachings. My study enabled me and hopefully readers to understand better the broader picture of Baptists in the development of the "believer's church" category within the history of Christianity, and the future challenge of Baptists to address the Controversy[133]

**The Origins of Baptist Associations Among the English Particular Baptists**: Once again I reached back into my dissertation as the source for this article. For my effort, I received the Norman W. Cox Award for the best article published by the Historical Commission in 1988. It appeared in the April, 1988 issue of *Baptist History & Heritage*.

The accepted view of the origin of Baptist associations was presented by the English Baptist historian, W. T. Whitley,[134] and supported by Robert G. Torbet,[135] an American Baptist historian. These two established Baptist historians concluded that Baptist associations were rooted in Oliver Cromwell's New Model-Army from the English Civil War. Cromwell organized his troops into "associations" to raise money and recruit troops. Many of his soldiers were Baptists, and this theory concluded that these Baptists transferred his method to church organization in 1653 in Ireland.

I rejected this view and followed B. R. White,[136] who traced the origin of Baptist associations to Henry Jacob, founder of the moderate Separatist church in Southwark in 1616. Jacob's writings and the church's confessional statement in 1616 advocated a form of voluntary associational cooperation.[137] Additionally, a non-authoritative voluntary classis, a term used in the Dutch Reformed movement, organized in the 1620s in Holland. Many followers of Henry Jacob, or "Jacobites," participated in the organization. One of the persons active in the group was John Davenport, who had a close association with the Southwark congregation. Therefore, Jacob not only presented an associational theory, but a sectarian model existed based upon efforts of English exiles. One final example was the production of the first London

---

[133] Slayden Yarbrough, "The Believer's Church," *Southwestern Journal of Theology 38* (Summer 1986): 33-44.
[134] See W. T. Whitley, *A History of English Baptists* (London: Charles Griffin, 1923).
[135] Robert G. Torbet, *A History of Baptists*, 3rd ed. (Valley Forge, PA: Judson Press, 1973), 44.
[136] B. R. White, "The English Particular Baptists and the Great Rebellion," *Baptist History & Heritage* 9, no. 1 (1974): 20-24.
[137] Slayden A. Yarbrough," The Origins of Baptist Associations Among the English Particular Baptists," *Baptist History & Heritage* 23, no. 2 (1988): 14-24.

Confession of Faith in 1644, based upon voluntary cooperation by seven Particular Baptist churches.

Baptist associations began to meet as early as 1624. They gathered for fellowship, evangelistic cooperation, and discussion of Baptist beliefs and practices. By 1655, the term "association" was common among both General and Particular Baptists. The voluntary nature of their organizations varied somewhat, but the foundation presented by Jacob found expression in the actions of these cooperative efforts. The direct teachings of Jacob, and the indirect examples and involvement in voluntary cooperative church efforts of those connected to the Southwark church, provide a documented trail of voluntary associational polity that appeared among the early English Baptists.

**The Ecclesiology of Henry Jacob**: I previously discussed this article. It described Jacob's understanding of congregational church polity. In 1616 Jacob organized a nonconformist, independent congregation in Southwark, England. Church members freely discussed issues of disagreement, including baptism and a move toward becoming an early Particular Baptist Church under the pastoral leadership of Henry Jessey in 1645.

Jacob's views of both congregational church government and associational cooperation were deeply imbedded in the Baptist tradition in the years that followed. My study of his congregational teachings shaped my own understanding of the Baptist tradition in these areas. I was especially impressed by Jacob's tolerance and respect for other viewpoints. Furthermore, Jacob's views provided a solid foundation as the Controversy resulted in an erosion of congregational autonomy when the denomination moved through crisis and into division in the twenty-first century.

**The Influence of Plymouth Colony Separatism on Salem: An Interpretation of John Cotton's Letter of 1630 to Samuel Skelton**: This article may well be my most academic contribution in the field of church history. I certainly achieved one of my publishing goals which I established at the beginning of my professional career. I published this article in *Church History*, the journal of the American Society of Church History.[138]

---

[138] Slayden Yarbrough," The Influence of Plymouth Colony Separatism on Salem: An Interpretation of John Cotton's Letter of 1630 to Samuel Skelton," *Church History* 51, no. 3 (September 1982): 290-303.

Once more, I turned to my doctoral dissertation for the basic contents of this article. I challenged the traditional position that New England congregationalism followed the "non-Separatism" tradition of Henry Jacob. Earlier twentieth-century church historians had traced the origin of New England congregationalism to English Separatists, who rejected the congregations and the Church of England as true churches. Although Jacob established a congregational church in Southwark in 1615, he did not reject the validity of the churches of England.

In 1912 Champlain Burrage proposed the "non-Separatist" theory, which was soon adopted by Perry Miller, a renowned church historian. His views were adopted by subsequent generations of New England Congregational historians. Challenges began to appear in the 1960s, often rooted in a letter from John Cotton to Samuel Skelton. While not rejecting the "non-Separatist" interpretation, they attributed a greater influence to the Plymouth Colony Separatists.

I thoroughly studied the ecclesiological positions of John Robinson, pastor of the Plymouth Colony church (even though he remained in England) in my dissertation. I compared his views with those of Henry Jacob. I concluded that Robinson developed a more moderate view of Separatism. In examining Cotton's positions in his letter to Skeleton, I concluded that his congregationalism was the same as that of Robinson and the Plymouth Colony church. I termed Robinson's views as "moderate Separatism," which made their position with the Church of England much more compatible than the "Rigid Separatists," who rejected the validity of the English congregations.[139] Unfortunately, I have not found any contemporary historians who have adopted my position—at least not yet. But I have always been optimistic. Surely some young church historian will discover my article and see the light shining on New England Congregational origins.

**Tying Up Loose Ends**: Two Articles at my final SBHS meeting as Executive Director: As the Society officers and I planned what would be my final annual meeting as executive director of the SBHS, we decided to meet at William Jewell College in Liberty, Missouri. The college had an excellent Baptist history center and, of course, Liberty was the home of President Harry S Truman and First Lady Beth Truman. We included an evening

---

[139] Yarbrough, "Influence of Plymouth Colony," 301.

session in the Truman Library. President Truman was a Baptist, and the site was most appropriate for our group.

As a final contribution for my tenure, I prepared two articles, which were later published in *Baptist History & Heritage*. Both in one way or another reflected the Controversy and the restructuring of the Society, and expressed my observations and visions of what might be in store for the future.

"The History of Southern Baptist History: Restructuring of the New SBHS" began with an historical overview of the history of the Society.[140] It began in 1938 with its home on the campus of Southern Seminary. Collecting historical materials and publications and preserving and communicating the task of the Society shaped it early years. In 1951 the Historical Commission was established in Nashville, and the Society became an auxiliary of the agency. I highlighted the contributions of the Commission, as the Society took on a more support role.

I then traced developments that contributed to the decision to include the Commission among those agencies to be dissolved. Controversy over two small matters (in my mind) brought attention to the Commission. The first was the publication of the Nolan P. Howington "Who Are Southern Baptists?" pamphlet, which pointed out that some groups had chosen to support some Southern Baptist work outside the Cooperative Program. It mentioned the Cooperative Baptist Fellowship, a moderate organization created to provide an outlet for disenfranchised Southern Baptists who no longer felt at home in the Southern Baptist Convention. The pamphlet was criticized, and the Commission trustees voted to withdraw it. They chose to rewrite it without the reference to the Cooperative Baptist Fellowship. The other issue was a demand by the Executive Committee of the Southern Baptist Convention to "request" that all agencies refuse to accept contributions from organizations not affiliated with the convention.

I will deal with these two issues in greater depth in Chapter 10, when discussing the success and the failures of the Controversy in the convention. Included in this discussion will be new material related to the bullying tactics of Judge Paul Pressler, a member of the Executive Committee, against Dr. Lynn E. May Jr., executive director of the Historical Commission. Pressler

---

[140] Slayden A. Yarbrough, "The History of Southern Baptist History: Restructuring of the New SBHS," *Baptist History & Heritage* 34, no. 3 (Summer/Fall 1999): 108-20.

threatened to close the entity (which came to fruition in the restructuring of denominational agencies). Dr. Charles Deweese provides a passionate, firsthand description of the confrontation.

The second disagreement was an extension of the pamphlet controversy. The Commission trustees voted in 1994 in Memphis to continue accepting Cooperative Baptist Fellowship gifts. Only two trustees dissented against the motion. The trustees also reaffirmed commitment to the Cooperative Program, acknowledged the sacred right of all Baptists to give voluntarily as they felt led, and opposed efforts to do harm to the Cooperative Program.

Such efforts came to naught. In 1994 during the annual meeting held in Orlando, the messengers voted 4,730 to 3,342 to request that all denominational agencies discontinue receiving designated funds from moderate organizations. The Historical Commission yielded to the pressure, and notified the Cooperative Baptist Fellowship that it would no longer accept the organization's gifts.[141]

Appeasement with the Executive Committee proved unsuccessful. Several commissions, including the Historical Commission, were numbered among the agencies dissolved by the Southern Baptist Convention in June 1997. The "Covenant for a New Century" was adopted. It resulted in the most significant restructuring of the Southern Baptist Convention in its history.[142]

During the period that led to the dissolution of the Historical Commission, I planned my return to OBU. The SBHS elected me as executive director, and moved its operation to Shawnee, Oklahoma. OBU provided office space for the Society.

Janis, my wife, was hired as the part-time administrative assistant. I hired her at minimum wage to avoid any appearance of nepotism. She was worth much more to me and the Society and kept the office operational during my tenure as executive director. I served as both the executive director of the Society, and as professor of religion on the faculty at the University. The Society continued to provide published materials on Baptist history to churches,

---

[141] Yarbrough, "Restructuring," 110.
[142] Yarbrough, "Restructuring," 112.

associations, and state conventions, publish *Baptist History & Heritage,* and make long-term plans.

Subsequent to these events the Program and Structure Study Committee was organized. Dr. Mark Brister, pastor of First Baptist Church of Shreveport, Louisiana, served as chair of that committee during my two years as executive director of the Historical Commission. Interestingly, Dr. Brister later become president of OBU. We worked together well at the university. I even invited him to speak in my Baptist history class on the restructuring, when I was away at a professional meeting.

I concluded the article with my concerns related to the restructuring of the Commission. I noted five issues. I addressed current issues for the Society and challenges for the twenty-first century. Challenges remain after a quarter of a century, but so does the Society. I believe that any historian wishing to understand what was going on within the Historical Commission and the Society during these difficult days would benefit from a review of this article.

"Baptist History in the Twenty-First Century: Dreams and Visions: At the same I prepared another article that was forward looking in relation to the Society. I learned a lot in my various roles, where I interacted with the Commission, the Society, and both historical organizations and Baptist historians. I titled the article "Baptist History in the Twenty-First Century: Dreams and Visions."[143] I provided an overview on my introduction to and involvement with Baptist history. Drawing from many years of experience at a variety of levels, I provided a rationale of the need for commitment to Baptist history in the twenty-first century.

I put on my prophetic hat once again. An overview of developments raised the question in terms of where the SBHS should go in the future. What would shape the role of the organization in terms of service, preservation, and recording of Baptist history? Controversy and conflict would not go away, and the organization needed to be a respected and active organization in maintaining the integrity of Southern Baptist and Baptist history.

I addressed the concern of the name—the SBHS. I advocated the name remain for the near future. My rationale was to continue to make available

---

[143] Slayden A. Yarbrough, "Baptist History in the Twenty-First Century: Dreams and Visions," *Baptist History & Heritage* 34, no. 3 (Summer/Fall 1999): 95-107.

historical resources for individuals and churches in the Southern Baptist Convention for as long as possible. But I was also certain that the Society would soon have to change its name. This took place in 2001, when the organization adopted the name "The Baptist History & Heritage Society." I followed with challenges and changes related to the twenty-first century.

I also presented opportunities for the Society. Finally, I concluded with a quote from Genesis 16:7-8. An angel of the Lord asked the pregnant Hagar, who had fled hostility from Sarah, Abraham's wife, a question relevant for all generations: "Where have you come from, and where are you going?" Over a quarter a century after the radical changes in the Southern Baptist Convention disenfranchised so many who loved Baptist history, and the organizations which led the way in collecting, preserving, and interpreting denominational history, the former SBHS and now the current Baptist History & Heritage Society continues to answer these questions.

I believe that these two articles are not only a fitting conclusion to my role as an active participant in the work of Baptist history, but also contain important insights into the events in Southern Baptist life and the work of history at the agency and the society levels, and hopefully the future as well. I also believe that the collective energy and struggle of so many committed Baptist historians was well worth it. Baptist history is worth knowing, worth fighting for, and worth commitment to in the years ahead. It is the work not just of professionals and teachers, but lay persons and ministers who wear the moniker "Baptists."

## Articles and Denominational Periodical Writings

Introduction: I produced numerous articles for journals, encyclopedias and dictionaries, and other denominational publications. I wrote many of these for academicians, researchers, and individuals interested in Baptist history, especially considering the Controversy in the Southern Baptist Convention. In many articles I focused on the importance of pastors to understand and appreciate the contributions of educators serving in denominational institutions. I was committed to providing resources and direction on the issues that church leaders faced during convention conflict. The articles were much more than simply addressed to assigned topics. My writings, directly or indirectly, were intended to provide examples of the validity and usefulness of solid, biblical research, and historical and theological contributions to the understanding and application of the faith in the denominational setting of the Southern Baptist Convention.

Slayden A. Yarbrough

Heresy-hunting conservatives increasingly attacked professors by a microscopic examination of their publications. A longstanding saying for college and university professors was "publish or perish." In the battle-scarred Southern Baptist Convention, it seemed more like a warning of "publish and perish." I state this based upon my experience at SWBC. My goal in publishing therefore was to refute easily made charges of heresy in the classroom and among denominational leaders. Providing information and practical examples to be used in the pulpit based upon my teaching documented my commitment to the mind as an essential tool in addressing shallow charges. Southern Baptists effectively taught me this lesson. It was a principle often neglected and frequently attacked by the right wing of the convention.

Many of these articles related directly to the issues arising from the Controversy. Others simply provided evidence that good, academic research when applied to subjects that were tools for pastors and lay persons, elevated the understanding of both teachers and students. Once more, I sought to demonstrate the Southern Baptist emphasis on education and application, which I had been taught in college classrooms at three denominational schools and enhanced as a religion professor during my academic career.

***Biblical Illustrator.*** Interpreting the Faith to Laity: I wrote nine articles for *Biblical Illustrator*. This wonderful publication was produced for Sunday School teachers and included topics related to Sunday School lessons. It provided important historical and biblical background material for lay teachers. The content of my articles ranged from geography, Rome and warfare, the early church, and biblical and extrabiblical personalities.

Chronologically, the titles of the articles were "Pontus and Bithynia," (Summer,1984), "Centurions and Soldiers: The Roman Army" (Winter, 1986), "Early Christianity's Exclusivism" (Winter, 1987), "Judea" (Summer, 1988), "The Judaizers" (Spring, 1989), "Barabbas" (Winter, 1991), "Nero and the Christians" (Spring, 1994), "The River Chebar" (Summer 1995), and "Persecution in the Early Church" (Spring 2000).

I thoroughly enjoyed writing for *Biblical Illustrator*, which was edited by Bill Stephens. The quarterly journal was an effective way to take the academic classroom approach to the Sunday School teacher. Again, it was an opportunity for me to contribute to the dialogue over what it means to be a Baptist, even if I did not mention that rationale in my numerous contributions.

Reflecting on these articles, I concluded that each one demonstrated to Sunday School teachers the value of sound, biblical scholarship, which considered the history, politics, culture, and geography as a context for the biblical narrative being studied each Sunday morning. Add to this, the high-quality photographs provided by Stephens with each article enabled the readers to visualize the geography, architecture, archaeological discoveries, ancient writings, and artistic images of the people and places being discussed. In its own way, publications such as the *Biblical Illustrator* addressed the importance of academic and critical thinking in interpreting the written Word in a way that respected the role of lay people and their backgrounds. To me, this was a subtle but invaluable contribution in the struggle for the soul of the denomination.

Another important element in researching topics related to subjects examined by Sunday School teachers was the awareness that my research also opened the opportunity to evaluate my own positions. For example, in the article "The Judaizers" I began my research to gather information based upon my belief that the Judaizers in Galatia were Jewish Christians, who insisted that Gentile converts to Christianity follow the Jewish law. The most important emphasis was that male converts be circumcised. Paul vigorously opposed this requirement.

However, as I studied available information, I discovered that in the Roman world Gentiles who accepted the Jewish faith were often said "to Judaize." The male "Judaizers" underwent circumcision to qualify as converts to the Jewish faith. In the New International Version, Paul angrily made his case in Galatians 5:11-12, stating [11] But as for me, brothers and sisters, if I still preach circumcision, why am I still persecuted? Then the stumbling block of the cross has been eliminated. [12] I wish that those who are troubling you would even emasculate themselves (NASB)." I suddenly realized that Gentile converts to Judaism and then to Christianity, having been circumcised, would likely be upset that new converts to Christianity would not have to endure the same affliction that they had undergone. These Judaizers therefore demanded that Gentile converts to Jesus also be circumcised.

Assuming I was correct in my new understanding of the Judaizers, the value of research and openness to new possible interpretations was an important part of the Baptist heritage. The movement's tradition of calling for both education and freedom in the quest for knowledge and its application was essential for both the growth, understanding, and application of the Scriptures for the people called Baptist. Such a commitment was essential for relevancy in the present and the future generations. Furthermore, the Baptist principle of diversity is made evident with this appreciation of what Shurden calls the "Baptist identity."

***Proclaim:*** Presenting the Faith in the Pulpit: In the January-February-March 1985 issue of *Proclaim*,[144] my first sermon appeared in this pastors' quarterly published by the Sunday School Board. The title was "How Can We Believe in the Resurrection of Jesus?" I began asking how the early followers of Jesus believed in the resurrection, and then followed up with the same question for contemporary Christians. I seldom use alliteration, but made an exception in this case. I divided the answers in each question into head, history, and heart. In other words, the early disciples used their intellectual or rationale skills, and their emotions and passion. They also believed in the resurrection in the history of their personal journeys, and their ministries.

As an example of the times, one semester a student in my New Testament class complained to Dr. Bob Agee, president of OBU, that I did not believe in the resurrection. Dr. Agee called me in and informed me of the accusation. We discussed my approach to the topic. I sent him a copy of the sermon in *Proclaim*. The issue was dismissed. I must add that Dr. Agee walked the narrow path between denominational politics and faculty integrity very effectively. He always supported me, even when I stepped out on a limb with my comments or publications. For a religion faculty member during the days of the Controversy, I was always appreciative of his ability to affirm both academic integrity and faculty support.

While teaching at OBU, I concluded that I could apply my career skills as a teacher to assist pastors in proclaiming the biblical and historical faith to the people in the pews. At the same time, I believed I could address the concerns being raised over biblical integrity with substance that affirmed commitment to the Scriptures and the application of good biblical scholarship to the task of interpretation. Having been influenced by Buddy Shurden's monologue on the Bible, I prepared my own version with an emphasis on the development of canon, text, and translations, followed by common-sense application of this knowledge. In so doing, my hope was that both ministers and laity would better understand how we got the Scriptures in the current forms available in the vernacular of the readers. I published my monologue

---

[144] Slayden A. Yarbrough, "How Can We Believe in the Resurrection?" *Proclaim* 15, no. 3 (1985), 30-31.

"I Am the Bible" in the May-June-July issue of *Proclaim*.[145] As a result, I received letters from pastors who expressed appreciation for my contribution to the "Sermon Summaries" section of the publication.

One of my favorite monologue presentations was "I Am Christmas."[146] It can be characterized as a dramatic reading, a combination eventually of about ten different characters in the Christmas narratives. Each character presented a monologue telling the Christmas story from his or her unique perspective. I soon enlisted readers for each of the parts. I presented the dramatic reading in multiple churches throughout my career and retirement (in which I have served as interim pastor on numerous congregations). *Proclaim* published the reading in the October-November-December 1986 issue. Following the Christmas break one year, a student from Janis's home church, Pleasant Grove Baptist Church, a rural congregation outside Bucklin, Missouri, told me that the congregation presented my program. Rev. Steve Long, the church's pastor, identified me as the author, and *Proclaim* as his source. He did not know at the time that Janis grew up in the church, and that we were married in his church in 1964.

In the January-February-March issue of *Proclaim*, I published an article in the "Pulpit Performance" section entitled "The Pastor as Church Historian."[147] I discussed the pastor as a student of church history and included useful resources to include in a good pastor's library. I addressed the responsibility of the pastor as a teacher of church history. And finally, I challenged the pastor to be a proclaimer of church history. I encouraged the pastor to build biographical sermons around influential and colorful personalities, and to do historical studies of theological, ethical, and mission issues. As a part of this I recommended monologue sermons, which by now I was presenting on a variety of figures, as an effective way to communicate the stories of important historical and biblical figures.

I also submitted to *Proclaim* a monologue entitled "John and the Apocalypse." It was a way of teaching my amillennial interpretation to this challenging book. I was pleased to have the article accepted, and quickly cashed the check for a little under $40. I anxiously awaited the publication on this fun topic.

---

[145] Slayden Yarbrough, "I Am the Bible," *Proclaim* 16, no. 3 (1986): 27-twenty-nine.
[146] Slayden A. Yarbrough, "I Am Christmas," *Proclaim* 17, no. 1 (1986): 31-32.
[147] Slayden A. Yarbrough, "The Pastor as Church Historian," *Proclaim* 17, no. 2 (1987): 42-43.

Alas, I am still waiting. It was never published. Eventually and sadly *Proclaim* ceased publication. My unpublished monologue perished with it.

**Report from the Capitol:** Defending Religious Liberty: I submitted a sermon to *Report from the Capitol* on the subject of "Religious Freedom: Right and Responsibility."[148] For me, the most unexpected change in Southern Baptist life was the radical shift on church and state from the historic Baptist position of separation to a position that became known as "accommodationist." This change resulted in the eventual defunding of the Baptist Joint Committee. As noted previously, it took six years to finally accomplish this defunding during the annual Southern Baptist Convention meetings. I firmly believed in the separationist principle and in religious liberty for all. I prepared a sermon and submitted it to the BJC for consideration. It was published in 1986. I outlined the sermon to include the following sections: "Freedom as Citizens," "Freedom as Baptists," and "Freedom in Christ." It does not get any more Baptist than that. When the opportunity presents itself, I continue to preach this sermon with revisions around July 4. I seek to remind my listeners on the importance of liberty, both religiously and politically.

Rev. Kathy Palen, a good friend from my SWBC days, served on the staff of the Baptist Joint Committee. A committee was established by the conservative party during the Controversy to examine publications in convention-affiliated organizations for heresy. Kathy informed me that in one of their sessions dealing with the Baptist Joint Committee, my sermon on "Religious Freedom" was provided as an example of heretical teachings. I was astounded, since I considered the sermon to be a very conservative statement of the traditional Baptist view.

**The Baptist Messenger.** Baptist History Vignettes: I produced twenty-six vignettes on Baptist history for Oklahoma's denominational newspaper, *The Baptist Messenger*. My goal was to provide an historical foundation of the Baptist heritage for readers of the publication. In the *Baptist Messenger*, I contributed to Southern Baptists' understanding of their history on a variety of topics, which I believed was essential to address issues arising out of the conflict. In so doing I added to my credentials as a good Baptist historian.

---

[148] Slayden A. Yarbrough, "Religious Liberty: Right and Responsibility," in *Report from the Capital* (July-August, 1986), 10-11.

## Conclusion on publications:

In summary, throughout and beyond my career as a university professor of religion, I produced at least the following number of publications. I wrote and updated seven books. My journal publications included articles in *Church History, Baptist History & Heritage* (7), *The Quarterly Review, Perspectives in Religious Studies, The Oklahoma Baptist Chronicle* (12), *The Biblical Illustrator* (9), *Proclaim* (4), *The Southwestern Journal of Theology*, and other journals. Book Reviews appeared in *Baptist History & Heritage* (7), *Journal of Church and State* (8), *Church History, The Theological Educator, Southwestern Journal of Theology,* the *Oklahoma Baptist Chronicle, and* twenty-six vignettes in *The Baptist Messenger* (the official newspaper of the Oklahoma Baptist Convention).

## Awards

During my career I received several awards, including those related to the discipline of Baptist history. They are listed as follows.

Norman W. Cox Award: for the best article published by the Historical Commission in 1988: "The Origin of Baptist Associations Among the English Particular Baptists," was published in *Baptist History & Heritage* in April.

W. O. Carver Distinguished Service Award: received from the SBHS in 2000. This award recognizes and pays tribute to individuals who have made outstanding contributions to the cause of Baptist history. Recipients have exhibited rare and unusual dedication to the cause of Baptist history through writing, teaching, denominational service, archival and library development, historical center and society work on national and state levels, communicating Baptist heritage, and interpreting the history of Baptists.

The Carolyn Blevins Meritorious Service Award: presented to me and Janis, my wife, and office administrator of the Baptist History & Heritage Society during its time in Shawnee, Oklahoma. The award was presented in 1999. It was named after the distinguished church history professor at Carson-Newman College, whose career at the institution spanned thirty years, and who is now retired as associate professor of religion emerita. The award is presented by the Baptist History & Heritage Society during its annual meeting to an individual or organization considered to have provided commendable and exemplary service to the society and is an expression of the organization's genuine appreciation for contributions made to the success of the society in its ministry and service.

Slayden A. Yarbrough

Oklahoma Baptist Historical Society Distinguished Service Award: presented in 1995.

Gaskin Church History Award. presented to me by the Oklahoma Baptist Historical Commission. It was part of the Baptist General Convention of Oklahoma competition for 1992. The award was the result of my work, *The Lengthening Shadow*, the centennial history of First Baptist Church, Shawnee, Oklahoma.

Distinguished Service Award for Effective Service in Higher Education - Hannibal-LaGrange College: This award came in 1988. I graduated from the school in 1965. I also met Janis Lane there on the back row of an economics class. We married in 1964. Interestingly, Bill Dudley who led the campaign to get me fired at SWBC, was a trustee at H-LG, and nominated me for the award.

Hobbs Lecturer, Oklahoma Baptist University: The lectureship is named after Herschel Hobbs, the distinguished pastor of First Baptist Church of Oklahoma City, and elder statesmen in the Southern Baptist Convention throughout his many years of service and ministry. In 1990 I presented the lecture "Baptists and Freedom: Conviction and Contradiction."

## Moving Day from Nashville to Oklahoma Baptist University

One interesting story relates to the move of the SBHS to OBU. The narrative of my publication contributions resulted in a new dimension with the closing of the Historical Commission. I rushed to have a picture taken as the last executive director of the Commission. Surprisingly, it hung in the Southern Baptist Historical Library and Archives located in the Southern Baptist Convention building in Nashville for several years. I find that ironic, considering my identification as a heretic during my early years at Southwest Baptist.

As the agency closed, I loaded up a U-Haul truck (a very old one), which towed a trailer (even older than the truck), and headed west from Nashville to Shawnee on I-40. I was loaded down with all the possessions of the Society, including primarily its inventory of pamphlets, journals, and other publications. A little over halfway home, as I had turned north on I-40 out of Little Rock, Arkansas, I looked in the side mirror and saw what seemed to be flames coming from the trailer. In actuality, the trailer tongue had collapsed under the weight of the trailer and its holdings and was causing sparks to fly from the pavement. The temperature was in the mid-90s, I had no cell phone in those days, and I walked to a nearby state park to find a pay phone.

Along the way, I stepped on a piece of melted, previously chewed, discarded gum, which stuck to my shoe sole. I am sure I uttered some Old Testament epitaph, which placed a curse upon the children of those who had led to the dissolution of the Historical Commission in their quest for authority over all aspects of denominational life. I located a phone and contacted U-Haul. I soon helped two workers in sweltering heat unload the cargo from the collapsed trailer into a new one, and once more headed toward Shawnee. I do not recall that the officers of the Society mentioned this responsibility when they enlisted me as executive director of the organization. I arrived the next day with a commitment to preserve the historical work of Baptist history for both Southern Baptists and other organizations which had arisen during the Controversy. The society approach was once more the voluntary method for doing the work of Baptist history.[149]

---

[149] Yarbrough, "Restructuring," 113.

# Chapter Ten

# The "Controversy:" Success or Failure for the Southern Baptist Convention?

### E. Y. MULLINS ON CONFESSIONS OF FAITH

"Religious liberty excludes the imposition of religious creeds by ecclesiastical authority. . . When they [confessions of faith] are laid upon men's consciences by ecclesiastical command, or by a form of human authority, they become a shadow between the soul and God, an intolerable yoke, an impertinence and a tyranny."[150]

### Introduction

The interpretation of the events following the Controversy, restructuring, and revision of the *Baptist Faith and Message* are based upon my twenty-nine-year experiences as a professor of religion in two Baptist educational institutions, my activity as a trustee and executive director of the Historical Commission, my role as executive director of what is now the Baptist History & Heritage Society, and my contributions as a writer who published book, articles, denominational materials, and edited *Baptist History & Heritage* for several years. Some may disagree with my reflections, but that is simply evidence of what it means to be Baptist. We are better off when we can have "meaningful dialogue" when discussing events and principles which characterize the movement. The lack of dialogue results in stagnation.

The Controversy and the restructuring of the Southern Baptist Convention from 1979 to 2000 was the most significant internal conflict in the history of the denomination. Agency battles, politics, publications, and personal assaults were evident each year, reaching peak fervor during annual sessions of the convention every June. Busloads of messengers arrived every year in the host cities to appoint trustees, affirm budgets, and receive reports from every denominational board, commission, and institution, and to debate motions over controversial issues. Of course, messengers were exposed to a

---

[150] Record of Proceedings, Third BWA Congress (Nashville: Baptist Sunday School Board, 1923), 68.

barrage of sermons throughout the sessions delivered by well-known personalities.

The strategy of the conservatives swiftly shifted from the call for parity to "winner takes all." Early calls for compromise were cast aside as the right-wing orchestrated success after success in electing the convention president at the annual meetings. By 1995, conflicts on the convention floor were over. With the revision of the *Baptist Faith and Message* in 2000, including significant changes to the preface which strengthened denominational control and weakened the autonomy of the local churches, the Controversy came to an end. There would be no more efforts to change the direction of the Southern Baptist Convention. The conservatives rejoiced, and the moderates were completely disenfranchised. Calls for doctrinal purity were on the horizon.

The moderates responded to the takeover of the Southern Baptist Convention by establishing new denominational organizations and institutions.[151] Moving forward they devoted their energy and resources in new directions. The first organization established by alienated Southern Baptists was the Southern Baptist Alliance, founded in 1987. Dr. Stan Hastey, an OBU graduate, was elected to lead the movement. Other Baptist groups identified with the Alliance, and it expanded its outreach. A new name, the Alliance of Baptists, was adopted in 1993.[152]

The Cooperative Baptist Fellowship was formed in 1991.[153] The defeat of Dan Vestal by Morris Chapman for president of the convention in New Orleans in 1990 led to the withdrawal by many moderates and the formation of the Fellowship. Cecil Sherman was chosen as its first coordinator. The Cooperative Baptist Fellowship is the largest and most successful of the moderate organizations connected to disenfranchised Southern Baptists. The Cooperative Baptist Fellowship serves, as Jesse Fletcher describes, as an umbrella for other initiatives, such as the Alliance, Women in Ministry, and the publication *Nurturing Faith Journal* (formerly *Baptists Today; SBC Today*).[154]

---

[151] The establishment of moderate organizations is summarized in the concluding chapter of Yarbrough and Kuykendall, *Southern Baptists*, 172-73.
[152] Fletcher, *Southern Baptist Convention*, 349; Morgan, *New Crusades*, 83-84. See Andrew Gardner, *Reimagining Zion: History of the Alliance of Baptists* (Macon, GA: Nurturing Faith, Inc., 2015).
[153] Walter B. Shurden, "CBF's 'An Address to the Public,'" *The Baptist Identity*, 97-102, in Shurden and Shepley, *Going for the Jugular*, 266-70; Richards, *History of Southern Baptists*, 339-40.
[154] Fletcher, *Southern Baptist Convention*, 312. See Terry Maples and Gene Wilder, *Reclaiming and Re-Forming Baptist Identity: Cooperative Baptist Fellowship* (Macon, GA: Nurturing Faith, Inc.,

Other moderate entities arose out of the Controversy. They include the Baptist Theological Seminary at Richmond, Baptists Committed, Smyth and Helwys Publishing, and *Associated Baptist Press* (now *Baptist News Global*).[155] These entities are possible links for the larger group of current and former Southern Baptists to engage, debate, and coexist. Nevertheless, after over forty-five years since the Controversy officially began, no efforts at reunion with Southern Baptists have materialized.[156]

Moderates also established new divinity and theological schools. Colleges, universities, and societies were forced to choose sides. They either strengthened ties with the convention or established new relationships with moderate groups. Independent, voluntary societies, such as the Baptist History & Heritage Society, revised their scope to continue their missions outside the Southern Baptist Convention. The success of the Takeover did not eliminate the influence of the moderates. It simply established new avenues to carry on their traditional ministries.

## The Success of the Conservatives and the New Southern Baptist Convention

Overall, it was obvious that the strategy of the conservative element of the convention had proven overwhelmingly successful. Early conservative calls for "parity" and defense of "designated giving" were hurriedly set aside. Initially, there seemed to be a willingness to work together with moderates with some changes. That attitude did not last long. Success in election after election of the president of the Southern Baptist Convention invigorated the conservatives to purge the convention of all moderates, either by resignations, retirements, or firings.

The one exception in the strategy to elect presidents committed to the conservative cause was Dr. Jim Henry, pastor of First Baptist Church of Orlando, Florida. He was a conservative theologically, and led his church in contributing to the Cooperative Program more than any other convention congregation. He was not a participant in the effort to seize control of the

---

2017); Aaron D. Weaver, ed., *CBF at 25: Stories of the Cooperative Baptist Fellowship* (Macon, GA: Nurturing Faith Inc., 2016).

[155] Editor Walter Shurden's book, *The Struggle for the Soul*, relates the origin of many of these new entities. Baptists Committed ceased operations in 2017, and The Baptist Theological Seminary at Richmond closed in 2019.

[156] When moderates left the Southern Baptist Convention, the dissenting voice within the denomination went with them. The lack of balancing positions resulted in the Southern Baptist Convention becoming even more conservative and authoritative than anticipated.

denomination. Remarkably, he was elected over against a more radical candidate, and served as president two terms from 1994-1996. Hopes for a more conciliatory future, however, did not last.

On a personal level, I developed genuine appreciation for Dr. Henry. When I decided to make a motion on the convention floor to save the Historical Commission from dissolution, I initially asked Dr. Henry to stop by my office when he was in Nashville for a meeting of the Executive Committee. At the time he had a full schedule and could not honor my request. But the next time he was in town, he unexpectedly stopped by. I asked how I should go about making a motion at the annual convention. He went through the procedures. He told me to sit next to the Southwestern Seminary student who was in the area where I was sitting and who was manning a notification light for messenger recognition. The call for motions was announced, the student immediately punched the button, his light came on, and I was the first messenger to make a motion. I presented my careful and diplomatic motion calling for the preservation of the Historical Commission. Unfortunately, but not unexpectedly, my motion failed. As previously mentioned, Dr. Bob Agee, my president at OBU, was on the platform. He probably experienced great anxiety when I stepped up to the microphone. Fortunately, I did not embarrass him or the university. But I also expressed my freedom as a Baptist in making my case.

Sometime later, Dr. Henry contacted me to write an introduction for an anniversary history of First Baptist Church of Orlando. I delightfully accepted. Dr. Henry was a person of great respect and integrity in my opinion. I am convinced if more presidents of the convention were like him, we might have remained together, and continued to practice the traditional "unity in diversity," which I had been taught about Southern Baptists from my teenage years. But like the moderates, his kind was also in the minority. His tenure as convention president was only a blip on the radar of those dedicated to taking control of the convention.

The strategy of electing presidents committed to the conservative agenda resulted in the success of the movement. They succeeded in nominating and electing only conservatives to the boards and commissions of the denomination. They also irreparably divided the convention. Only one party would win. There was no room for compromise. If the conservatives had failed in their power play, I am certain that they would have initiated a split.

Strikingly, this strategy is obvious in American politics in the twenty-first century. A line is drawn down the middle. You are on one side or the other. I am also convinced that outside interference by hostile nations contributed greatly to dividing our nation. They have not had to fire a shot in their effort to defeat democracy. Division, not cooperation, is a strategy that now dominates all areas of life not only in religious organizations and our nation, but throughout the world. Southern Baptists were an example of this strategy very early on. My first year as a professor at Southwest Baptist provides evidence of this approach. But, like the dog who finally catches the car, what would they do with it?

Beginning in 1995 and continuing into the middle of the 2020s, major restructuring and control now rested with the conservative group. They achieved their goal of ridding the convention of heretics, like myself. However, I survived my firing, and as a freedom-loving Baptist, I left of my own volition upon retirement from OBU in 2001. The conservatives succeeded in the institutionalization of their agenda. In this regard, they were completely successful. The "conservative resurgence" or the "takeover" was final. Opponents were removed one way or another. Agencies and institutions were either eliminated or reshaped with the conservative agenda adopted. At the same time, the question of success calls for further evaluation, when analyzed by the history and principles of the denomination, and evaluated by the promises of more glorious days for Southern Baptists once the purge was completed.

**The Failures of the Takeover**

In 2021 Dr. Michael Kuykendall and I edited and updated an earlier publication of mine on Southern Baptist history. In the "Conclusion" of *Southern Baptists: A History of a Confessional People*, Mike contributed a section called "Final Reflections and Future Challenges." At the time Mike was teaching the Baptist history course at what is now Gateway Seminary on the campus in Vancouver, Washington. He continued to study developments in the convention, and although a New Testament specialist, is an excellent Baptist historian.

Mike pointed out that although the Controversy had ended, several issues that "had sparked or perpetuated" the conflict were never fully resolved. They included the status of women in the denomination, issues over the gifts of the Spirit, the surge of Calvinism, the decline of baptisms and membership, and the challenge of multiculturalism.[157] A few of these in no particular order are worth noting for this volume.

**Failed Leadership: Orthodoxy Does Not Ensure Integrity:**

The architects of the conservative takeover were Dr. Paige Patterson and Judge Paul Pressler. They fiercely championed and led the movement to seize control of the convention. Pressler developed the strategy aimed at electing presidents, who then appointed only agenda-driven members to the nominating committee. Patterson fired up the base to attend annual meetings, vocalize concerns at the state, institutional, associational, and church organizations of Southern Baptists, and seek out heretics at all levels.

However, once successful, theological orthodoxy did not guarantee success in terms of personal piety nor ethical purity. In recent years their reputations as convention leaders have been severely tarnished by their own actions. In both cases the evidence pointed to flawed individuals who excelled in pointing out the theological deficiencies of others. At the same time both revealed personal weaknesses which affected not only their reputations, but also the reputation of the denomination.

Dr. Paige Patterson: Patterson used his notoriety as the theological leader in the political struggle for power initially to become president of Southeastern Baptist Theological Seminary (1992-2003), and then achieve the pinnacle of his career as president of Southwestern Seminary (2003-2018). The movement he led, of course, resulted in the firing of Dr. Russell Dilday, the highly respected president of the school. Southwestern was the largest seminary in the world during Dilday's tenure from 1978 to 1994. It trained more than half of all Southern Baptist missionaries during his term as president. When he was fired for opposing the conservative takeover, a photo of the locks being changed on his office doors appeared in denominational newspapers throughout the convention, and demonstrated the political side of the Controversy.[158] Immediate successors at Southwestern did not result in the achievement of greater glory for the institution. In fact, the rapid and significant decline at this seminary in terms of the number of students, finances, and influence is astounding.

---

[157] Yarbrough and Kuykendall, *Southern Baptists*, 174-78.
[158] Scott Collins and Russ Dilday, "Russell Dilday, Baptist Statesman," *Baptistnews.com*, 21 June 2023.

Patterson became president of Southwestern in 2003. He was fired by trustees in 2018 after reports of his insensitivity to issues raised by women over abusive behavior by students at the seminary was revealed. Under Patterson's leadership, Southwestern was charged with "ignoring female students' complaints of sexual harassment and stalking behavior by male student-employees." An article in *Baptist News Global* describes in detail the story of one female student, who met with the president to discuss her continued rape by a seminary employee, who was a plumber on campus, and Patterson's insensitivity to her problem.[159]

On May 22, 2018, the seminary's trustees voted to remove Patterson as president, but to appoint him as president emeritus with pay. However, a new story appeared in the *Washington Post*, which claimed that a student at Southeastern Seminary charged that Patterson while president at that seminary had mishandled her rape report. A week later Patterson was terminated without pay, based upon new evidence that questioned his answers related to the Southeastern incident. In an email in which he had described meeting with the student privately, Patterson stated that he met with her alone so that he could "break her down."[160]

Questions of impropriety did not end with the firing of Patterson. Three years later the seminary charged the Pattersons with taking items from the Southwestern and improperly contacting donors to the seminary to transfer funding to the Pattersons' personal nonprofit organization.[161] In the 2021 *Southern Baptist Convention Book of Reports*, the seminary stated that "The Pattersons have continued to use institutional records for their own personal benefit and to the detriment of the Seminary," and that "The Pattersons' actions have caused substantial financial harm to the Seminary."[162]

The seminary charged that following Patterson's termination "the Pattersons had improperly removed boxes of documents that belonged to the Seminary from the President's Home" including "confidential donor information, student records, institutional correspondence, financial records, historical

---

[159] Bob Allen, "Lawsuit Reveals Details about Paige Patterson's 'Break Her Down' Meeting with Woman Alleging Campus Rape," *Baptistnews.com*, 24 June 2019.
[160] Allen, "Lawsuit Reveals Details."
[161] Brian Kaylor, "Southwestern Accuses Pattersons of Theft, Improper Donor Solicitation," *Wordandway.org*, 28 May 2021.
[162] Kaylor, "Southwestern Accuses Pattersons."

files, and meeting and convention records." Requests for return of the documents has not occurred at the time of this book's writing.

The seminary accused Patterson of "misappropriation of confidential donor information." The report stated the Pattersons used that confidential list of all donors to the school and "undertook a scheme" to "contact Seminary donors to divert donations and gifts away from the Seminary." An example stated that a $5 million gift was made by donors to the school prior to Patterson's termination. The report added that after his firing, Patterson convinced the donors to "revoke their substantial gift and to instead donate those funds to Sandy Creek Foundation," which was the Pattersons' personal nonprofit organization. The report also stated that the foundation purchased a "roughly $1 million home" in August 2018 for the Pattersons, apparently "made possible" by the $5 million gift. As further evidence, *Word & Way* examined financial reports from Sandy Creek Foundation, which substantiated Southwestern Seminary's accusation. The foundation started the 2018 with only $82,292 in net assets, but finished the year with $5,295,210 in net assets.[163] Additional charges of misuse of the seminary's donor list, and of removal of artwork, antiques, and taxidermy from a donated collection also took place.[164]

Southwestern Seminary's conflict with Patterson confirms that there is much more to one's Christian witness than simply holding to orthodox theology. Conduct is essential to one's faith. Although everyone has personal flaws and shortcomings, the egregious failure of Patterson's response of vulnerable women to sexual assault, and charges of unethical actions related to his firing from the seminary raise serious concern about the place of theology on understanding the Christian witness.

I have stated before that my conviction is that for Baptists "theology is not a test of faith, but rather the result of faith." Stated another way is that we should not define our faith by our theology. Rather our theology should be confirmed by the way we live our lives as believers." In other words, "what you believe is revealed in what you do, not simply what you say."

Judge Paul Pressler: Even more concerning than Patterson's shortcomings was the moral failure charges leveled against Judge Pressler. In March, 2024, in an article by Mark Wingfield in *Baptist News Global*, the story of Paul

---

[163] Kaylor, "Southwestern Accuses Pattersons."
[164] Kaylor, "Southwestern Accuses Pattersons."

Pressler's abuse of young men appeared. Wingfield surprisingly praised *Baptist Press*, the official news arm of Southern Baptists, for reporting on Pressler's moral failures. Pressler claimed and deserved credit (or blame) for orchestrating the conservative takeover of the Southern Baptist Convention.

But Pressler apparently had a hidden secret during the years of the Controversy that has now come to light. *Baptist News Global* and *Baptist Press* have chronicled the story. In summary, the *Baptist Press* story reported in detail allegations of Pressler's sexual abuse of boys and young men. The allegations happened while the judge was leading the charge for the takeover of the convention. Wingfield frames the *Baptist Press* opinion piece, "A word in praise of Baptist Press," in the context of Pressler's commitment to control the Southern Baptist press arm of the convention.[165] Back in 1990, the most controversial event related to news publishing was rooted in the firing of two of the writers for *Baptist Press*, the official news agency of the convention. Dan Martin and Al Shackleford were dramatically fired by the Executive Committee. Armed security guards at the meeting shocked many Southern Baptists. The firings of Shackleford and Martin resulted in the organization of *Associated Baptist Press*, which later became *Baptist News Global*.[166]

Another event which provides evidence of the aggressive approach of Pressler, a member of the Executive Committee, occurred when I was chairman of the trustees of the Historical Commission. The story demonstrated the bullying tactics of Pressler in attempting to intimidate an agency leader during the struggle for control of the convention. The background can be framed in the context of the initial call for "designated giving" by conservative leaders. They later rejected that approach after seizing momentum in the takeover battle. Initially, conservatives justified supporting their favorite causes outside the Cooperative Program. Once they had the power, they attacked the same defense by the moderates.

Pressler and the Nolan P. Howington pamphlet: A controversial pamphlet in a series on Baptists published by the Historical Commission set the stage for Pressler's pressuring tactics. Nolan P. Howington wrote the pamphlet "Who Are Southern Baptists?" In his effort to be both historically accurate and diplomatic, Howington presented a strong and supportive statement of the Cooperative Program. He also described the voluntary nature of giving by

---

[165] Mark Wingfield, "A Word in Praise of Baptist Press," *Baptistnews.com*, 11 March 2024.
[166] See Yarbrough and Kuykendall (*Southern Baptists*, 90-92) for a discussion of this event, as well as other conflicts between the conservatives and moderates over education and publications.

Southern Baptist churches. He affirmed that the Southern Baptist Convention enabled churches to pool and distribute their money for supporting ministries at home and around the world through the plan called the Cooperative Program. Howington then added an historically correct statement, writing that "Some churches also give money for missions education, and other causes through such channels as the Cooperative Baptist Fellowship."

Howington was describing the reality based on the earlier defense of "designated giving" voiced by conservative leaders of the Controversy. The Historical Commission had received as much as $10,000 in designated gifts during previous years. The Executive Committee of the Southern Baptist Convention informed the Historical Commission that it had received "numerous complaints" (an undefined number) about the pamphlet.[167]

Word came that one of the agency's board members was in a conversation during the 1993 Southern Baptist Convention meeting in Houston, Texas. A warning was made by two members of the Executive Committee that if the pamphlet was not withdrawn and rewritten with the offending statement removed, then funding to the Commission could be reduced. Since the Executive Committee recommends budget allocations to the Southern Baptist Convention, this was no idle threat.[168]

Dr. May informed me as chair of the trustees of the events. In consultation with him, the board chose not to fight this issue, and voted to withdraw and rewrite the pamphlet. The action was approved at a cost of around $1,500 to the Commission. This was not an insignificant amount to a small commission of the Southern Baptist Convention.[169]

In a December 7, 2023, email exchange with Dr. John Finley (current executive director of the Baptist History & Heritage Society), he shared with me a story which I was not aware, and which I believe is significant and insightful information related to my comments about the Howington pamphlet. John wrote:

Charles Deweese told me a few years ago about the confrontation between Paul Pressler and Lynn May over the HC's decision to publish a resource that

---

[167] Slayden A. Yarbrough, "The History of Southern Baptist History: Restructuring and the New SBHS," *Baptist History & Heritage* 34, no. 3 (Summer/Fall 1999): 108-20.
[168] Yarbrough, "Restructuring and the New SBHS," 110.
[169] Yarbrough, "Restructuring and the New SBHS," 110.

spoke favorably about Cooperative Baptist Fellowship. As Charles describes it, the spirit and tone of Pressler's visit was that he was enraged at the Commission's action and was there to issue a threat. He left the impression with Charles that he had the power to shut the agency down. In the end the convention followed his lead and that of others who spear-headed the movement. The Southern Baptist Convention adopted the Restructuring Committee's recommendation and dissolved the Commission and several other agencies.[170]

I decided to verify John's story. On December 9, 2023, I sent an email to Charles, a long-time friend, asking him about the event, and its relationship to the pamphlet. I received an email from Charles on the same day. Charles's words can describe what happened much better than I can. In a lengthy email he wrote:

"When Nolan Howington submitted his manuscript to the Commission, Lynn May suggested that we delete the reference to Cooperative Baptist Fellowship. I convinced him that we retain it since it simply mentioned the organization without advocating it. Lynn agreed to go along with my suggestion. After the pamphlet was published, Paul Pressler became aware of it. One day afterwards, when the Southern Baptist Convention Executive Committee was meeting in the Southern Baptist Convention Building, I was talking with Shirley Rose at her receptionist desk when Pressler barged into the office and abruptly asked where Lynn's office was. Shirley told him and, without an invitation, he marched down the hall toward Lynn's office. Sensing trouble, I followed him because Lynn's battle with Parkinson's had already started and he had asked me to assist him in special ways.

Without knocking, he opened Lynn's door and walked right in. I followed him and shut the door behind us. In the course of five or fewer minutes, he verbally blistered Lynn specifically because the Commission had published Nolan's pamphlet including a Cooperative Baptist Fellowship reference. In intimidating fashion, he threatened to terminate the Commission because of that reference. And then he left. And then the Commission was terminated in 1996.

In one sense I felt a little remorse for having encouraged Lynn to include the Cooperative Baptist Fellowship reference. In my more mature moments, however, I recognized that this was just one of many precipitating factors

---

[170] John Finley, email to Slayden Yarbrough, December 9, 2023.

that eventually led to the demise of the Historical Commission, Education Commission, Stewardship Commission, Brotherhood Commission, etc. If it had not been the Howington reference, it would have been something else. Right-wing, authoritarian advocates in Southern Baptist life simply were and are simply a part of the authoritarian impulses in American religion and politics today."[171]

Combining Charles's narrative with my experience as chair of the trustees of the Historical Commission, a complete record of this confrontation and its consequences for the agency is now available. Threats and intimidation are evidence of the willingness of the conservative party in the Southern Baptist Convention to obtain total control of all agencies and institutions of the convention. Compromise and parity were simply meaningless words that were rapidly forgotten by the new order.

A second disagreement arose following the pamphlet controversy, which I conclude was a continuation of the narrative related to Pressler's intimidating visit to Dr. May. The Commission trustees voted in 1994 in Memphis to continue accepting Cooperative Baptist Fellowship gifts. Only two trustees dissented against the motion. The trustees also reaffirmed commitment to the Cooperative Program, acknowledged the sacred right of all Baptists to give voluntary as they felt led, and to oppose efforts to do harm to the Cooperative Program. Such efforts came to naught. During the annual meeting of the convention in Orlando, the messengers voted to ask all agencies to discontinue receiving such designated funds. The Historical Commission yielded to the pressure, and notified the Cooperative Baptist Fellowship that it would no longer accept the organization's gifts.[172]

Pressler's intimidation of Dr. May and his threat to dissolve the agency was confirmed with the adoption of the restructuring report in Atlanta. In the end, such efforts at appeasing Pressler and the Executive Committee proved unsuccessful. The Historical Commission was one of the agencies dissolved by the Southern Baptist Convention in June 1997.[173] This appellate judge as a defender of orthodoxy used his power to carry out his threats to dictate what the denomination's historical agency could publish and what it could not, and ultimately determined whether the agency should even exist.

---

[171] Charles Deweese, email to Slayden Yarbrough, December 9, 2023.
[172] Yarbrough, "Restructuring and the New SBHS," 110.
[173] Yarbrough, "Restructuring and the New SBHS," 112.

Wingfield's article on *Baptist Press* provides a detailed overview of the activities of Pressler, which were taking place behind the scenes of the public controversy in the convention. The basic charges against him summarized by Wingfield are that he not only abused "church boys and young interns committed to his care, he abused an entire denomination and hundreds of faithful clergy and denominational leaders along the way. There is no other single person who has done more damage to more Southern Baptist leaders and Southern Baptist churches than Paul Pressler."[174] As a Baptist historian who also participated in the decades long struggle, and based on the available evidence, I identify with Wingfield's assessment.

Wingfield highlighted several important conclusions and observations in the *Baptist Press* article related to Pressler's sexual abuse charges. Here are the summaries he presented, which include events, evaluations, and questions:

"Hints of a darker side to Pressler, a former Texas state judge, began to emerge two decades ago. The church where he served as a deacon, Houston's First Baptist Church, rebuked Pressler for being nude at his home with a young man from the congregation."

"Also in 2004, Pressler settled a lawsuit by Duane Rollins that alleged assault by Pressler, according to more recent court filings. In exchange for confidentiality and the destruction of 'all tapes, affidavits or other written or audible information,' Pressler agreed to pay $1,500 per month until 2029—nearly half a million dollars."

"Evidence in the (Rollins) case included affidavits by multiple men who claimed Pressler engaged in inappropriate sexual behavior with them."

Danny Akin, president of Southeastern Baptist Theological Seminary: "I am grieved beyond measure at the revelations of what the evidence seems to be overwhelmingly clear that he did for many, many years. . .. What he did can only be called evil, wicked and distasteful in the highest degree."

"Jim Guenther, an attorney who represented the SBC and its Executive Committee until his resignation in late 2021, wrote in a 2021 email to a then-EC vice president that all codefendants in the Rollins lawsuit, including the SBC, believed a full investigation into Pressler's conduct likely 'would have

---

[174] Wingfield, "Word in Praise of Baptist Press."

produced a lot of evidence of the truthfulness of the fundamental allegation by the plaintiff that Pressler had sexually abused him for many years.'"

"Current SBC attorney Gene Besen echoed Guenther's assessment, tweeting in January that Pressler is a 'dangerous predator who exploited boys based on his power and his false piety,' and adding, 'The man's actions are of the devil. That is clear.'"

Heather Evans, a licensed social worker and adviser to the SBC's Abuse Reform Implementation Task Force: "Why are there leaders that remain silent and don't publicly call out the evil of what was done, even though there are ways (Pressler's) work is celebrated and revered? Why are they silent on this issue? That silence speaks so loudly to survivors. It re-harms survivors, and not just the survivors directly hurt by Pressler, but all survivors in both a watching convention and beyond."

Marshall Blalock, pastor of First Baptist Church in Charleston, South Carolina, and former chairman of the SBC Abuse Reform Implementation Task Force stated: "Typically, we don't comment on lawsuits while they are under adjudication. I understand that. I get that. But we came to a settlement, and no one who has the real information has explained the whole perspective of why we did what we did: why we settled, what was involved, when the information came forward. None of that has been officially presented to people."[175]

My advice as previously noted to my students when discussing Baptist theology that "if I want to know what you really believe, I will look at what you do, not what you say." The stories of Patterson and Pressler provide poignant examples of this conviction. Pressler was in assisted living facility in Houston when he died on June 7, 2024. His story once again is a reminder that theological orthodoxy is not the measuring rod of faith. Rather, the most important statement of one's beliefs is rooted in the commitment to and practice of a living faith. To evaluate the contributions of the judge from Houston requires an awareness of the greater story of his life, not just what he claimed to believe theologically.

---

[175] Wingfield, "Word in Praise of Baptist Press."

## Failed Promises:

Conservatives in the convention promised that purging the moderates and liberals would result in denominational purity, which would increase growth in churches, baptisms, and membership. On the one hand, the number of churches cooperating with the SBC has grown in the years following the takeover. However, membership consistently continued to decline. Since 2006, the SBC lost 1.5 million members. Furthermore, baptisms also declined, with almost 30 percent fewer than in 2007.[176]

I might add, that in my Baptist and biblical view, baptism is a symbolic confession of faith, not a purification right of orthodox theology. The most visible spokesman for conservatives is the president of Southern Seminary, Dr. R. Albert Mohler. He described the decline of baptismal numbers as "both remarkable and lamentable."[177] Doctrinal purity and heretical purging did not result in the anticipated surge of membership and baptisms. Even considering the effects of COVID, the overall record for Southern Baptist membership and Baptists reflects significant decline in the two plus decades following the takeover.

As further evidence of the failure of the conservative promise of growth, a 2020 article by Kate Shellnut in *Christianity Today* carried the title "Southern Baptists See Biggest Drop in 100 Years."[178] In the annual statistical report of the convention in 2023, baptisms had increased while at the same time remaining well below 2019 levels, further reflecting a decline that started in 1999. At the same time membership continued to drop with the largest decline in a century.

The return to the conservative heritage has produced neither membership growth nor prevented actual decline in membership and baptisms overall since 2000. Of course, all mainline denominations have experienced decline. Southern Baptists have not been immune to that trend, despite their "doctrinal purity." In fact, religion researcher Ryan Burge, one of the foremost authorities in America on the demographics of religion, stated that

---

[176] Carol Pipes, "Giving Increases for SBC in 2018, Baptisms, Attendance Continue Decline," blog.lifeway.com, 23 May 2019; Kate Shellnut, "Southern Baptists See Biggest Drop in 100 Years," *Christianity Today*, 4 June 2020.
[177] See R. Albert Mohler Jr., "The Future of the Southern Baptist Convention: The Numbers Don't Add Up," Albertmohler.com, 31 May 2019.
[178] Mark Wingfield, "In SBC Annual Statistics, Even the Good News Isn't that Good," *Baptistnews.com*, 11 May 2023.

"The decline the SBC is experiencing is at a scope and scale that has not been seen in any other Protestant denomination in American history."[179] Membership in the convention peaked in 2006 at 16.3 million. In 2023 it had fallen back to 1978 levels, at 13.2 million.[180] Once more, my conclusion is that the commitment to doctrinal orthodoxy along with other factors diminished a focus upon missions and ministry, diversity, traditional Baptist principles, and relevancy for the twenty-first century.

**Southern Baptists and Calvinism:**

In our book on Southern Baptists, Mike Kuykendall discussed the issue related to the rise of Reformed Baptists in the convention.[181] Many conservative participants in the Controversy were committed to Calvinist theology. This tradition appeared in the rise of Particular Baptists in seventeenth-century England. In America, it can be traced to the Philadelphia Association that arose in 1707. There has always been a minority of Reformed leaders throughout the history of Southern Baptists. A resurgence in Calvinism has appeared in the Southern Baptist Convention in the past forty-plus years. During this time span a few Southern Baptist seminaries have produced numerous Reformed pastors, who have been vocal in their theological commitments.

However, the fact is that many Southern Baptists are troubled by the theological trend. The quest for theological orthodoxy apparently has not led to doctrinal uniformity, nor peace. A 2006 report by LifeWay research, which stated that 10 percent of convention pastors accepted five-point Calvinism. That number grew to about 30 percent by 2013. At the same time, as many as 60 percent were concerned about the impact of the movement in the convention.[182]

The debate over Calvinism resulted in Frank Page, president of the convention, to appoint an advisory committee to study the topic. The report of the committee issued in 2013 paradoxically called for cooperation among Southern Baptists among the diverse positions.[183] I find this ironic and an

---

[179] Wingfield, "SBC Annual Statistics."
[180] Wingfield, "SBC Annual Statistics."
[181] Yarbrough and Kuykendall, *Southern Baptists*, 175-76.
[182] Greg Horton, "Are Southern Baptists Predestined to Fuss over Calvinism?" *Baptist Standard*, 6 June 2013.
[183] Michael Foust, "Calvinism Committee Issues Report, Urges SBC to 'Stand Together' for Great Commission," *Baptistpress.org*, 31 May 2013.

example of "selective theology." Diversity is allowed on this major and controversial issue. Yet diversity was not allowed on the battle over the Bible during the Controversy. The same concern is also evident over the role of women in ministry, especially in terms of the complementarian controversy, which became the orthodox standard for the denomination in actions taken by the messengers to the convention in 2023. Diversity on this issue is not acceptable in the current Southern Baptist Convention.

The debate over the Reformed tradition is still evident in the convention. In response to Calvinism, a growing number of "traditional" Southern Baptists expressed concern. In 2017, an increasing number of churches and ministers in the denomination urged "loyal opposition" to Calvinism's encroachment on the denomination.[184] Rumors of another split in the convention circulated, but abated for the time being. Once again, however, disagreement over theology contributed to divisiveness rather than unity in diversity within the denomination.

I might also raise an important theological question. If theological purity promised growth in the denomination, then why have baptisms and membership rolls declined during the last decade plus? If the Calvinists are right, does this mean that God has chosen fewer sinners to be among the elect? Or, if the non-Calvinists are right, has the conflict over controversy in the current generation sapped the energy of evangelism, which once characterized the convention?

One final observation may be made from my Baptist history teaching days. I have never met a Calvinist who was not one of the "elect." There may have been a small number in this category through the ages, but not to my knowledge.

## Women and Ministry: A New Purge of Churches and Pastors:

An explosive issue during the Controversy was the role of women in leadership positions. Historically, many leading Southern Baptist churches ordained women as deacons. In 1973 it was reported that two to three

---

[184] David Roach, "Connect316 Urges 'Loyal Opposition' to Calvinism," Sbcannualmeeting.net, 22 June 2017. See the video provided in this link for Roach's view: https://www.bing.com/videos/search?q=David+Roach%2c+"Connect316+Urges+'Loyal+Opposition'+to+Calvinism%2c"&qpvt=David+Roach%2c+"Connect316+Urges+'Loyal+Opposition'+to+Calvinism%2c"&FORM=VDRE

hundred churches in the convention had women deacons.[185] Conservatives sought restriction and moderates defended the roles of women both as deacons and pastors.

First Baptist Church of Shawnee, Oklahoma, my home church, decided to ordain women as deacons. From this action threats from the Pottawatomie-Lincoln Association arose, seeking the removal of my church. As previously discussed, I recall one instance where Rev. James Paul Maxwell, one of many good associational ministers caught in the middle of the conflict, met with our pastor, Dr. Joe Brown, to discuss the issue. Joe reminded him that our church provided most of the funding for the association and unsurprisingly, the issue quietly disappeared. The issue of women deacons did not gain enough traction for removal of churches on a significant scale. It seems that the rules for doctrinal orthodoxy were one thing and the acceptance of financial contributions from an offending congregation were another.

In 1964 the Watts Baptist Church of Durham, North Carolina, ordained Addie Davis as a minister of the Gospel. By 1988, more than 500 women had been ordained as ministers in the denomination.[186] This set the stage for increasing conflict over women in the role of pastors in the convention.

Organized activity on the issue by both parties developed rapidly during the Controversy. Southern Baptist Women in Ministry arose from the moderate wing. From the conservative element, motions against women in ministry appeared at both state and national levels. A good summary of these activities is discussed in *Southern Baptists* by myself and Mike Kuykendall.[187]

As discussed in an earlier chapter, the 2023 Southern Baptist Convention annual meeting took official action to seize the authority of the local congregation in theologically expressing its faith. In New Orleans, messengers approved the first reading of a constitutional amendment which prohibited women from serving as pastors. They adopted two supportive resolutions on the issue. They also voted to remove two churches from the convention—Saddleback Church in California and Fern Creek in Kentucky. Al Mohler defended the action on biblical grounds. However, retired Saddleback pastor Rick Warren and Fern Creek pastor Linda Barnes Popum

---

[185] Yarbrough and Kuykendall, *Southern Baptists*, 82.
[186] Yarbrough and Kuykendall, *Southern Baptists*, 83.
[187] Yarbrough and Kuykendall, *Southern Baptists*, 83-85.

cited the same Bible and defended the practice of their respective congregations.

Not only were women senior pastors rejected. The title of pastor was not to be used for women, who served as children's pastor, youth pastor, associate pastor, and missions pastor. Both Warren and Popum affirmed their conservative principles. "Complementarianism," however, ruled the day. There was no room for negotiation or compromise. Southern Baptist orthodoxy on the role of women as pastors became a requirement for all the churches affiliated with the convention.

The vote was overwhelming. Freedom under the Lordship of Jesus was determined by the messengers. Fern Creek was rejected as a part of the convention by a 91 percent majority. Strikingly, Saddleback, the largest church in the Southern Baptist Convention, was cast out by an 88 percent majority.[188] In 2023, historic Baptist principles found in the *Baptist Faith and Message* meant nothing to leadership intent on enforcing their brand of orthodoxy on the churches of the denomination.

Less than a month after the expulsion of Saddleback Church and Fern Creek Church, Elevation Church in North Carolina notified the Southern Baptist Convention that it was withdrawing its affiliation with the denomination. Elevation is a megachurch, which draws thousands of worshippers to multiple campuses. Its influence upon Christian music resulted in expanded reach far beyond Southern Baptists. Holly Furtick, wife of pastor Steven Furtick, preaches regularly to men and women. The letter of withdrawal does not mention the reason, but the assumption is the issue of women pastors. It is anticipated that other congregations may also separate from the convention over the complete rejection of women pastors.[189]

As previously mentioned, the Southern Baptist Convention has been in membership decline for nearly two decades but remains the largest Protestant denomination in America. In statistics released in 2023 by Lifeway Research, the denomination fell to 13.2 million members in 2022. That is the lowest level since the late 1970s. Rates of baptisms are also in long-term decline. Instead of growing because of doctrinal orthodoxy, could it be that some of

---

[188] Mark Wingfield. "Anti-Egalitarian Forces Make Clean Sweep at Southern Baptist Convention Annual Meeting," *Baptistnews.com*, 14 June 2023.Anti-egalitarian forces make clean sweep at Southern Baptist Convention annual meeting,"
[189] Maina Mwaura, "Another Megachurch Leaves the SBC," *Baptistnews.com*, 30 June 2023.

the numerical decline is the result of an increasing and more narrowly defined orthodoxy demanded by the denominational leadership?

The proposed constitutional amendment opposing women in ministry required a second reading at the 2024 Southern Baptist Convention annual meeting. Just how restrictive will the Southern Baptist Convention become if messengers to this annual meeting approve a second reading of a proposed constitutional amendment against women in ministry? It depends on who is doing the explaining. Challenges arose to the "Law Amendment," named after Virginia pastor Mike Law. He proposed an amendment to the SBC Constitution that would add a sixth item to Article III, Paragraph 1, regarding the friendly cooperation of SBC churches: "Affirms, appoints, or employs only men as any kind of pastor or elder as qualified by Scripture." The amendment narrowly failed on June 12, 2024, during the annual SBC meeting.

Complementarianism describes the separation of the roles of men and women, and justifies prohibiting women to be ordained as pastors. Rigid interpretation of this position calls for not only limiting pastoral roles for women, but also prohibiting women from teaching men in any setting. The most extreme views of Complementarianism establish a gender hierarchy. Further evidence of the scope of this trend occurred several years ago, when complementarians attacked popular Bible teacher and author Beth Moore. She subsequently became an Anglican, leaving the Southern Baptist Convention behind.[190]

Putting on my prophetic hat again, I anticipate that the denomination's rigid view toward women will lead to significant irrelevancy in succeeding generations. Young women will reject the authoritarianism of male-only leadership and will demand recognition of their spiritual gifts for ministry. Many will follow the example of Beth Moore, and look to church groups that do not discriminate against women in pastoral ministry. I often told my female students (and my male students) that the call to ministry was not a question of gender, but rather a question of gifts. I continue to hold that view today. If I am correct, Southern Baptists in the efforts to limit the role of women as pastors are failing in the responsibility to affirm the personal nature of the calling to ministry in Baptist churches. I consider the action related to

---

[190] Mark Wingfield, "As SBC Moves Toward Second Vote on Law Amendment, Debate Continues on Just What It Means," *Baptistnews.com*, 1 December 2023.

women by the denomination a failure to recognize the leadership of God in the question of gender.

## Autonomy of the Local Church versus the Authority of the Convention and Baptist Confessional Theology versus Creedal:

Two developments took place during the Controversy and restructuring that confirmed a revision of confessional theology toward creedalism. In 1998 the addition to the *Baptist Faith and Message* of Article XVIII on "The Family" was adopted. This was followed with major revisions in the adoption of the 2000 *Baptist Faith and Message*. Both changes reflected movement away from traditional Baptist confessional theology approach toward more authoritative, creedal interpretations of doctrinal statements. Decisions were based not upon history and tradition, but by majority vote. Creedalism became the new norm in the Southern Baptist Convention, although leadership continued to use the term "confessions" as revised by their imposed limitations on the freedom of Baptists and Baptist churches.

I appeal once more to the two volumes which I published as Baptists moved into in the twenty-first century. Both were predicated on my commitment to address the changes resulting from the Controversy and the restructuring of the Southern Baptist Convention. In 2000, I published *Southern Baptists: A Historical, Ecclesiological. and Theological Heritage of a Confessional People*. In 2021 with the assistance of Michael Kuykendall, we edited and updated my earlier volume, and published *Southern Baptists: A History of a Confessional People*. Mike added the history of Southern Baptists between 2000 and 2021. These two books cover thoroughly the following topics. The chapters on "A Heritage of Conflict (the Controversy)," "A Heritage of Change (The Restructuring of the Southern Baptist Convention)," and "A Theological Heritage (A Confessional People)" are essential sources in the following discussion, and in other parts of this volume. They chronicle the context of my own pilgrimage and my interpretation of so much of not only my journey, but developments within the Southern Baptist Convention. Anyone wanting to understand the history of the denomination and its restructuring in the 1990s is encouraged to read these chapters, plus the conclusion, where Mike predicts the issues currently facing the contemporary convention.

During these challenging days I made my choices with whom I identified. I observed what was going on in Baptist life. I understood Baptist history, and applied that understanding to the courses which I taught at SWBC. During my subsequent years at OBU, I identified with the moderate movement in the Southern Baptist Convention. Those critical of me considered me a bleeding-heart liberal out to destroy the faith of my students. My colleagues and friends understood me to be a Southern Baptist committed to a rich denominational heritage, a capable Baptist historian, and an outspoken defender of both biblical and Baptist principles. The major context of my career was shaped by what is the Controversy, which influenced every important principle and practice related to Baptists and their history. It certainly was evident in my understanding of Baptist confessional theology.

The three versions of the *Baptist Faith and Message* (1925, revised 1963, revised 2000) begin with statements in the preface, which detail the nature, function, and limitations of such confessions. Although I have discussed this issue earlier in my book, it is worth reviewing in this section. The confessional statements clearly protect the freedom of Baptists and Baptist churches to confessionally express their faith. The bottom line is that:

That they constitute a consensus of opinion of some Baptist body, large or small, for the general instruction and guidance of our own people and others concerning those articles of the Christian faith which are most surely held among us. They are not intended to add anything to the simple conditions of salvation revealed in the New Testament, viz., repentance towards God and faith in Jesus Christ as Savior and Lord.

That we do not regard them as complete statements of our faith, having any quality of finality or infallibility. As in the past so in the future Baptists should hold themselves free to revise their statements of faith as may seem to them wise and expedient at any time.

That any group of Baptists, large or small, have the inherent right to draw up for themselves and publish to the world a confession of their faith whenever they may think it advisable to do so.

That the sole authority for faith and practice among Baptists is the Scriptures of the Old and New Testaments. Confessions are only guides in interpretation, having no authority over the conscience.

That they are statements of religious convictions, drawn from the Scriptures, and are not to be used to hamper freedom of thought or investigation in other realms of life.[191]

---

[191] Lumpkin and Leonard, *Baptist Confessions*, 409-10.

The prefaces of the 1925 and 1963 confessions also state that "Baptists are a people who profess a living faith. This faith is rooted and grounded in Jesus Christ who is the 'same yesterday, today, and forever.' Therefore, the sole authority for faith and practice among Baptists is Jesus Christ whose will is revealed in the Holy Scriptures."[192] When one examines the central teachings of Baptists and Southern Baptists, the Lordship of Christ is the theological foundation of each group. The authority of the living Lord supersedes all other authority.

Significantly, these principles were deleted in the preface of the 2000 *Baptist Faith and Message*. The removal of the position that "the Lordship of Christ and his will as revealed in the Bible is the supreme authority for faith and practice among Baptists," and that confessions have "no authority over the conscience" was apparently intentional. Members of the committee also added that "Baptist churches, associations and general bodies have adopted confessions of faith as a witness to the world accountability. We are not embarrassed to state before the world that these are doctrines that we hold precious and essential to the Baptist tradition of faith and practice."

Critics of the 2000 *Baptist Faith and Message* interpreted these changes to be more creedal than confessional. The change expressed concern that the Bible would replace Christ as the ultimate authority for faith and practice for believers. When applied, the understanding of Christ and his leadership in the lives of believers would be restricted to the Bible only. I point out that there was no agreement on the New Testament canon until Athanasius, bishop of Alexandria, Egypt, in an annual Easter letter to his congregation listed all twenty-seven books of the New Testament, no more and no less, in A.D. 367. Until that time disagreement took place over the potential canon list. And believers followed the leadership of the Spirit in determining their faith and ministry.

The leadership of the Spirit in dealing with contemporary issues not discussed in the Bible would be relegated to an inferior position below the Scriptures, and the interpretation of what the Scripture means on any given teaching. These changes resulted in the 2000 *Baptist Faith and Message* being used as a creedal document to determine the orthodoxy or heterodoxy of any person or church, and as such a significant radical application of theology as a test of faith.

---

[192] *Baptist Faith and Message*, 1963, 5.

One final change is notable in the preface. The 2000 version of the *Baptist Faith and Message* includes the statement that Baptists "have adopted confessions of faith as a witness to the world, and as instruments of doctrinal accountability." Southern Baptist leaders have used the revision to insist upon "doctrinal accountability." The issue of women as pastors is an example of this creedal application.

I often asked my students in my Baptist history class at OBU, "who decides what is doctrinally accountable?" I always volunteered to make those decisions for the denomination but got no takers. Vocal leaders in the current convention have assumed the authority to determine what is acceptable and what is heretical. I frequently added to my comments what I have previously stated, and what I consider to be consistent with Baptist principles: "If you ask me what I believe, I will tell you. If you tell me what I must believe, I will ask when did you stop being Baptist?" To state this another way, my position is that for Baptists, "theology is not a test of faith, it is the result of faith." As such, it should always be growing and changing, if it seeks to be relevant.

## The Secular Politicization of the Southern Baptist Convention

I would add to Mike's list the politicization of the Southern Baptist Convention. In many ways, the new SBC has become a wing of one political party in the United States. A good example of political transformation by a Southern Baptist leader is Al Mohler. He initially opposed Donald Trump as the Republican candidate for president of the United States. Then the pressure came. He has since changed his tune.

When I was growing up in First Baptist Church of Washington Park, Illinois, I thought that most Southern Baptists were Democrats. That was probably because our congregation was composed primarily of laborers. I began to notice that other factors could come into play when my pastor spoke out against John F. Kennedy as a candidate for president. I was not old enough to vote, and the influence of my parent's caused me to favor Kennedy. But my pastor was concerned that the Democrat would have to follow the teachings of an infallible Pope, and that was taboo for Southern Baptists. However, I was not easily swayed and questioned my pastor's position.

I also have vigorously defended the responsibility of all people to hold and defend their own political views. I believe that this is essential for a free society. But this has radically changed in the twenty-first century. Additionally, I have taught throughout my career that churches should not be overly close to politicians since they will always be used for political purposes in the end. History and the contemporary situation in American politics justifies my belief in this matter.

MAGA (Make America Great Again) became a test of faith in Southern Baptist life. In my opinion the Southern Baptist Convention has become a major wing of the Republican party. The influence of the largest Protestant denomination in the country is an attractive source of support for politicians. The question that I ask is "Who is selling their birthrights for a mess of political pottage?" I will not dwell on this issue, but I will conclude that the mission and ministry of a once proud denomination has been redefined to be simply an advocate of right-wing politics. I cherish the freedom of all Baptists to determine how they vote, including those who disagree with me. But when one's political views becomes a test of faith, we have crossed a line which negates the spiritual nature of individuals and churches. Finally, what we seem to have now is both theology and politics that are considered tests of faith. That is sad and spiritually risky.

The danger for any denomination is to lose its spiritual identity to a political one. This is evidently what has become of the Southern Baptist Convention. Not only have rigid requirements, such as no women pastors, become a test of faith. Political affiliation also seems to be high on the purity list for individuals and churches. The freedom to decide and to vote should rest with the individual, not with denominational leadership, not even one's pastor.

**The Executive Committee, Sexual Abuse Scandals, and the Future**

As I completed editing the footnotes for this book, the announcement came that Dr. Jeff Iorg was to be named the new president of the Executive Committee of the Southern Baptist Convention. The Executive Committee's reputation, major problems and financial challenges facing it over sexual abuse cases, and the failure to choose a new executive for two-and-a-half years, had tarnished the reputation of what had become an excessively powerful force in the denomination during the Controversy.

During my years as trustee, and then executive director of the Historical Commission, I experienced firsthand the bullying tactics of the Executive Committee. The controversy over Nolan Howington's pamphlet and Paul Pressler's threats required my leadership as chair of the trustees. After consultation with Dr. May, I reluctantly recommended to the board withdrawal of the pamphlet. The trustees soon faced the Committee's demand to discontinue receiving contributions from moderate organizations. Failure to do so would have resulted in punishment of the Commission, probably in the form of reduced funding and the continued threat of dissolution of the historical agency.

Indirectly, I followed a path which went around the Executive Committee's attempt to dictate to the agencies. I discovered while reading the SBHS minutes a very interesting fact concerning the Society's collection of books and materials. The Society was organized in 1938. In 1951 the Historical Commission was established, and was assigned operation of the Southern Baptist Historical Library and Archives. The Society had led in the collection of Baptist historical books and materials over the years. After the Commission arose, the Society assigned the agency as "custodian" of its collection to the Southern Baptist Historical Library and Archives (SBHLA), which was now being operated under the authority of the Commission.

As the interim executive, with the task of dissolving the agency, I led the Commission trustees to accept the position of the Society to designate that the SBHLA continue to serve as "custodian" of the Baptist history books and materials. Bill Sumners, director of the SBHLA at the time, and I initiated an inventory of the Society's holdings, which totaled about 3,000 volumes. Bill and I talked with a lawyer, thanks to Carolyn Patton, administrative assistant for the Commission, who arranged the meeting. Carolyn was an unspoken hero in the transition period while the dissolution of the Commission was being implemented. The lawyer confirmed the legitimacy of the Society's claim. I believe he also recommended that in anticipation of the dissolution of the Commission, I ask the Society to reaffirm its appointment of the SBHLA as "custodian" of its collection. I followed his recommendation and had the Commission trustees vote to accept the role of the SBHLA to continue serving as the custodian of the collection. The trustees willingly agreed.

After the dissolution of the Commission and the continuation of the SBHS, the SBHLA continued under the supervision of the seminary presidents. After Charles Deweese became executive director of the Society, I reminded him of the action taken by the Society and the trustees of the Commission in renewing the agreement and appointing the library as the custodian of the Society's books and materials. Charles initiated conversations with Bill Sumners.

The Society did not have available space for the collection, nor did it have the resources for hiring a staff member to administer the collection. An agreement was reached with the SBHLA, and the collection was sold to the library, which continued to make the holding of the Baptist history materials available to interested Baptist history researchers.[193] The work of the Society in obtaining the books in the collection continued through this agreement. The combined efforts of Charles Deweese, Bill Sumners, Carolyn Patton, and myself insured the peaceful transition of this valuable Baptist history collection to the SBHLA with little notice.

While seemingly unimportant, I also sought and received Historical Commission trustee approval to transfer some office equipment to the Society. This included computers and other items, which had resulted from donations by Society members over the years. More significantly, during the dissolution of the Commission, the trustees approved assigning endowment funds which had been donated by Society members and designated to the Society's holdings rather than the Commission's. The Alf-Wardin endowment was the largest of these. Dr. Albert Wardin, who administered the fund, transferred it directly to the Society the day following the initial vote to dissolve the Commission in Atlanta.

I also remember being contacted by Dr. Robert Gardner and his wife, Anne, devoted Society members, to transfer their contributions to the control of the Society. Robert sent me a box with copies of numerous canceled checks to verify their gifts. All of them were written to the "SBHS." The Gardners were avid Society supporters, attending every annual meeting of the organization. Their passion for Baptist history was contagious.

One final note concerning the relationship of the Commission and the Executive Committee. The Committee appointed small teams of its trustees to work with the respective agencies that were being dissolved. I did not take a passive approach to the meetings that I had with them. I initially reminded them that as executive director of the Commission, that I was appointed by the trustees to the position, and that the trustees were elected by the messengers at the annual meetings of the convention. The Executive Committee could advise, but only the trustees could approve. My position of the issue was the rationale that I used when seeking and following trustee action on the previously described actions, along with others. I opposed the Executive Committee's assumption that it had unlimited authority over the agencies.

In the years following the implementation of the restructuring, the Executive Committee assumed power in directing the convention and its agencies. It

---

[193] Dr. Charles Deweese, email to Dr. Slayden Yarbrough, March 25, 2024.

now functions as the legal representation of the Southern Baptist Convention between annual meetings. During the annual sessions, messengers make decisions in business meetings to guide the denomination. The Executive Committee coordinates the agencies. It also receives and distributes offering funds from churches and state conventions.[194]

In so doing, the issues described in the preceding paragraphs resulted in tensions and conflict in the denomination. The Committee directed actions related to women in ministry, use (and misuse, it seems) of financial resources, and insensitivity to churches and state conventions in shaping the convention. Without going into detail, its record on many issues led to the disruptive activities up to the present. The actions and inactions of the Executive Committee have resulted in a failure to lead the convention during divisive and troubled times.

The selection of Dr. Jeff Iorg may not resolve all the tensions related to the Executive Committee. There continues to be calls for dissolution of the Committee which I find ironic, having witnessed the Historical Commission and other agencies dissolved in the restructuring thanks to the influence of the Executive Committee. However, the selection of Iorg provides the possibility of more positive days for the agency and the convention.

Dr. Iorg brought a successful record as a pastor and as a seminary president. He was planning to retire in 2024, when elected president of the Committee. He had an established record of constructive leadership. He will be the first executive for the Committee from the West, breaking the hold on the position of president by Southerners. His election by unanimous vote provides him with a mandate to set a new direction in terms of style and spirit for the office of president.

Iorg is president of Gateway Seminary. He is the first permanent staff member of the Committee in the last two-and-a-half years. He is credited with saving Golden Gate Seminary (as it was previously known). He led in the sale of the prime real estate in Mill Valley, the movement of the main campus to central California, and produced financial stability for the school and its multiple campuses in the West.[195]

---

[194] Mark Wingfield, "Iorg Elected Unanimously to Lead SBC Executive Committee," *Baptistnews.com*, 21 March 2024.
[195] Wingfield, "Iorg Elected."

He is viewed as a one who emphasizes the positives rather than the negatives. He has a reputation as a unifier. And he will lead the agency and the convention in terms of accountability, while facing issues directly. He will not move the convention away from its conservative positions, but he will not take a confrontational approach. In this regard, he has the opportunity and the challenge to reshape the direction of the denomination in a much more positive sense.

From the perspective of disenfranchised moderates, I know of no one who seeks a return to the Southern Baptist Convention. The denomination has not and will not return to its former days and previous structures, which united it for so long. The theological issues will not be healed. At the same time, possibly the tone and commitment of the denomination might be redirected. Perhaps some of the significant principles which united Baptists might be rediscovered and, in some ways recovered. Perhaps Iorg can contribute to a more positive convention. Or, possibly once more Southern Baptists may choose the way of division over any attempts at unity.

## Conclusion

Buddy Shurden's historic definition of Baptist freedoms and prophetic warnings of the dangers in losing them are presented in his extremely popular *The Baptist Identity: Four Fragile Freedoms*. He examines four essential freedoms. They are Bible freedom, soul freedom, church freedom, and religious freedom. Although he discusses theological freedom in another context, I have added this freedom to his list of four. I believe that a major emphasis on theological freedom is especially relevant in the twenty-first century, and deserves greater emphasis. I base this position upon both the history of Baptists and my own personal journey.

For me, the bottom line for being a Baptist—and a Christian—is freedom. Paul teaches in Galatians 5:1, "It is for freedom that Christ set you free." The context is the debate over the Jewish law. But the principle is relevant for every generation and every believer, and expands to a variety of historic principles. Galatians 5:22-23 describes the fruit of the Spirit. None of the nine listed have to do with theology. They have to do with the application and practice of one's faith.

I have concluded that the conservatives won the battle for control of the convention. But in so doing, they have failed in preserving those very principles which would define the movement for the twenty-first century. The desire for short term gain will have long term consequences. Loss of these freedoms will make Southern Baptists more and more irrelevant for the upcoming generations. They will continue to exist. But their message will restrict their influence in a changing world. The demand for orthodoxy has replaced the desire for orthopraxy. People will judge their views not by what they say, but by what they do. "What would Jesus think?" seems to be the convention's motto, not "What would Jesus do?"

# Conclusion

# A Young Professor's Defense of Diversity

"A little heresy is good for the soul!"

"Yesterday's heretics are tomorrow's heroes." Quotes from Slayden Yarbrough[196]

**Final Thoughts**

I begin my conclusion with a question, "Was Jesus a heretic?" I believe that he was in relation to the authorities of his day, both religious and political. In Matthew's Sermon on the Mount, Jesus discusses the law. In chapter 5, Jesus stated "you have heard that it was said. . . but I say unto you. . ." Does not this position challenge the religious authorities? He then provides examples which reinterpret the purpose of the law.

Note as well that this important collection of teachings of Jesus begins with the Beatitudes, the "blessings." These are not theological statements. They are ethical teachings and spiritual relationships with God and humanity. He then used metaphors to describe his followers, or citizens of the Kingdom of Heaven. They are salt, light, a city on a hill, and a candle open to light the room. Note that he does not describe his followers as theologians.

Instead, he encourages his followers to set aside the *lex talionis*, the law of retaliation. He advises them to go beyond the law, to turn the other cheek, to give to the one who sues you both your coat and cloak, and to go the second mile. He is saying that the definition of your faith is found in how you relate with others, how you go beyond the expected, and how you define your neighbor to include your enemies.

Because of his teachings, Jesus became a threat to the religious powers. In a dangerous union between the established religious leaders in Palestine and the Roman civil authorities, Jesus was arrested, tried, and convicted. His

---

[196] Statements made by Slayden Yarbrough in a church history class, SWBC, 1972.

teachings were described as blasphemy by the religious leaders. And he was sentenced and executed by crucifixion. He went against the teachings of the religious establishment. He was considered a heretic by the religious authorities in Jerusalem. But they charged him with political crimes before Roman officials.

In summary, he rejected the authority of the Sanhedrin, the ruling council of the Jews in Palestine. He challenged narrow views, ancient traditions, and hypocritical leaders. His heresy could not be tolerated, and it was not. But in the end, Jesus won. Believers in the twenty-first century know the story well.

My personal journey was framed in the context of the Controversy and restructuring of the Southern Baptist Convention. I experienced charges of heretical teaching and lost my job at my alma mater because of these charges. However, I survived to teach at OBU. I also found myself with unexpected opportunities to be a leader in the work of Southern Baptist history. I served as a trustee and then the last executive director of the Historical Commission. I became the first executive director of the SBHS newly independent organization following the restructuring of the convention. How a convicted heretic could slip through the cracks of the Controversy and be in such positions to contribute to and affect future developments of the important work of Baptist history is remarkably ironic, to say the least.

I also found the opportunity to write extensively in the field of Baptist history, and directly and indirectly in other fields of study. I even had the wonderful privilege to serve as editor of *Baptist History & Heritage*. Because of unexpected opportunities, I along with so many others who loved the history of Baptists was able to build upon the historic foundation of the denominational heritage.

In the end, I chose to walk away from Southern Baptists. Janis and I became American Baptists. However, the principles and the influences of so many of those Baptists who nurtured me continue to be relevant in my continuing journey. At the same time, I witnessed the erosion of their teachings by those who demanded theological purity based upon their personal beliefs. And, I became a contributor and a proponent for the good of the heritage which influenced my life and career.

Freedom, education, questioning, and relevancy are all important traits or principles of the people called Baptists. They provide the foundation for my own understanding and commitments as a Baptist. Adherence to them opens the possibility of success in the journey of faith. Deviation from them results in a corruption of the faith which leads to heterodoxy in theology, and failure in continuing the tradition of a kind and caring movement of people trying to find meaning in a rapidly changing world.

I have no regrets from my pilgrimage. In fact, I feel honored to have been a part of a conflict which forced me to take sides, to examine my foundations, and to trust the freedoms which I found in my Christian faith and my Baptist heritage. I believe that I know myself better, that I recognize the good of all of those who influenced me, and that I was fortunate to have the opportunity to make a difference for current and future generations. From my journey I have concluded that "Being Baptist: it certainly isn't boring!"

Finally, I recognize that my story is only one of countless others who traveled together drawing from our past and shaping our future. Many I knew or continue to know personally. Others I have observed from a distance. Still others, I am certain, stood along all the rest of us, standing firm to the principles from their Baptist roots, which could not be purged by convention votes and aggressive denominational politics. We taught, served, wrote, and defined what the struggle meant not only to ourselves but to a very rich tradition. Together, we made our marks.

When woven together, our stories reveal that we made a difference to our heritage and our hope for the years to come. I continue to believe that the goodness and the principles of the people called Baptist will prevail in the hearts and minds and actions of my fellow pilgrims. Perhaps this book might influence others to keep the faith, and just maybe be called "heretics" by those who sacrificed the biblical and historic principles of the people called Baptist for a mess of theological pottage. If this should happen, welcome to a society of committed Baptists.

# Bibliography

**Books**

Baker, Robert A. *The Southern Baptist Convention and Its People, 1607-1972*. Nashville: Broadman Press, 1974.

Barnes, W. W. *The Southern Baptist Convention: 1845-1953*. Nashville: Broadman Press, 1954.

Brackney, William H. *A Genetic History of Baptist Thought*. Macon, GA: Mercer University Press, 2004.

_____. *Baptists in North America: An Historical Perspective*. Malden, MA: Blackwell, 2006.

Cothen, Grady C. *What Happened to the Southern Baptist Convention?* Macon, GA: Smyth & Helwys, 1993.

Chute, Anothy L., Nathan A. Finn, and Michael A. G. Haykin. *The Baptist Story: From English Sect to Global Movement*. Nashville: B & H, 2015.

Criswell, W. A. *Why I Preach That the Bible Is Literally True*. Nashville, TN: Broadman Press, 1969.

Davies, G. Henton. "Genesis." *Broadman Bible Commentary*, Vol. 1. Nashville, TN: Broadman Press, 1969.

Durso, Pamela R. and Keith E. Durso. *The Story of Baptists in the United States*. Brentwood, TN: Baptist History and Heritage Society, 2006.

Hankins, Barry. *Uneasy in Babylon: Southern Baptist Conservatives and American Culture*. Tuscaloosa, AL: University of Alabama Press, 2002.

James, Robison B. *The Takeover in the Southern Baptist Convention*. Decatur, GA: Southern Baptist Convention Today, 1989.

Early, Joe Jr. *The Life and Writings of Thomas Helwys*. Macon, GA: Mercer University Press, 2009.

Elliott, Ralph. *Message of Genesis*. Nashville: Broadman Press, 1961.

Fletcher, Jesse C. *The Southern Baptist Convention: A Sesquicentennial History.* Nashville TN: Broadman & Holman, 1994.

Francisco, Clyde T. "Genesis." *Broadman Bible Commentary,* Vol. 1. rev. ed. Nashville, TN: Broadman Press, 1972.

Gardner, Andrew. *Reimagining Zion: History of the Alliance of Baptists.* Macon, GA: Nurturing Faith, Inc., 2015.

Garrett, James Leo Jr. *Baptist Theology, A Four Century Study.* Macon, GA: Mercer University Press, 2009.

Hefley, James C. *The Truth in Crisis.* 5 vols. Dallas: Criterion Publications; Hannibal, MO: Hannibal Books, 1986-1990.

_____. *The Conservative Resurgence in the Southern Baptist Convention.* Hannibal, MO: Hannibal Books, 1991.

Leonard, Bill. *Baptist Ways: A History.* Valley Forge: Judson, 2003.

_____. *God's Last and Only Hope: The Fragmentation of the Southern Baptist Convention.* Grand Rapids: Eerdmans, 1990.

Maples, Terry and Gene Wilder. *Reclaiming and Re-Forming Baptist Identity: Cooperative Baptist Fellowship.* Macon, GA: Nurturing Faith, Inc., 2017.

McClellan, Albert. *Meet Southern Baptists.* Nashville: Broadman Press, 1978.

Morgan, David T. *The New Crusades: Conflict in the Southern Baptist Convention, 1969-1991.* Tuscaloosa: University of Alabama Press, 1996.

Patterson, Paige. *Anatomy of a Reformation: The Southern Baptist Convention 1978-2004.* Fort Worth, TX: Seminary Hill Press, 2004.

Patterson, W. Morgan. *Baptist Successionism: A Critical View.* Valley Forge, PA: Judson Press, 1979.

Pressler, Paul. *A Hill on Which to Die: One Southern Baptist's Journey.* Nashville: Broadman & Holman, 1999.

Record of Proceedings. Third BWA Congress. Nashville: Baptist Sunday School Board, 1923, 68.

Richards, Roger C. *History of Southern Baptists*, Rev. ed. Nashville: CrossBooks Publishing, 2015.

Shurden, Walter B., ed. *The Baptist Identity: Four Fragile Freedoms*. Macon, GA: Smyth & Helwys, 1993.

_____. *Not a Silent People: Controversies That Have Shaped Southern Baptists*. Nashville, TN. Broadman Press, 1972. Revised edition. Macon, GA: Smyth & Helwys, 1994.

_____. *The Struggle for the Soul of the Southern Baptist Convention: Moderate Responses to the Fundamentalist Movement*. Macon, GA: Mercer University Press, 1993.

Shurden, Walter B., and Randy Shepley, eds. *Going for the Jugular: A Documentary History of the Southern Baptist Convention Holy War*. Macon, GA: Mercer University Press, 1996.

Sutton, Jerry. *The Baptist Reformation: The Conservative Resurgence in the Southern Baptist Convention*. Nashville: Broadman & Holman, 2000.

Torbet, Robert G. *A History of Baptists*. 3rd ed. Valley Forge, PA: Judson Press, 1973.

Weaver, Aaron D., ed. *CBF at 25: Stories of the Cooperative Baptist Fellowship*. Macon, GA: Nurturing Faith Inc., 2016.

Whitley, W. T. *A History of English Baptists*. London: Charles Griffin, 1923.

Yarbrough, Slayden A., and Michael Kuykendall. *Southern Baptists: A History of a Confessional People*. Jefferson, NC: McFarland & Company, 2021.

Yarbrough, Slayden, J. M. Gaskin, Eunice Short, and Helen Thames Raley. *The View from Bison Hill*. Shawnee, OK: Oklahoma Baptist University, 1985.

Yarbrough, Slayden A. *Henry Jacob: A Moderate Separatist and His Influence on Early English Congregationalism*. Unpublished Ph.D. Dissertation. Baylor University, 1972.

_____. *I Am: Storytelling in Worship*. Rapid City, SD: New Harbor Press, 2020.

Slayden A. Yarbrough

_____. *Southern Baptists: A Historical, Ecclesiological, and Theological Heritage of a Confessional People*. Nashville, TN: Fields Publishing, 2000.

_____. *We Coulda Been Killed! Two Brothers and Others Growing Up*. Vancouver, WA: Self-Published, 2023.

_____. *Southern Baptists: Who Are We?* Oklahoma City, OK: Oklahoma Baptist Historical Commission, 1984, edited 1985, and edited 1990.

_____. *The Lengthening Shadow: The Centennial History of FBC, Shawnee, OK.* Shawnee, OK: First Baptist Church, 1992.

## Articles, Pamphlets, and Reference Works

A Report from the Board of Trustees of Oklahoma Baptist University to the Baptist General Convention of Oklahoma, 12 November 1980.

*Baptist Faith and Message*. Nashville, TN: Sunday School Board, 1963.

Carroll, J. M. *The Trail of Blood*. n.c.: n.p., January, 1, 1931.

Druin, Toby. "Patterson Group Seeks Long Range Control of Southern Baptist Convention." *Baptist Press*, 21 April 1980, 1-5.

Foust, Michael. "Calvinism Committee Issues Report, Urges SBC to 'Stand Together' for Great Commission." *Baptistpress.org*, 31 May 2013.

"Garrett Out at SWBC." *Bolivar Herald-Free Press*, 19 February 1978, 1-C.

Horton, Greg. "Are Southern Baptists Predestined to Fuss over Calvinism?" *Baptist Standard*, 6 June 2013.

Pipes, Carol. "Giving Increases for SBC in 2018, Baptisms, Attendance Continue Decline." blog.lifeway.com, 23 May 2019.

Shellnut, Kate. "Southern Baptists See Biggest Drop in 100 Years." *Christianity Today*, 4 June 2020.

Shurden, Walter B. "Southern Baptist Responses to Their Confessional Statements." *Review and Expositor* 76, no. 1 (1979): 80-81.

White, B. R. "The English Particular Baptists and the Great Rebellion." *Baptist History & Heritage* 9, no. 1 (1974): 20-24.

Wills, Gregory A. "Progressive Theology and Southern Baptist Controversies of the 1950s and 1960s." *Southern Baptist Journal of Theology* 7, no. 1 (2003): 12-31.

Yarbrough, Slayden. "Baptists and Academic Freedom in Academic Freedom and Southern Baptist History." *Baptist History & Heritage* 39, no. 2 (2004) 45-47.

_____. "Baptist History in the Twenty-First Century: Dreams and Visions." *Baptist History & Heritage* 34, no. 3 (Summer/Fall 1999): 95-107.

_____. "Biblical Authority in Southern Baptist History, 1845-1945." *Baptist History & Heritage* 27, no. 1 (January 1992): 4-12.

_____. *Biblical Illustrator* articles: "Pontus and Bithynia" (Summer 1984); "Centurions and Soldiers: The Roman Army" (Winter 1986); "Early Christianity's Exclusivism" (Winter 1987); "Judea" (Summer 1988); "The Judaizers" (Spring 1989); "Barabbas" (Winter 1991); "Nero and the Christians" (Spring 1994); "The River Chebar" (Summer 1995); and "Persecution in the Early Church" (Spring 2000).

_____. "How Can We Believe in the Resurrection?" *Proclaim* 15, no. 3 (1985): 30-31.

_____. "I Am Christmas." *Proclaim* 17, no. 1 (1986): 31-32.

_____. "I Am the Bible." *Proclaim* 16, no. 3 (1986): 27-29.

_____. "Is Creedalism a Threat to Southern Baptists?" *Baptist History & Heritage* 18, no. 2 (April 1983): 21-32.

_____. Articles in Bill J. Leonard, ed., *Dictionary of Baptists in America*. Downers Grove, IL: InterVarsity Press, 1994: "Jones, Samuel, 1735-1814"; "Landrum, William Warren, 1853-1926"; "New Connection Baptists"; "Oklahoma Baptist University"; and "Orthodox Baptist Movement."

_____. "Premillennialism Among Baptist Groups." *Encyclopedia of Southern Baptists*. Vol. IV. Nashville: Broadman Press, 1982.

Slayden A. Yarbrough

_____. "Religious Liberty: Right and Responsibility." *Report from the Capital,* July-August, 1986, 10-11.

_____. "The Believer's Church." *Southwestern Journal of Theology* 28, no. 3 (Summer 1986): 33-44.

_____. "The Ecclesiastical Development in Theory and Practice of John Robinson and Henry Jacob." *Perspectives in Religious Studies* 5, no. 3 (1978): 196-210.

_____. "The Ecclesiology of Henry Jacob." *The Quarterly Review* 40, no. 2 (January-March 1980): 66-78.

_____. "The History of Southern Baptist History: Restructuring of the New SBHS." *Baptist History & Heritage* 34, no. 3 (Summer/Fall 1999): 108-20.

_____. "The Influence of Plymouth Colony Separatism on Salem: An Interpretation of John Cotton's Letter of 1630 to Samuel Skelton." *Church History* 51, no. 3 (September 1982): 290-303.

_____. "The Origins of Baptist Associations Among the English Particular Baptists." *Baptist History & Heritage* 23, no. 2 (1988): 14-24.

_____. "The Pastor as Church Historian." *Proclaim* 17, no. 2 (1987): 42-43.

**Editorials in Baptist History & Heritage**

Carter, Rosalyn. Guest Editorial. "Baptists and the White House: Strengthened by our Faith in Baptist and the White House." *Baptist History & Heritage* 32, no. 1 (January 1997).

Taulman, Jim. "Wars and Rumors of War: Guest Editorial, in Baptists and the Civil War." *Baptist History & Heritage* 32, nos. 3-4 (July/October 1997).

Yarbrough, Slayden A. Guest Editorial. "Dr. Lynn E. May, Jr.:" in "The Spirit of Baptists, 1845-1995." *Baptist History & Heritage* 30, no. 3 (October 1995).

_____. "Atlanta 95: Celebration and Sorrow in Living According to God's Word." *Baptist History & Heritage* 30, no. 4 (October 1995).

_____. "*Baptist History & Heritage* Publication Principles" in "Two Ways to be Baptist." *Baptist History & Heritage* 32, no. 2 (April 1997).

\_\_\_\_\_. "Church and State in Baptist History" in "Changing State of Church and State." *Baptist History & Heritage* 33, no. 1 (Winter 1998).

\_\_\_\_\_. "In Memoriam: Lynn E. May, Jr." in "Southern Baptist Identity." *Baptist History & Heritage* 31, no. 4 (October 1996).

\_\_\_\_\_. "Is This Good Ground?" in "Texas Baptists and the Southern Baptist Convention." *Baptist History & Heritage* 33, no. 3 (Autumn 1998).

\_\_\_\_\_. "Issues Shaping Baptist Identity" in "Southern Baptist Identity." *Baptist History & Heritage* 31, no. 4 (October 1996).

\_\_\_\_\_. "Living God's Word" in "Living According to God's Word." *Baptist History & Heritage* 31, no. 4 (October 1996).

\_\_\_\_\_. "Southern Baptists and Worship" in "Southern Baptists and Worship." *Baptist History & Heritage* 31, no. 3 (July 1996).

\_\_\_\_\_. "The Last Will and Testament of the Historical Commission of the Southern Baptist Convention: A Report and Observations on the Dissolution of the Historical Commission, in Baptist and the Civil War." *Baptist History & Heritage* 32, nos. 3-4 (July/October): 117-23.

## Websites

Allen, Bob. "Lawsuit Reveals Details about Paige Patterson's 'Break Her Down' Meeting with Woman Alleging Campus Rape." *Baptistnews.com*, 24 June 2019.

Butler, Anthea. "Faith Could Bring Us Together. But Too Often It Divides Us." *CNN.com*, 24 November 2019.

Collins, Scott, and Russ Dilday. "Russell Dilday, Baptist Statesman." *Baptistnews.com*, 21 June 2023.

Kaylor, Brian "Southwestern Accuses Pattersons of Theft, Improper Donor Solicitation." *Wordandway.org*, 28 May 2021.

Koonce, Brian. "1961 Controversy over 'The Message of Genesis' Gets Baptist Historians' Reflections." *Baptistpress.org*, 16 September 2013.

Mohler, R. Albert Jr. "The Future of the Southern Baptist Convention: The Numbers Don't Add Up." Albertmohler.com, 31 May 2019.

Mwaura, Maina. "Another Megachurch Leaves the SBC." *Baptistnews.com*, 30 June 2023.

Richard Rogers and Oscar Hammerstein II. *Oklahoma!* 1943.

Roach, David. "Connect316 Urges 'Loyal Opposition' to Calvinism." Sbcannualmeeting.net, 22 June 2017, See the video provide in this link for Roach's view.

Simon, Paul. "The Boxer." Columbia Records. Recording released 21 March 1969.

Wingfield, Mark. "A Word in Praise of Baptist Press." *Baptistnews.com*, 11 March 2024.

_____. "Anti-Egalitarian Forces Make Clean Sweep at Southern Baptist Convention Annual Meeting." *Baptistnews.com*, 14 June 2023.

_____. "As SBC Moves Toward Second Vote on Law Amendment, Debate Continues on Just What It Means." *Baptistnews.com*, 1 December 2023.

_____. "In SBC Annual Statistics, Even the Good News Isn't that Good." *Baptistnews.com*, 11 May 2023.

_____. "Iorg Elected Unanimously to Lead SBC Executive Committee." *Baptistnews.com*, 21 March 2024.

_____. "Ralph Elliott, Author of Genesis Commentary that began the Southern Baptist Convention's Battle for the Bible, Dies." *Baptistnews.com*, 27 October 2022.

https://www.criswell.edu.about/history-and-heritage/.

## Letters, Telephone Conversations, and Memos

Charles Deweese, email to Slayden Yarbrough, December 9, 2023.

Collection of Letters of Rev. Bill Dudley to and from Southwest College President Dr. James Sells,

Collection of memos between Academic Dean Dr. G H Surrette, Dr. Slayden Yarbrough, et al., 1976-1980, maintained by Slayden Yarbrough, Vancouver, Washington.

Letters between Doyle Shepherd, Chair of Deacons, First Baptist Church, Monett, MO, and Southwest College President Dr. James Sells, April, 1979.

Letters to Amanda from Sargent Major Marion Hill Fitzpatrick, Company K, 45th Georgia Regiment, Thomas' Brigade, Wilcox Division, Hill's Corps, CSA to his wife Amanda Olive White Fitzpatrick, 1882-1865.

John Finley, email to Slayden Yarbrough, December 9, 2023.

G H Surrette, memo on tenure to Slayden Yarbrough, March 7, 1978.

\_\_\_\_\_, memo to Dr. Slayden Yarbrough, May 28, 1978.

Rev. Bill Dudley, personal note of November 20, 1978, of Bill Dudley recalling a phone conversation with Dr. G H Surrette on March 2, 1978.

Rev. Bill Dudley, letter to Rev. Roy Jerrell, November 27, 1978.

Rev. Dave Williams, letter to Dr. James Sells, February 2, 1977.

Yarbrough, Slayden, memo to Dr. H. K. Neely, March 3, 1978, which he forwarded to Dr. G H. Surrette.

\_\_\_\_, memo to Neely, March 3, 1978, containing direct quote from the Faculty Handbook on tenure.

\_\_\_\_\_, memo to G H Surrette, April 19, 1978.

## Index

Adams, Larry 89

Agee, Bob 95-99, 156, 165

*Baptist Faith and Message* 9, 33-34, 36-38, 66, 79, 89, 113-14, 162-63, 182-85

*Baptist History and Heritage*, editor and articles 10, 125-40, 152, 193

*Baptist New Global* 11, 170, 174-70, 180-81, 189

*Baptist Press* 94, 170, 174

Beck, Rosalee 101, 129

Belcher, Dick 27-28, 34, 58, 136

*Biblical Illustrator* 98, 104, 154-55

Bibliography includes listing of all of Slayden Yarbrough's publications discussed in chapters 7-9, in Bibliography 195-203

Brister, Mark 98-99, 152

Blevins, Carolyn 130, 159

*Broadman Bible Commentary* 35, 81, 145

Brown, Joe 79, 114, 179

Burgess, Bob and Joy 96

Carolyn Blevins Meritorious Service Award, The 159

Carroll, B. H. 28

Carroll, J. M. 28, 58, 82

Carter, First Lady Rosalyn 132

Cochran, Dan 72

Complementarianism 40, 130, 181

Criswell, W. A. 25, 35

Dalglish, Edward 31

Darnell, Nancy 19

Davies, G. Henton 35, 82, 145

Davis, Addie 179

Deweese, Charles 10-11, 84, 138, 140, 144, 171-73

*Dictionary of Baptists in America* 124

Dilday, Russell 167

Distinguished Service Award, Hannibal-LaGrange College 160

Dudley, Bill 11, 24-25, 44-52, 54-55, 57-58, 64-66, 120

Dunn, James 137

Elder, Lloyd 36

Elevation Church, Holly and Steven Furtick 180

Elliott, Ralph 33-36, 66, 77, 81-82, 91, 145

*Encyclopedia of Southern Baptists* 123-24

Faught, Jerry 35

Finley, John 121, 171-72

Fletcher, Jesse 129-30, 163

Francisco, Clyde 36

Galeotti, Gary 48

Gardner, Robert and Anne 188

Garrett, Howard 52

Gaskin Church History Award 160

Gaskin, J. M. 73, 87, 104, 111-12, 114, 142

Graves, Charles 89

Gunnin, Gerry 63

Hall, Eugene 95

Hall (Yarbrough), Betty 14, 62

Hall, John L. 14, 62

Hawkins, Merrill M., Jr. 126, 141

Hastey, Stan 163

Helwys, Thomas 87, 118

Henry, Jim 97, 165

"Heresy Paper" 74, 88-90

Hilburn, Glenn O. 1

Hobbs, Herschel; Lecture 160

Holcomb, Dan 63, 74

Honeycut, Roy 5

Horton, Greg 177

Howington, Nolan P. 146, 170-71, 186

Hunt, Harry B., Jr. 48, 50, 91-92

Huser, Carl 49

*I Am: Storytelling in Worship* 110, 116-18

Ingram, Joe l. 84, 89, 95

Iorg, Jeff 186, 189-90

Jerrel, Roy 49-51

Jones, Shirley 95-96

King, Martin L., Jr. 30

Koonce, Brian 34

Kuykendall, Michael 3, 8, 40, 67, 75, 78, 103, 118-19, 166, 177, 179

Krause, Lewis 55

Law, Mike, "Law Amendment" 181

Lefever, Alan 129

Leonard, Bill J. 38, 80, 93, 108-09, 124-25, 131

Lumpkin, Bill 38

MAGA 186

Martin, Dan 94, 170

Martin, Ron 68, 125

May, Lynn E., Jr. 10. 84, 126, 131, 144, 171-73

Maxwell, James Paul 79, 114, 179

McBeth, H. Leon 36, 82, 108, 123, 130, 133, 145-46

McCartney, Richard 84-85

McMillan, W. Lynn 29

McWilliams, Warren 3, 63, 74, 106

Meade, Gen. George 72

*Message of Genesis, The* 34, 66, 77, 81-82, 144

Mohler, R. Albert 39, 176, 179, 185

Moore, David 50-51, 93

Mullins, E. Y. 33, 162

Neely, H. K. 27-28, 44, 46-47, 49, 52-54, 64-65, 111-112

Norman W. Cox Award 159

Oklahoma Baptist Historical Society Distinguished Service Award 160

Palen, Kathy 158

Page, Frank 177

Patterson, Paige 25, 46, 82, 115, 167-69

Patterson, Morgan 61-62, 129

Patton, Carolyn 129, 187-88

Pence, Glen 55

Popum, Linda Barnes 40, 179-80

Pratt, Tom 48

Pressler, Paul 25, 37, 72, 82-83, 85, 167, 169-75

*Proclaim* 104, 156-58

*Report From the Capitol* 92, 158

Robison, James 91

Rogers, Richard, and Oscar Hammerstein 71

Sells, Jim 25, 46-48, 51, 56

Shackleford, Al 94, 170

Shellnut, Kate 176

Shepherd, Doyl 56

Sherman, Cecil 163

Shurden, Walter B. 1, 20-21, 37, 108-09, 190

Simon, Paul 45

Southern Baptist Alliance, Alliance of Baptists 163

Stanley, Charles 5

Sullaway, Jerry 88

Sumners, Bill 187-88

Surrette, G H 1, 25, 45, 48, 50-52, 54-56, 99

Taulman, Jim 132, 134-35

Terry, Bob 51

Timberlake, James 63

Toy, Crawford Howard 8-82

Truett, George W. 61, 133

*View from Bison Hill, 1961-1983, The* 114-15

Vestal, Dan 163

Wardin, Albert 129, 188

Warren, Rick 40, 179-80

Waterson, Bill 5

Whitsitt, William 28, 146

Williams, Dave 48

Wills, Gregory 81

Wingfield, Mark 34, 40, 175-77, 180-181, 189

W. O. Carver Distinguished Service Award 159

Wooley, Davis C. 123

Yarbrough, Janis 18-19, 31, 67, 110, 112, 119, 151, 159-60, 193

Yarbrough, Slayden A., publications of books, articles and practical writings primarily discussed in chapters 7-9